CONTENTS / INHALT

CONTENTS / INHALT

EXTRA PAGES

Com = Communication Ex = Exercise **Follow** = Follow up **Intro** = Introduction **List** = Listening **Proj** = Project
Read = Reading **Rev** = Revision Sit = Situation **TYE** = Test your English **W & P** = Words and pictures

Go Ahead 9

für die Jahrgangsstufe 9 an sechsstufigen bayerischen Realschulen

erarbeitet von John Eastwood, Street, Somerset
Klaus Berold, Kulmbach
Elke Zahn, Bayreuth

unter beratender Mitarbeit von Gerlinde Eberhardt, Surberg
Werner Epp, Kempten
Gisela Fiedler, Nürnberg
Günter Geiß, Weiden
Renate Grieshaber, Kempten
Renate Heidemeier, Eichstätt
Konrad Huber, Maisach
Jürgen Kanhäuser, Rain
Reinhold Schnell, Frickenhausen

Verlagsredaktion Stefanie Gröne, Katja Hartmann

Projektleitung Helga Holtkamp

redaktionelle Mitarbeit Sigrid Janssen, Rob Packer, Fritz Preuss

Design und Layout David Graham (*Units*), James Abram (*Anhänge*)

Bildredaktion Uta Hübner

zum Schülerbuch sind erhältlich **Workbook, CDs**

Hinweise zu weiteren Bestandteilen im Lehrerhandbuch.
Bild-, Text- und Musikquellen auf Seite 168.

www.cornelsen.de

1. Auflage, 11. Druck 2016

Alle Drucke dieser Auflage sind inhaltlich unverändert
und können nebeneinander verwendet werden.

Druck: Mohn Media Mohndruck, Gütersloh

ISBN 978-3-464-02843-8

PEFC
PEFC/04-31-1033

PEFC zertifiziert
Dieses Produkt stammt aus nachhaltig bewirtschafteten Wäldern und kontrollierten Quellen.
www.pefc.de

GO AHEAD

9

Cornelsen

3

George III was King from 1760 to 1820. It was a time of growing trade but also of war both in Europe and in the colonies. The battle of Waterloo, which England won, ended the Napoleonic Wars in 1815.

4

Queen Victoria ruled the British Empire from 1837 to 1901. During this time, Britain became an industrial society known as 'the workshop of the world'. But In Victorian times many factory workers were children. They worked long hours and were often treated badly.

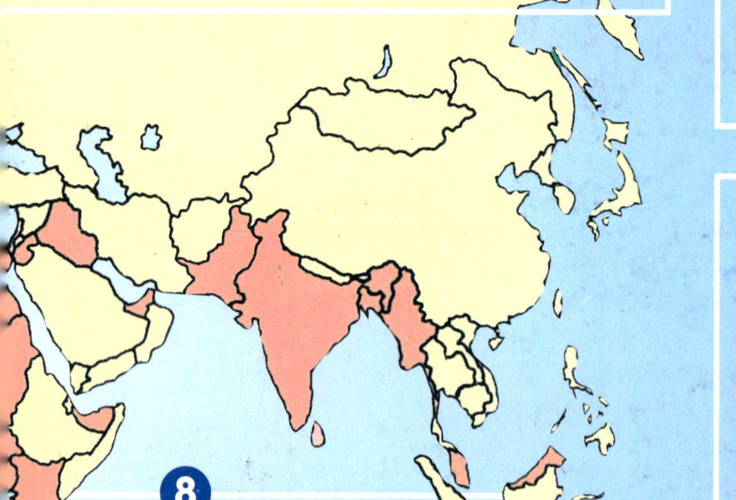

8

In 1922, after 750 years of English rule, most of Ireland became the Irish Free State, but the religious problems still haven't been solved today.

10

In the 1930s the British Empire began to turn into the Commonwealth of Nations and today has 54 members.

11

About 125,000 people from the Caribbean and many more from India, Pakistan and West Africa came to live in Britain between 1948 and 1958. Today, Britain is a society made up of many different races.

9

World War II changed everybody's life in Britain. More than 60,000 people were killed during the 'Blitz'.

UNIT 1

WHAT'S ON?

WORDS AND PICTURES

01

THEATRES

APOLLO VICTORIA
Box office 0870 4000 650
BOMBAY DREAMS
A poor boy dreams of becoming a movie star. 'A big show with wonderful songs, love and colour.'
Tues-Sat 7.45pm, Wed & Sat 3pm, Sun 4pm
www.bombaydreamstheshow.com

LYCEUM THEATRE
Wellington St, WC2 0870 243 9000
THE LION KING
Disney's musical is the popular story of Simba the young lion.
Tues-Sat 7.30pm, matinee Wed & Sat 2pm & Sun 3pm
online booking: www.disney.co.uk

PRINCE OF WALES THEATRE
Coventry St, W1 020 7839 5987
THE FULL MONTY
The successful film is now a stage musical. Once they were steel workers; now they take their clothes off.
Eves 7.45pm, Mats Wed & Sat 3pm
www.thefullmontymusical.com

FILMS

ATTACK OF THE CLONES (PG)
The new Star Wars movie.

THE FAST AND THE FURIOUS (15)
Action movie about boys in LA racing their fast cars. Great entertainment.

HARRY POTTER (PG)
The adventures of Harry and his friends at Hogwarts School of Magic.

LORD OF THE RINGS (15)
The story of a dangerous journey to find the ring.

OTHER EVENTS

SADLER'S WELLS
Rosebery Ave, EC1.
Box office 020 7863 8000
CIRQUE ÉLOIZE
Fri 7pm; Sat 3pm & 7pm; Sun 3pm
Acrobats, comedy and live rock music.

BRICK LANE MARKET
BRICK LANE FESTIVAL
Sunday 30th only, noon-10pm
Music and dance. Caribbean DJs, Asian drum bands, the London School of Samba and much more.

GIGS

Saturday 29
AMERICAN HIFI
200 Club, Acton Town. 8pm
FREESTYLERS
Camden Palace. 8pm
JAMES HUNTER
Rock House, Kensington High St. 9pm

SITUATION 1

02

Josh I like The Strokes.
Hannah So do I. Well, they're OK.
Josh They're a great band.
Hannah I haven't got this new CD of theirs.
Josh No, neither have I. And I haven't got enough money on me to buy it.
Hannah Nor have I, unfortunately. But I could lend you five pounds if you like.
Josh Thanks, but I still wouldn't have enough. I've only got three pounds myself.

So → page 100

I like The Strokes. – **So do I.**
My brother is in a rock band, and **so is my boyfriend.**
I can play the guitar. – **So can I.**

Neither / nor

I haven't got this CD. – **Neither / Nor have I.**
I'm not a country music fan. – **Neither / Nor am I.**
Charlotte didn't like the film, **and neither / nor did Kate.**

EXERCISE 1

Dominic and Natalie have answered a questionnaire in a magazine that tells you what kind of person you are.

➡	*Have you got lots of friends?*	*yes/~~no~~*
➡	*Do you worry about the future?*	*~~yes~~/no*
1	*Can you play a musical instrument?*	*~~yes~~/no*
2	*Are you a sports fan?*	*yes/~~no~~*
3	*Do you like buying clothes?*	*yes/~~no~~*
4	*Could you live without a mobile phone?*	*~~yes~~/no*
5	*Have you ever climbed a mountain?*	*~~yes~~/no*
6	*Would you like to travel round the world?*	*yes/~~no~~*

Dominic and Natalie have answered the questions in exactly the same way. What do they say?

We sometimes use *could* instead of *was / were able to*.

➡ *Dominic* I've got lots of friends.
Natalie So have I. And I don't worry about the future.
Dominic Neither do I. And …

Work in pairs and continue the conversation.

EXERCISE 2

Look again at the questionnaire and write six sentences like these.

➡ Dominic has got lots of friends, and so has Natalie.
➡ Dominic doesn't worry about the future, and neither does Natalie.

EXERCISE 3

Work with a partner and make a conversation from the notes. Partner **A** completes the sentence, and partner **B** answers with *so* or *neither*. Try to make a sensible conversation.

- I like the Harry Potter books.
- So do I. I've read all of them.

If you've got something different to say, you can answer like this.

- I like the Harry Potter books.
- Well, I don't. I think they're silly. Anyway, they're for little kids.

1 I'm going to ... on TV tonight.
2 I hate ... .
3 I'm a big fan of ... .
4 I did ... in the last English test.
5 I haven't seen ... yet.
6 I'd like to ... one day.

Now change partners. Practise the conversations with at least four other pupils.

SITUATION 2

03

Claire Are we going to see the new *ET* film at the weekend?
Hannah Yes, why not?
Natalie If Josh asks you out, you'll go with him, won't you?
Hannah Well, he hasn't asked me out.
Claire If you asked him, he'd go with you.
Hannah I'm not going to ask him.
Natalie It would be quicker if you did. He's slow, isn't he?
Hannah Look, shut up about Josh, will you?

If ... simple present ..., ... will / can / might / must / should ...

If we **go** to the cinema together, it**'ll be** more fun.
If Josh **buys** the CD, he **can bring** it to the party.

If ... simple past ..., ... would / could / might ...

If Josh **wasn't** so slow, he **would ask** Hannah out.
If we **went** to a club, we **could dance** all night. → page 100-101

EXERCISE 4

Complete the sentences. The notes in brackets will help you, or you can use your own words. Make sure you use the verb in the correct form.

1 If no one asks me out tonight, ... (I / watch / ... / on TV)
2 If I was a DJ, ... (I / play / ...)
3 If ... win their next game, ... (I / be / ...)
4 If I had my own TV chat show, ... (I / invite / ...)
5 My parents say I can go to the pop festival if ... (with / friend)
6 I could be a model if ...
7 If I had a few million euros, ...
8 It would be really great if ...

Let's go out

04

The Kelsey family – mum, dad, Chloe (17) and Tim (15) live in Cornwall. They're visiting their friends the Websters. The Websters live in Highgate, a suburb of north London. It's Saturday evening. Downstairs in the living-room, Jordan (17) and Rachel (16) are chatting to Chloe and Tim.

Rachel What are we going to do tonight?

Tim Let's go out somewhere. We could go to the West End and see a film or something.

Jordan I'll have a look in the paper. Cinemas, here we are. *Attack of the Clones*, *The Fast and the Furious*, *Harry Potter*, *Lord of the Rings*, ...

Tim I've seen that.

Chloe So have I, and it isn't very good.

Tim Oh, I liked it.

Chloe *The Fast and the Furious*? What's that about?

Jordan It's about racing fast cars. My friend Adam says it's good.

Rachel No way.

Jordan And it's on at our local cinema. We don't need to go into the West End.

Rachel I don't want to watch a film about cars.

Chloe Neither do I, really. And I'd rather go into the West End. Isn't that where it all happens? I really envy you – living in London with so much going on.

Rachel We don't really go to the West End very often. We have homework to do in the evening.

Jordan The West End is expensive.

Rachel We'll go there tonight of course, because you're here, and it's special.

Chloe We can see these films back in Cornwall. What about doing something different – something we can't do at home?

Tim It says here there's a circus.

Chloe Come on, Tim. The circus is for little kids.

Rachel Anyway, it's cruel to animals.

Tim I don't think they have animals. It says acrobats, comedy and live rock music. The next performance is at seven o'clock.

Chloe If you go to the circus, you'll be on your own, Tim. And it's no use arguing.

Rachel Is there anything in 'Time Out', Chloe?

Chloe It says here there's a festival, the Brick Lane Festival. Caribbean DJs, Asian drum bands and the London School of Samba. Sounds all right, doesn't it?

Rachel Brick Lane is miles away. It's in the East End.

Chloe Oh, it's on Sunday.

Jordan Well, maybe we can go over there tomorrow. If we ask mum and dad, they might take us in the car.

Rachel But what about tonight? If we can't think of anywhere to go, we'll just have to stay in.

Camden Palace

Chloe What about a gig?

Jordan Yes, why not?

Rachel Let me have a look at the magazine. American HiFi, Freestylers, James Hunter. I've never heard of any of them.

Tim I've heard of Freestylers.

Chloe So have I. They're good.

Rachel There's an article about them here. It says here they do all kinds of stuff: hip hop, electro, tech house, reggae, …

Chloe Something for everyone.

Jordan It might be worth going along. Where is it?

Rachel Camden Palace.

Jordan That's not far, is it? We can go to Camden Town on the tube.

Rachel But Chloe wants to go into the West End.

Chloe Oh, I don't mind. A gig would be great.

Rachel It starts at eight o'clock.

Chloe But the only thing is, I don't think I've brought anything I could wear to a gig.

Rachel Well, fortunately, we're about the same size, aren't we? Let's go upstairs and look in my wardrobe. I'm sure we'll find something.

Chloe Oh, thanks, Rachel.

Rachel In fact I've got a top that will be absolutely perfect for you.

Tim What about tickets? Will we be able to get some?

Jordan I expect so. But I'd better ring just to make sure.

Rachel Come on, Chloe.

EXERCISE 5

Look at the text and complete these sentences in your own words.

1 Jordan is looking in the newspaper to see … .
2 Tim liked *Lord of the Rings*, but Chloe … .
3 If Chloe and Tim wanted to watch *The Fast and the Furious*, they could …, so they wouldn't need … .
4 Rachel and Jordan think the West End is too …, and anyway … in the evenings, so … .
5 Chloe doesn't … because she thinks … younger children.
6 They might … tomorrow if Mr and Mrs … give them … .
7 A band called … are doing … at a … in … .
8 Chloe hasn't got any … that she could …, but Rachel … her something.

EXERCISE 6

Find the right word for the explanation in brackets.

➡ The music was live. (played in front of an audience and not recorded)

1 The young people are sitting around and … . (talking in a friendly way)
2 This sweater looks the right … for you. (how big something is)
3 Some people think it's … to race horses. (wanting to hurt a person or an animal)
4 Jordan plays football for a … team. (in the area where he lives)
5 Rachel's … is very full. (cupboard for clothes)
6 The first … of the school play is on Monday. (doing something in front of an audience)
7 My cousin lives in a West London … . (part of a city outside the central area)
8 Chloe … her friends. (wishes she had the same opportunities as)

The Freestylers …

… and going out in the West End

EXERCISE 7

Sometimes you need to use exactly the right word, and sometimes you can be vague. For example, you can use 'stuff' or 'things' when it is clear from the situation what you mean. Choose the most likely meaning of 'stuff' or 'things' in these sentences.

1 The band play all kinds of stuff.
a) games b) music c) instruments
2 When I've put my things in the car, we can go. a) bags b) oil c) passengers
3 My sister likes soap operas and stuff like that.
a) activities b) books c) TV programmes
4 The Tourist Board sent us some stuff about things to do. a) information b) jokes c) stories
5 Unfortunately, there are lots of things I have to do this weekend. a) free time b) fun c) jobs

EXERCISE 8

05

Listening

Josh is inviting Hannah to go to a musical with him. Listen to their conversation.

This poster for the musical has eight mistakes in it. Write the words for a new poster with the correct details. Try to design a poster for the event.

EXERCISE 9

Look at these sentences with *had better* and *would rather.*

> **You'd better** get ready now, or we'll be late.
> **We'd better** not lose our way.
> **We'd rather** go into the West End than stay here in Highgate.
> **I'd rather not** see a horror film. I'd prefer to watch a comedy.
> **Would** you **rather** watch Brookside or EastEnders?
>
> → page 119

You'd better get ready means that you should get ready.
We'd rather go out means that we would prefer it (like it better) if we went out.

Complete the sentences using *had better* or *would rather*.

➽ I just want to dance. I'd rather go (I / go) to a disco than a concert.
1. I love reggae. ... (I / listen) to reggae than soul.
2. If we want to know what's on tonight, ... (we / buy) a paper.
3. My brother doesn't really like going out. ... (he / stay) at home and read a book.
4. ... (you / not / take) any drugs. They're bad for you.
5. Circuses are cruel. ... (I / not / go) to one if you don't mind.

EXERCISE 10

Look at these sentences.

> It might be **worth going** along to the gig.
> **What about doing** something different?
> It's **no use arguing**.
>
> → page 118

We can use an *ing*-form after *worth*, *what about* and *no use*.

Combine the two sentences in brackets. Use an *ing*-form.

➽ (Let's watch it. It might be worth it.)
The film won three Oscars. It might be worth watching.
1. (We'd have to get some tickets. What about it?)
It's the Liam Gallagher concert next month. What ...
2. (Don't buy them. They aren't worth it.)
These pop videos are very expensive. They ...
3. (Don't try to switch it on. It's no use.)
The computer isn't working. So it's ...
4. (We could watch a video. What about it?)
There's nothing on television. So ...
5. (Why ring them? It's no use.)
They never answer the phone at the box office. ...
6. (I'm going to read it. It might be worth it.)
This magazine has an article about pop festivals. ...

EXERCISE 11

When they were back home in Cornwall, Chloe and Tim both wrote to Mr and Mrs Webster. On the right is Chloe's letter.

Imagine you have just been to London for two weeks on an exchange visit. You stayed with Stephen and Joanna Draper and their children Rebecca and Luke at their house in Wood Green, north London. The Drapers showed you some of the sights of London and helped you with your English. Write a letter of thanks to Stephen and Joanna. In your letter you should mention two of the sightseeing trips that you enjoyed. (Choose two sights and invent the details.)

15 Larkhill Rd
Camborne
Cornwall

7 Sept

Dear Helen and Andrew,

Thank you very much for having us to stay in Highgate and looking after us and cooking all those wonderful meals. It was good to see you all, and we had a great time. The gig in Camden Town was excellent. It all makes Cornwall seem very boring.

Thank you also for taking us to Brick Lane on Sunday. I really enjoyed the festival, even though I was a bit tired after the gig.

We're looking forward to seeing you both and Jordan and Rachel when you come down here later in the year.

Many thanks again for a lovely weekend.

Love, Chloe

SITUATION 3

06

Hannah Where's Josh? We said half past seven, and it's quarter to eight now. He's going to miss the film.

Claire He might have forgotten all about it.

Dominic He could have got on the wrong bus.

Claire Or come on the wrong day. You know he's a pretty mixed-up kid. He might have come here the day before yesterday. Or maybe he'll be here the day after tomorrow.

Dominic Maybe he's changed his mind and decided not to come.

Hannah He wouldn't have done that. He's got a mobile. He would have rung. What could have happened, I wonder?

EXERCISE 12

Complete the conversation. Put in *might have*, *could have* or *would have* and a past participle.

Might have / could have / would have + past participle

Josh **might have forgotten** about the cinema.
Something awful **could have happened**.
He **wouldn't have left** home without his mobile phone. → page 102

Darren I can't find my ticket for the game on Saturday. I don't know what I could have done (could / do) with it. I thought I ... (might / leave) it on the kitchen table.

Mum When was this?

Darren Yesterday afternoon.

Mum I can't remember. But I don't think I ... (would / throw) it away.

Darren But I ... (might / not / leave) it there. I'm not sure.

Mum Well, think. Where ... you ... (would / put) it?

Darren In my desk, probably. But it isn't there. I expect I've lost it. It ... (could / fall) out of the back pocket of my trousers. Or someone ... (might / steal) it. They ... (could / take) it out of my pocket.

Mum That doesn't seem very likely.

Darren Or maybe I put it in a different pocket. Yes, I think I did. I'll just go and have a look.

Mum I think I ... (might / wash) your school trousers this morning.

Darren What! Oh no! Mum, tell me it isn't true.

EXERCISE 13

Look at the pictures and say what you think might or could have happened.

➽ That girl is very wet. She might have fallen in the swimming-pool.

SITUATION 4

07

Next week Josh and Hannah and their classmates are going on a trip to the Globe Theatre in London to see a Shakespeare play. In school they're reading about life in Shakespeare's time.

Life then was very different from what it is for young people today. Imagine if you had lived 400 years ago. Actually you would have been lucky to survive because more than half of all children died at birth. If you had become ill, you could easily have died. People didn't know much about hygiene in those days. Poor families lived in terrible conditions. If your family had been poor, you would have lived in a cold and dirty slum. If you'd lived in the country, your home would have been a one-room cottage. If you'd been rich, you would have gone to school and learned Latin. But instead of going to school, most children had to work as early as six years old. Parents and employers were very strict, and children were beaten for bad behaviour. You might have gone to the theatre if you'd lived in London, because there were several theatres in or near the city. If you'd lived outside London, you might have seen a play at your local market. The plays were performed by groups of actors who travelled around the country.

If … past perfect…, … would have / might have / could have …

If I had read the play first, I would have enjoyed it even more.
If you had been born 400 years ago, you might not have survived.
If Dominic hadn't been ill last week, he could have come on the trip.

… would have / might have / could have … if … past perfect …

I would have enjoyed the play even more if I had read it first.
Your home might have been a one-room cottage if you'd lived in Shakespeare's time.
We couldn't have got in if we hadn't had tickets.

→ page 101

EXERCISE 14

Complete these sentences about the Kelseys' visit to the Websters two weeks ago.

➽ Chloe didn't want to stay at home during the Easter holiday. If she had stayed at home she would have been bored.

1 The gig was in Camden Town. If it … in the West End, Chloe would … even more excited about it.

2 Chloe didn't bring her new dress. If she … it, she could … it to the gig.

3 Rachel and Chloe were the same size. If they … different sizes, Chloe couldn't … Rachel's clothes.

4 Someone mentioned the film *Lord of the Rings*. They might … it if most of them … it already.

5 Tim wanted to go to the circus. He could … if the others … to go with him.

6 It took ages to get home. If there … so much traffic on the roads, they would … home a lot quicker.

Shakespeare and the Globe

08

The new Globe was built to look just like the old one.

The old Globe Theatre

The Globe Theatre was built over 400 years ago. In those days the theatre was a new form of entertainment, and it was very popular. Thousands of people went to the theatres every afternoon. Even the Queen, Elizabeth I, enjoyed watching plays.

However, the Mayor of London didn't like theatres because people went there and enjoyed themselves instead of working. The theatres were set up just outside the city walls, and so outside the Mayor's control. If they had been inside the city, he would have closed them.

The first London theatre was started in 1576 by an actor-manager called James Burbage. His company was a great success. It included an actor and writer called William Shakespeare. In 1599 the company built a new theatre on the south bank of the River Thames. It was called the Globe. It was a round wooden building partly covered by a thatched roof and partly open to the sky. It held about 3,000 people.

The company performed plays by Shakespeare and other writers. Everything went well until one day in 1613. During a performance of 'Henry VIII', a cannon was fired, and the thatched roof caught fire. The whole building was burned to the ground. Fortunately everyone managed to get out, and no one was injured, although one man's trousers caught fire. It could have been serious if he hadn't managed to pour beer over the flames and put them out.

William Shakespeare (1564–1616)

William Shakespeare came from Stratford-on-Avon in the English Midlands. His father was quite an important person and became Mayor of Stratford in 1568. William went to school, where most of the time he learned Latin. When he was 18, he married Anne Hathaway. Anne, the daughter of a farmer, was eight years older than her husband. The couple had two daughters and a son.

We don't know many details about Shakespeare's life. He left his family in Stratford and went to London, where he joined a theatre company. For twenty years he wrote and acted. He wrote comedies, tragedies, history plays and poems.

Shakespeare had a successful career and made a lot of money. He had no financial problems. He bought a large house in Stratford, and in 1610 he went back to his home town. When he died, he left everything to his daughter Susanna's children. To his wife Anne he left only his 'second-best bed'. No one knows what this could have meant.

Hamlet

Shakespeare's famous tragedy 'Hamlet' was first performed in 1601 or 1602.

Hamlet is the Prince of Denmark. (The plot is complicated, so please concentrate.) Hamlet's father, also called Hamlet, was King of Denmark. He died not long ago, and his brother Claudius has taken the throne. (Claudius is the bad guy.) Uncle Claudius has also married Old Hamlet's widow, Gertrude. Young Hamlet sees a ghost that tells him Claudius killed Old Hamlet. The news is a big shock for the boy. His uncle killed his dad and married his mum! He ought to kill Claudius and get revenge for his father's murder, he thinks. And what about his mother? Does he love her or hate her? No wonder he seems such a crazy mixed-up kid. He even thinks about killing himself. 'To be or not to be: that is the question.'

Things go from bad to worse. Hamlet's girlfriend Ophelia is found dead in the river after Hamlet's behaviour has driven her crazy. Her brother Laertes is furious with Hamlet, and they have a big sword fight which kills both of them. As Hamlet is dying, he manages to kill Claudius. Queen Gertrude drinks a cup of poison that Claudius had prepared for Hamlet. So at the end more or less all the main characters are dead.

Well, I warned you it's a tragedy and not a comedy.

The new Globe Theatre

In 1949 an American actor called Sam Wanamaker was in London, and he decided to visit the site of the famous Globe Theatre. But the theatre had gone. It became Sam Wanamaker's dream to build a replica of the Globe Theatre. It was almost fifty years before the dream came true.

The new Globe was built in the 1990s not far from the old site. The idea was that the new theatre should be just like the old one, and traditional building methods were used.

Today you can go and watch a Shakespeare play at the Globe. If you don't want to buy an expensive ticket, you can stand near the stage. The performance continues even if it rains, so if you're standing, you might get wet.

Not everything is the same as it was in Shakespeare's day. In his time the audience would have eaten and drunk all through the performance, and they would have shouted comments at the actors, like a football crowd today. The theatre also held twice as many people as are allowed today – and they didn't wash very often.

Scenes from Hamlet at the Globe

The Globe on the River Thames

EXERCISE 15

Here are some answers to questions about Shakespeare and the Globe. What are the questions?

➡ She thought it was good entertainment.
What did the Queen think about the theatre?

1 Because outside the city they were safe from the Mayor. Why were the theatre ~~out~~ buildt outside the city walls.
2 He started the first London theatre.
3 Yes, but not completely. It was partly open to the sky.
4 The roof caught fire, and the theatre burned down.
5 Stratford-on-Avon.
6 They had two daughters and a son.
7 His daughter Susanna's children.
8 I think he hates her because she married the man who killed his father.
9 They all die.
10 He found nothing there.
11 No, it continues in all kinds of weather.
12 It was crowded, there was a lot of noise and there was probably a terrible smell.

2. What did James Burbage do?

3. Was the globe covered?

EXERCISE 16

Complete the explanations of words from the text. Put in the words *burn, copy, gun, ill, laugh, opinion, place, ready,* ~~*well*~~.

➡ If you are a success, you have done well.

1 A cannon is a big ... .
2 If something catches fire, it starts to ... .
3 A comedy is a play that makes you ... .
4 If you drink something with poison in it, you may become ... or die.
5 If you prepare a meal, you get it ... .
6 The site of an old building is the ... where it once was.
7 If you make a replica of something, you ... it exactly.
8 If you make a comment about something, you give your ... of it.

EXERCISE 17

Look at these sentences.

He's such a crazy mixed-up kid.
Shakespeare's father was quite an important person.
The performance starts in half an hour.

We usually put *a* or *an* after *such*, *quite* or *half* and not before it.

Put the words in brackets into the correct order.

➡ We ate half a box of chocolates (a / box / half / of / chocolates) while we were watching the play.

1 It took ... (a / long / quite / time) to complete the Globe project.
2 Hamlet is ... (a / complicated / play / such).
3 The man poured ... (a / beer / bottle / half / of) over his trousers.
4 It was ... (a / long / quite / way) to Stratford.
5 We were lucky it was ... (a / evening / such / warm).
6 Anne was ... (a / bit / older / quite) than William.

EXERCISE 18

Look at these three kinds of sentences with *if* again.

I'm going to stand out in the open. If it rains, I'll get wet. But I don't mind.
I'm not going to stand out in the open. If it rained, I'd get wet. I'd rather stay dry, thank you.
I stood out in the open. If it had rained, I'd have got wet. But luckily it didn't rain.

Compare the three sentences with *if*. Which one is about a past situation? Which one is about a real situation? Which one is about an imaginary situation?

Now look at this sentence.

At every performance there are people out in the open. If it rains, they get wet.

This sentence is about a situation that happens lots of times. In what way are the form and meaning different from the first sentence above?

Complete the sentences. Put in the correct form of the verb.

➡ The Shakespeare family were quite rich. If the family had been (be) poor, William wouldn't have gone to school.

1 The Globe? No, it isn't far. If you turn right here, you ... (see) it on your right.
2 In those days people didn't know much about hygiene. The smell wouldn't have been so bad if they ... (wash) more often.
3 It's no good. If I ... (ring) the box office, I just get a recorded message. It's the same every time.
4 You can't shout comments at the actors now. They ... (not be) very pleased if you did that.
5 You must take a trip to Stratford. If you ... (go) there, you'll be able to see a play at the Royal Shakespeare Theatre.
6 I've got a film of *Romeo and Juliet* on video. If you ... (want) to watch it, you'd enjoy it, I'm sure.
7 The Queen went to the theatre because she enjoyed watching plays. If she hadn't enjoyed them, she ... (not go).

Useful words and phrases

09

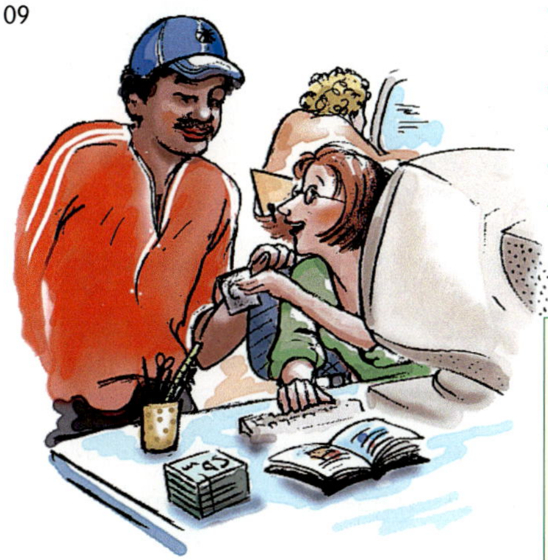

Julie You know we've been having problems with the computer?
Nick Uh-huh.
Julie Well, now it's really crashed, unfortunately.
Nick What? Oh no! That means we've lost all our project work.
Julie Don't worry. I saved it. It's all on this disk.
Nick Oh, well, that's a relief.

Look at how these expressions work in the conversation.

- **Uh-huh** shows that Nick understands or agrees.
- **Unfortunately** signals bad news.
- **Oh no!** expresses emotion.
- **Don't worry** reassures Nick.

EXERCISE 19

Say what work each expression in italics does. Choose from these answers in the box.

1 How do you like my new dress?
– *Wow!* It's great.
2 Let's hope we haven't missed the bus.
– *I'm afraid* we have. It's just going, look.
3 Is your dad giving you a lift?
– No, he can't drive a car. He's disabled, *you see*.
4 Are you tired? Do you want to sit down and have a rest?
– No, *it's OK*. I'm fine.
5 That boy's riding your bike, look.
– *Hey!* What are you doing?
6 We ought to leave now.
– *Right*. Let's go then.
7 What time should we meet?
– *Let me see*. Quarter past seven?
8 You take a ticket from the machine and then wait until your number is called.
– Oh, *I see*. Thank you.

- agreeing
- explaining
- expressing emotion
- getting someone's attention
- giving yourself time to think
- reassuring someone
- showing that you understand
- signalling bad news

EXERCISE 20

What's on TV tonight?

Work with a partner. Partner **B**: Please look at page 96.
Partner **A**: Ask partner **B** what the missing programmes are.

BBC 1	BBC 2	ITV	Channel 4	Channel 5
8.00 ?????	8.00 ?????	8.00 The Bill *Police drama series*	8.00 ?????	8.00 International Football *Germany v Argentina live from Stuttgart*
8.30 The Family *Situation comedy*	10.00 Teenagers *Documentary about young people and drugs*	9.00 ?????	9.00 The West Wing *Drama series about the US President*	10.00 ?????
9.00 ?????		9.30 Film: For a Few Dollars More - *Western with Clint Eastwood*	10.00 ?????	
10.00 News				

- Find out if there's a quiz show on.
- You don't want to watch the Western on ITV. Ask if there's another film on.
- Ask about documentaries.
- Find out if the football on Channel 5 is the only sport on.
- Find out what else is on tonight and what kind of programmes they are.

Bollywood

Bombay (or more correctly 'Mumbai') is the centre of the biggest and most successful film industry in the world. 'Bollywood' produces 800 films every year – far more than Hollywood ever did. A daily audience of 15 million Indians watch Bollywood films. These are people of different castes and religions, but they come together in their love of Indian musical cinema.

A Bollywood film is usually a simple story of romance. The films are very long – often as long as three and a half hours. There's lots of singing and dancing against a background of mountains. Sometimes the background and the costumes change in the middle of a song. One moment the characters are on a beach in Australia, and the next they're in front of a castle in Scotland. A Bollywood film creates an imaginary world; it isn't about real life. It's family entertainment with a boy-meets-girl plot.

Have you seen the film *Titanic* with Leo DiCaprio and Kate Winslet? This romance between a poor boy and a rich girl could almost be a Bollywood movie.

Bollywood is big in Britain too, where there are two million people of Asian origin. In Birmingham there's a 30-screen cinema with six screens that show only Bollywood films. It's mostly Asian people who watch the films, of course. But there are signs that Bollywood and Hollywood are coming closer together.

The Bollywood film *Lagaan* was a big success in Britain – and not only among Indians. The 'lagaan' was a tax on the Indians at the time of the British Empire. The film has Indian and British actors. It's about the poor people of an Indian village, their fight against the tax and the game of cricket they play against the British. There's romance too, of course. But the serious plot breaks with Bollywood traditions and makes it a more western kind of film.

British films have become more open to Asian influences. *East Is East* is a comedy about Asian families in the north of England. *Bend it Like Beckham* is about an Indian girl who wants to become a professional footballer but whose mother thinks it's more important to find a good husband. The British audiences for these films are not only people of Asian origin.

1 Look at these questions. In which paragraph of the text can you find the answer?

1 Is there a Hollywood film which shows Bollywood influences?
2 Where is Bollywood, and what does it do?
3 Are there British films with Asian themes?
4 What is a Bollywood film like?
5 What sport is the film *Lagaan* about?
6 Can you watch a Bollywood film in Britain?

2 Complete each sentence with a word from the text.

1 The story isn't complicated; it's really very s… .
2 If you look at this photo of me, you can just see the castle in the b… .
3 The actors in those Indian movies wear wonderful c… .
4 The film is about a family on holiday by the sea; when it starts, they're lying on the b… .
5 The events in the film didn't really happen; they're completely i… .
6 Could you explain the p… of Hamlet to us, please?
7 No one in the cinema could take their eyes from the s… .
8 The film is popular with people of Caribbean o… .

3 Complete these paragraphs. Use the words in brackets in their correct form and put in the right words.

Hollywood is a part of Los Angeles in California … the west coast of America. In the early years of the 20th …, film companies from New York … (begin) to come to Hollywood. California was … (sun), and people … able … make films outside. (… that time there were no lights strong … for inside scenes.) There were also different kinds of … (scene): the coast, the desert and the mountains, … example. Film directors … (can / shoot) scenes in all these places, and they … (not / have / travel) very far. Soon … were twenty film studios in the area.

The first sound film … (make) in 1927, and soon the musical … born. There were comedies, horror films and … (west). Hollywood became very good at … (make) … (success) films.

After the … (Two) World War, the film studios … (start) to move out, and after that many American films … (make) in other parts of the world. If you … (go) to Hollywood now, you can visit Universal Studios, the world's … (large) film studio and theme park.

4 Translate this information about Mumbai to go in a guide for German tourists.

Think of Mumbai / Bombay and you think of Bollywood films. But Mumbai is much more than that. It's a city of 18 million people and a centre of industry. It has one of the great harbours of the world. Unfortunately it also has some of the largest slums in Asia.

Mumbai is actually an island, but there are bridges to the mainland. Most tourists stay at the southern end of the island, where there are a number of hotels. The main street of this area is full of street sellers, shops and cafés. North of here is the business district. It is known as The Fort because there was once a British fort here.

If you'd like to walk along the shore, go to Marine Drive. It's also a good place to watch a sunset. From here you can see Malabar Hill. The expensive apartment houses on the hill have a wonderful view over the water.

The best time to visit Mumbai is between September and April, when it is cooler and drier. You could go in October or November for Diwali (the festival of light) and the fireworks.

5 A radio reporter is interviewing an Indian woman called Mrs Chatterjee. They are at Dunure Castle in the south-west of Scotland. Listen to the interview.

10-12

Part 1 (10)

Answer the questions.

1 Mrs Chatterjee is in Scotland with a group of people from India. Why have they come to Britain?
2 Which film was Dunure Castle in?

Part 2 (11)

Which six of these places does Mrs Chatterjee mention? Write them in your exercise book.

Edinburgh • Glasgow • Manchester • Blenheim Palace • Buckingham Palace • Tintagel Castle • Eilean Donan Castle • Windsor Castle • The Tower of London • Wales

Part 3 (12)

Choose the right answer.

1 Mrs Chatterjee is away for …
a) two weeks. b) three weeks. c) four weeks.
2 Mr Chatterjee is a …
a) tourist guide. b) film actor. c) factory manager.
3 The Chatterjees live in …
a) Mumbai. b) Hyderabad. c) Madras.

Adrian's little sister

This is from the diary of 15-year-old Adrian Mole. He lives with his mother in the English Midlands. His mother is expecting a baby, a first brother or sister for Adrian. His parents separated not long ago.

When I got home from school my mother's little suitcase was missing from the hall. She was nowhere in the house, but I found a note on the biscuit tin. It said:

I am in the labour ward of the Royal Hospital. Call a taxi. £10 note at the bottom of the spaghetti jar. Don't worry.
Love, Mum
PS Dog at Mrs Singh's.

Her writing looked very untidy.

The taxi ride was a nightmare. I was trying to get my hand free of the spaghetti jar all the way. The taxi driver said, 'You should have turned the jar upside down, you stupid idiot.' He parked outside the entrance to the hospital and looked at my hand in the jar in a bored kind of way. He said, 'You'll have to pay for the time I'm waiting here.' A hundred years passed, then he said, 'And I can't change a ten-pound note either.' I was almost crying when at last I managed to pull my hand free. I gave the taxi driver the ten pounds and ran into the hospital. Took the lift to 'Labour Ward'.

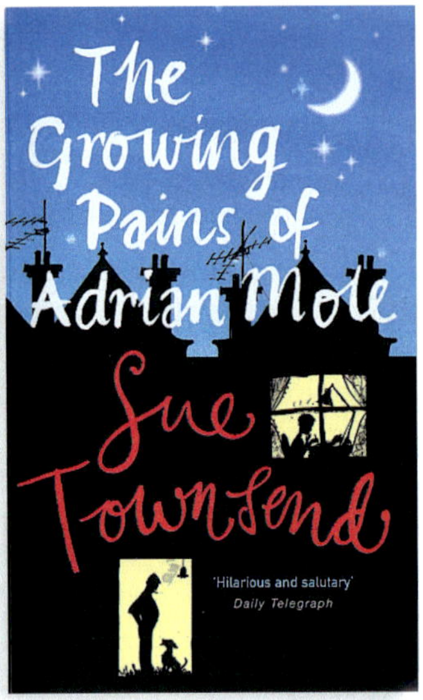

I came out into another world. It looked like the space control centre at Houston.
A technician asked, 'Who are you?'
I said, 'I'm Adrian Mole.'
'And you've got permission to visit the labour ward?'
'Yes,' I said. (Why did I say yes? Why?)
'Room 13.'

I pushed the door of Room 13 open and saw my mother lying on a high bed reading a book. She looked pleased to see me and then asked why I'd brought the spaghetti jar into the hospital. Then she screwed her face up and started singing.
After a bit she stopped singing and looked normal. She even laughed when I told her about the horrible taxi driver.

A black nurse came in and said,
'Are you all right, honey?'
My mother said, 'Yes. This is Adrian.'
After about half an hour my mother was singing more and talking less. She held my hand. The nurse came back in and to my relief told me to go out. But my mother wouldn't let go of my hand.
The pains started coming every minute, and my mother went crazy, and a lot of people ran in and started telling her to push. I sat in a far corner at the head end of my mother and tried not to look at the other end where doctors and nurses were doing something with metal things. My mother was panting. Soon everyone was shouting, 'Push, Mrs Mole, push!' 'Harder,' they shouted. My mother went crazy again, and the doctor said, 'I can see the baby's head!'
I tried to escape then, but my mother said, 'Where's Adrian? I want Adrian.'
Soon my mother had another crazy moment: then the doctors and nurses gave a kind of loud sigh, and I looked up and saw a skinny purple thing hanging upside down.
'It's a lovely little girl, Mrs Mole,' the doctor said.
The baby started crying in a bad-tempered way and she was put on my mother's flatter belly. My mother looked at her as if she was a beautiful piece of jewellery or something. She said, 'Say hello to your sister.'
The doctor stared at me and said, 'Aren't you Mr Mole, the baby's father?'
I said, 'No, I'm Master Mole, the baby's brother.'
'Then you've broken every rule in this hospital,' he said. 'I must ask you to leave. You could have all kinds of children's diseases.'
I went home and went to bed. It was only 7.30 but for some reason I was very tired. The phone woke me up at 8.15. It was my father gibbering about having a girl. He wanted to know every detail about her. I said she was like him. Not much hair and bad-tempered.

adapted from *The Growing Pains of Adrian Mole* by Sue Townsend

UNIT 2

LOOKING AHEAD

WORDS AND PICTURES

13 Here are some job advertisements in an English newspaper, The Milchester Express, dated 26 May.

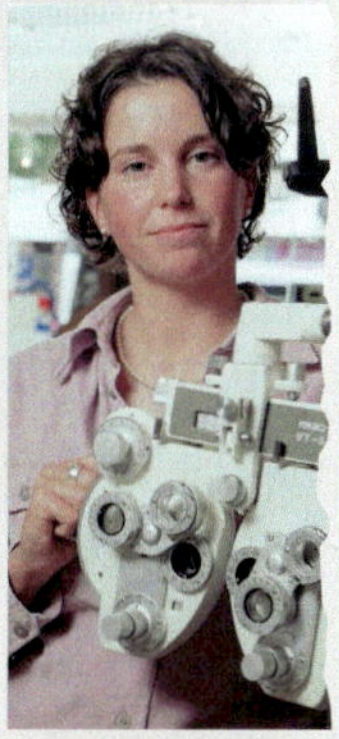

WEB DESIGNERS
are required to join our successful team. Full-time or part-time. Put yourself a step ahead financially. Call Interworld Communications on 01235 778413.

ENGINEERING TECHNICIAN
required by a mobile phone company to design and test telephone software. Must have a Higher National Diploma in electronic engineering or computer science. We are looking for a team player with an eye for detail. Jobwise Recruitment Agency 0450 33791

EXCITING OPPORTUNITY
to become an auto mechanic apprentice. Training on the job. Interested? Phone Paul Weeks on 01382 201470.

SALES ASSISTANT
We need a sales assistant at our city centre store to sell and help deliver TV and video equipment. We are looking for a smart, friendly person. Some Saturday work will be necessary. For details call Mike Dobson on Milchester 439216.

WORLDWIDE TRAVEL
requires an assistant to work in our Milchester travel agency. Excellent office communication skills are necessary as you will work with customers. Training will be given. 0370 233233

COMPUTER EXPERT
needed by Milchester Home Stores to work in our busy sales office. Experience with office software would be an advantage. 827439

SHIPPING ASSISTANT
Are you interested in joining our busy export team? We export shoes to many different countries, and your job will be to arrange shipping and to enter details into our computer. Full training will be given. A foreign language could be an advantage. Please send your CV to Brian Long, Export Department, Chic Shoes, Milchester MR5 6RS.

VETERINARY NURSE
wanted to work with small animals. Training can be given. Please apply to Kate Holmes at the Milchester Veterinary Centre 421778.

NURSERY ASSISTANT
needed for our Milchester nursery to work with 1–3 year olds. 8.45 am to 5.15 pm. 0370 722403

SITUATION 1

14

Darren is talking to one of his teachers about what he should do next year.

Darren I want to do electrical engineering.

Mr Taylor Well, you've done well in your GCSE exams, Darren. You can apply to do a course at the College of Further Education and get a qualification. I think that's what you should do. After a two-year course in electrical engineering, you'll be able to work as a technician.

Later, at home …

Mum Did you have your interview with Mr Taylor today?

Darren Yes, I told him I wanted to do electrical engineering. He said I'd done well in my GCSEs, and I could apply to do a course at the college. He thought that was what I should do. After a two-year course I would be able to work as a technician.

Reporting statements → page 102-104

Direct speech	Reported speech
'I want to do engineering.'	Darren **said** he **wanted** to do engineering.
'I don't know what I'm going to do next.'	Hannah **answered** that she **didn't know** what she **was** going to do next.
'Your results are excellent.'	The teacher **told** Emily that her results **were** excellent.
'You've done very well.'	She **told** me I**'d done** very well.
'Mrs Taylor gave me some advice.'	Darren **told** his mum that Mrs Taylor **had given** him some advice.
'You'll enjoy the course.'	The teacher **said** Adam **would enjoy** the course.

EXERCISE 1

Some pupils have had interviews with teachers about their careers. Afterwards they told their parents about the interviews. How did they report what was said?

- ➡ *James* Maths is my best subject.
  I said that maths was my best subject.
- ➡ *Mr Crosby* You have to start thinking about your future.
  Mr Crosby said I had to start thinking about my future.

1. *Mrs Hain* You need to take your exams again.
   Mrs Hay said I …
2. *Rebecca* I haven't thought much about a career.
   I said I …
3. *Mrs Snow* You won't have to pay for the course.
4. *Mr Pike* There's an Open Evening at the college next week.
5. *Jessica* I want to do modern languages.
6. *Mr Gilbert* You could do a course in business.
7. *Amy* I'm interested in communication technology.
8. *Joseph* I haven't got any idea what I should do next.
9. *Matthew* I don't think I did very well in my exams.
10. *Mrs Green* You will find it easier to get a job if you have a qualification.

EXERCISE 2

Read what Natalie and Sarah said to each other. Then work in pairs. Act out the conversation.

Natalie mentioned to Sarah that she was looking for a spare-time job. Sarah said that she worked at Silbury's Supermarket on Saturdays. She added that they needed people there. She thought that Natalie should apply. Maybe they could work together. Everyone was nice and friendly. Sarah said she enjoyed it at Silbury's. Natalie said that she had seen Sarah in there once or twice. But she really wanted something better than a supermarket job. Sarah answered that she thought Natalie was a real snob. She wouldn't find anything better because she didn't have any qualifications.

Begin like this.

Natalie *I'm looking for ...*

EXERCISE 3

Complete the sentences with *here, the day before, then, the next day, this, today.*

1 On Tuesday Ben said to Hannah, 'Mr Taylor is going to give us a test on Friday.' After the lesson on Friday, Hannah said to Ben, 'You said Mr Taylor was going to give us a test ..., but he didn't. Why did you say that?'

2 When Emma saw Oliver last week, he could hardly walk. 'I hurt my leg yesterday,' he explained. Today Emma's mum mentioned Oliver, and Emma remembered what he had told her. 'When I saw him last week, he told me he had hurt his leg ...,' she said to her mum.

3 Kirsty wanted to speak to Mr Pike at lunch time yesterday, but he said, 'I'm sorry. I can't talk to you just now, Kirsty.' Later in the day Kirsty told her parents, 'I saw Mr Pike at lunch time, but he said he couldn't talk to me just ... .'

4 Some time ago Tom lent Daniel some money. One day last week Daniel told Tom, 'I'll pay you back the money tomorrow.' Today Tom said to him, 'Where's my money? You told me last week you would pay it back ..., but you didn't.'

5 At school Kate said to Donna, 'Everyone has decided to meet at the cinema at eight o'clock tomorrow evening.' The next day, as they were walking past the cinema on their way home, Donna said to Tessa, 'Kate told me yesterday that everyone has decided to meet ... at eight o'clock ... evening.'

Careers abroad

15 This is Trevor from Radio Liffey Live again with a charming young lady at my side. Melanie Häfner, hello and welcome to my show Careers Abroad.

Hello, Trevor. Nice to meet you.

Well, Melanie, you've been working at a bank in Dublin for a year and a half, but you're from Germany, aren't you?

Yes, I'm from a village near Bayreuth in northern Bavaria.

Bavaria, yeah, I've heard about the Oktoberfest – but we're discussing careers, aren't we? Tell us, why did you choose to work in Ireland?

Well, a friend of mine was working in Dublin already and she said it had a lively atmosphere, and she told me about the advantages of working abroad. She suggested Ireland. She said there were lots of nice people here, and it would be easy to make friends.

Well, I hope our city is friendly to foreigners. Err, did you study business in Germany?

Well, I did banking. I went to the Johannes-Kepler-Realschule in Bayreuth, and then I went to a College of Further Education for two years. Then I worked at a bank and I finished my training there and got a further qualification. Someone told me it would be useful for my career if I spent a year abroad to improve my English. And I thought it was a good idea.

Your English is very good, Melanie.

Oh, thank you. I did a language course in London. I got a scholarship from the Carl Duisberg Gesellschaft in Cologne.

Oh, that was lucky.

And now I'm attending classes in English because I want to get another qualification, the Cambridge First Certificate.

I see, and how did you get the job in Dublin?

That was through an Irish recruitment agency that I applied to. They offered me this job at the bank – HVB Ireland.

Tell me, Melanie, what do you do at the bank?

Oh, I work in the credit administration department.

And is your job much different from at home?

Well, there's the whole world in my department – colleagues from the USA, France and Austria – so at first it was quite difficult to get to know the local Irish people!

Oh, don't you go out to the pub with Irish people?

Well, I would do if I liked beer – but I'm afraid too much beer doesn't agree with me.

OK, time for some music on Liffey Live and especially for the young lady at my side, it's U2 …

TEXT 1

Every year more than 100,000 Germans leave home to work abroad; most of them choose the USA, Poland or Spain. Before you go, you'll have to find a new job and – if your company does not work internationally – an employer. Ask around or look at job sites on the internet or the magazine 'Markt + Chance', where Melanie found a company for her training and practical work. If you decide to live and work outside the EU, you'll have to apply for a visa and a green card. But it's well worth it: your international work experience should look good on your CV and help you in your career.

And now tell us, Melanie from Bavaria, have there been any problems with living in Ireland?

Well, I share a house with a German girl and two Dutch boys. They're very nice people, but I must say all these annoying discussions about loud music, cleaning the bathroom and paying the telephone bill are getting on my nerves. And I'm missing my boyfriend and my family because there are so many new things I'd love to tell them about. And of course, there are ups and downs every day.

Well, nothing's perfect, is it? What things about Dublin and Ireland will you miss when you're back in Germany?

Oh, there are so many things I could mention. … First of all, I'll miss the entertainment Dublin offers, so when I get back to Germany, I'll probably move to a big city. Dublin has a great atmosphere, and there are so many exciting events, and I enjoy going to the beach in the evenings. And I'll miss my new friends!

And there's another thing I'd like to know: Would you go abroad again?

Yes, I certainly would! It's a great challenge. You have to speak a foreign language, experience a new way of life and get used to new working conditions. One of my friends from another bank has just moved to Australia – so you see, once you've been bitten by the bug of working abroad …

What advice would you give to somebody who plans to go abroad?

Try to get a scholarship because the money will be useful. If you're willing to start on a new adventure, go ahead and you won't regret it.

Well, thanks for the interview, Melanie, and we all hope you enjoy the rest of your stay in our friendly city.

EXERCISE 4

Answer the questions.

1 Where is Melanie working, and how long has she been there?
2 How did she hear that Dublin is a good place to go to?
3 What did Melanie study after she left school?
4 How did she get the job in Dublin?
5 What department does she work in at the bank?
6 Why doesn't Melanie go to the pub?
7 What does she like doing in her spare time in Dublin?
8 What does she think about the experience of working abroad. Does she regret it?

EXERCISE 5

Use the following notes and write a paragraph about Melanie Häfner.

- where from?
- place of work
- colleagues
- lives where?
- spare time
- enjoying herself?
- working abroad – her opinion

EXERCISE 6

How might Melanie finish the sentences?

➡ If I do well in English, I'll get my certificate.

1 I would go to the pub if …
2 It would make me ill if …
3 Life would be so much nicer if my boyfriend …
4 If they hadn't given me a scholarship, …
5 If anyone asks my advice about working abroad, …

EXERCISE 7

Complete these sentences. All the words are from the text and have something to do with education and jobs.

- ➡ You need to do six months training before you can do the job.
1. I'm going to take a course at a College of … Education.
2. The job sounds interesting. Are you going to … for it?
3. You should do a course to … your computer skills.
4. At the end of the course you get a … to say that you've completed it.
5. I got the job through a recruitment … .
6. My friend works in the company's export … .
7. I'm enjoying the job, and my new … are all very friendly.
8. I haven't worked in a shop before, and they want someone with sales … .

EXERCISE 8

Look at the idioms and find the right explanation. But be careful, there are more explanations than you need.

➡ 'I'm getting to know the place' means that I'm learning to find my way around.

I'm getting to know the place.
There are ups and downs.
It's getting on my nerves.
I'll get used to it.
It doesn't agree with me.
I've been bitten by the bug.

I've been bitten by the bug!*

*Käfer, Wanze

It makes me ill.
It's becoming annoying.
It won't always seem strange to me.
I'm learning to find my way around.
I'll succeed in the end.
I've become very interested.
Good and bad things happen.
I feel very happy.

EXERCISE 9

16-17

Listening

Dirk Walther comes from Bavaria. He is a hairdresser and make-up artist. A reporter is interviewing him about his career. Listen to the interview.

Part 1 (16)

Match Dirk's actions with the places.

1	Kulmbach	a)	first trained as a hairdresser
2	Bayreuth	b)	now lives
3	Berlin	c)	first worked with film actors
4	Munich	d)	attended school
5	Brixton	e)	now works
6	Covent Garden	f)	did some further training

➡ 1d) Dirk attended school in Kulmbach.

Part 2 (17)

Answer the questions.

1. What kind of people does Dirk sometimes go on tour with?
2. Dirk travelled with Victoria Beckham. Who else went to Rome, Paris and Scandinavia?
3. What did Dirk do to Victoria's hair?
4. Who came to see Dirk in Weimar?
5. Whose idea was the visit?

EXERCISE 10

Sophie Bates, 18, is applying for a job as a web designer.

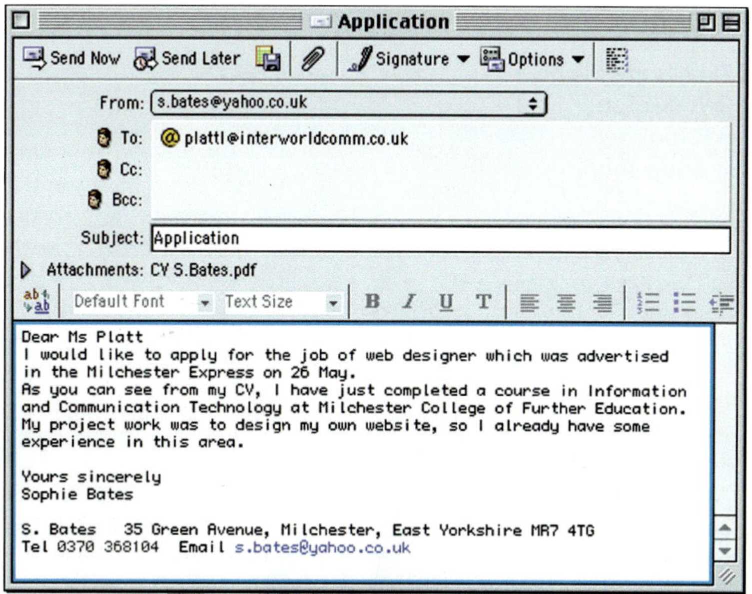
Application

Send Now | Send Later | Signature | Options

From: s.bates@yahoo.co.uk

To: plattl@interworldcomm.co.uk

Cc:

Bcc:

Subject: Application

Attachments: CV S.Bates.pdf

Dear Ms Platt
I would like to apply for the job of web designer which was advertised in the Milchester Express on 26 May.
As you can see from my CV, I have just completed a course in Information and Communication Technology at Milchester College of Further Education.
My project work was to design my own website, so I already have some experience in this area.

Yours sincerely
Sophie Bates

S. Bates 35 Green Avenue, Milchester, East Yorkshire MR7 4TG
Tel 0370 368104 Email s.bates@yahoo.co.uk

Write a similar e-mail to ask for details of one of the jobs on page 21. If you don't know the name of the person you are writing to, begin the e-mail 'Dear Sir or Madam' and end with 'Yours faithfully' and your name.

EXERCISE 11

This is Sophie's CV. Read it and then write your own CV.

CURRICULUM VITAE

Name	Sophie Bates
Address	35 Green Avenue, Milchester East Yorkshire MR7 4TG
Telephone	0370 368104
Nationality	British
Date of birth	20 May 1985
Marital status	Single
Education/Qualifications	
2002 – present	Milchester College of Further Education Expect to obtain Advanced Vocational Certificate of Education in Information Technology
1996 – 2002	King Alfred School, Milchester GCSEs in maths, computer studies, science, English, English literature, Spanish, geography
Spare-time jobs	
07/03 – 12/03	Office work at Chic Shoes
08/02 – 06/03	Waitress at Grand Hotel, Milchester.
Interests	Computers, basketball (school team), music, drama club

EXERCISE 12

Make a mind map about jobs. Find as many words as you can.

SITUATION 2

18

Mark is at college. He'll need to start looking for a job soon.

Reporting orders and requests → page 105

Direct speech	Reported speech
'You should write your answers on a piece of paper.'	The teacher told everyone to write their answers on a piece of paper.
'Don't look at your textbooks.'	He told us not to look at our textbooks.
'Can you lend me a pen, please?'	He asked Lucy to lend him a pen.
'It would be great if you didn't give us any extra work.'	We asked the teacher not to give us any extra work.
'The best thing to do is read all the questions first.	He advised us to read all the questions first.

EXERCISE 13

Mr Johnson has given advice to lots of college students about job interviews. What did he tell them? Use the verb in brackets to report what he said.

- 'You should wear something smart, Gemma.' (tell)
  He told Gemma to wear something smart.
- 'Please don't arrive late, James.' (ask)
  He asked James not to arrive late.

1 'It's best to be confident, Jody.' (tell)
2 'Think of one or two questions to ask, Emily.' (tell)
3 'Telling lies wouldn't be a good idea, Adam.' (advise)
4 'It's important to speak clearly, Charlotte.' (tell)
5 'It's no use being nervous, Lisa.' (tell)
6 'Could you come and tell me all about it afterwards, please, Mark?' (ask)
7 'Can you find out something about the company, Daniel?' (ask)
8 'You should look the interviewer in the eye, Nick.' (advise)
9 'Don't try to make jokes in the interview, Amy.' (advise)

SITUATION 3

19 A reporter is asking college students about their career plans.

Reporter What are you studying, Amber?
Amber I'm doing travel and tourism.
Reporter And have you applied for any jobs?
Amber Yes, I've applied for jobs in the travel industry, but I haven't been successful yet.
Reporter And what about you, Tyler? What kind of job do you want?
Tyler I'm doing business.
Reporter I see. And will the qualification be useful to you in your career?
Tyler Yes, I'm sure it will.

Later Amber told her mum about the reporter.

Amber Tyler and I were interviewed by a reporter today. He asked me what I was studying and if I'd applied for any jobs.
Mum A newspaper reporter?
Amber Yes, from the local paper. He's writing an article about careers.
Mum Well, we'll have to look out for it.
Amber Tyler was there too. The reporter asked him what kind of job he wanted. And he wanted to know whether his business qualification would be useful.

Reporting questions → page 105

Direct speech	Reported speech
How far have you got with your project work?	Ben's tutor **asked** him **how far** he **had** got with his project work.
'When will it be finished?'	He **wondered when** it **would** be finished.
'Is there a problem?'	He **wanted to know if / whether** there **was** a problem.

EXERCISE 14

Natalie had an interview for a job as a veterinary nurse. She was interviewed by a woman. Here are the questions she asked Natalie.

- ➡ Are you looking for a full-time job?
- ➡ What qualifications have you got?
1 Why did you drop out of college?
2 Have you had any experience with animals?
3 What pets have you had?
4 How far away do you live?
5 Can you drive?
6 Are you willing to work on Saturdays?
7 Why do you want the job?
8 Do you want to ask me any questions?

When Natalie got home, she told her parents about the interview and about the questions she had to answer. What did she say? Use *asked* or *wanted to know*.

- ➡ She asked if I was looking for a full-time job.
- ➡ She wanted to know what qualifications I had.

The richest man in the world

20

Bill Gates in the 1980s

Bill Gates is the most famous and most successful business person in the world. He started a computer software company and conquered the globe.

Bill grew up in Seattle, in Washington state. His father was a lawyer. As a teenager, Bill didn't spend a lot of time wondering what kind of career he was going to have. He was simply crazy about computers and computer programs. He wrote his first program when he was 13. At that time the only computers were large office machines, and most people had never seen one. In 1975, when Bill was 19, he heard about a new and much smaller computer called the Altair 8800. It was made by a company in New Mexico called MITS. It was a very primitive machine, and there was no software, so Bill and his friend, Paul Allen, decided to write a program for it. They used an existing computer language called BASIC. Paul phoned MITS boss Ed Roberts and told him that he and Bill had written the program, and he asked if he could come and show it to him. Paul then flew to New Mexico. (Between them, Bill and Paul had only enough money for one ticket.) Ed and his colleagues liked the program, and they bought it. Bill and Paul decided to set up a company – let's call it MS. Soon Bill dropped out of college to concentrate on the software business.

The big break came in 1980. At this time the leader in the computer world was an American company that made business machines. This company had decided to produce its first personal computer, and it asked Bill and Paul to create the operating system for it. The system was called MS-DOS. The company didn't pay much for it, but MS kept the right to sell the software to other computer companies. If they hadn't kept this right, the Bill Gates story would have been very different.

Soon the market for PCs started to grow very quickly. Other producers needed an operating system, and they chose the one that was already used in existing machines. Soon most PCs were sold with MS software already in them. The operating system was updated, and it became the computer user's window on the world. Its name was a household word.

The Gates' family house on the shore of Lake Washington, Seattle

Gates became fantastically rich. He married a woman who worked in his company, and they went to live in a $97 million hi-tech house on the shore of Lake Washington near Seattle. If you were a guest of the Gates family, electronic magic would do everything for you. It would turn the lights on and off as you entered or left a room. It would put your favourite pictures on the walls, and your favourite music would follow you through the house.

Gates's tactic was to make sure that his soft-ware was on your computer from the start so that none of his competitors had a chance. In this way MS won 90 per cent of the PC market.

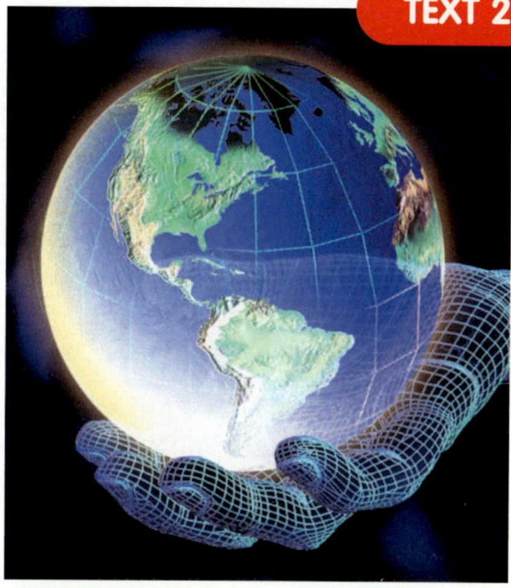

When the internet became popular in the 1990s, people needed software to use it. MS wasn't quick enough to see the importance of the internet, and one of its competitors had already produced some successful software. Gates decided to develop his own internet browser and then give it away with the operating system to stop people buying the rival browser. In 1998 the US government began a court action against MS because they didn't think that this tactic was fair.

In the world of Bill Gates there will be a computer in every home. The whole world will be connected through instant communication and instantly available information. It will be a global world.

The global world is where German kids spend their euros in American fast food places and talk to their friends on mobile phones made in Finland. It is a world of big companies, especially American ones. It's a place where everything moves around freely – people, money, jobs and information. And our journey to this world is called 'globalization'.

EXERCISE 15

Write a sentence to explain each of these.

➠ Seattle
Seattle is a city in Washington state.

1 The Altair 8800 was …
2 MITS was …
3 Paul Allen …
4 BASIC …
5 MS-DOS …
6 A PC …

EXERCISE 16

Put the sentences in the right order and tell the story of Bill Gates.

A Bill and his friend wrote a program for it and sold it to the company that produced the computer.
B But then he made a mistake.
C During his school days, Bill Gates developed an interest in computers.
D He was slow to develop software for the internet.
E This business tactic caused a few problems between the company and the government.
F This meant that Gates became very rich, and his company was very successful.
G When other companies started to produce PCs, Gates was able to sell them his system, and soon almost everyone was using it.
H While he was at college, the first personal computer came on the market.
I But their big break came when they sold a PC operating system to a big company.
J In the end he gave his browser away, just to stop people buying a competitor's product.

Begin like this. *During his school days, Bill Gates …*

EXERCISE 17

Imagine that in 1998 a reporter managed to ask Bill Gates a few questions about the court action against his company. Here is the conversation.

Reporter Mr Gates, do you agree that you have used unfair tactics?
Bill Gates No, I certainly don't agree.
Reporter What do you think will happen?
Bill Gates I'm confident we will win.
Reporter Do you have any comments to make?
Bill Gates No, I don't. And please don't put words into my mouth that I haven't said.
Reporter Is it the end for your company?
Bill Gates It's just the beginning.

The reporter wrote about his short meeting with Bill Gates. Complete the paragraph.

Luckily I managed to ask Mr Gates a few quick questions. First I asked him if he agreed that … . He said he … . Then I asked …

EXERCISE 18

In reported speech we often use *say*, *tell* or *ask*, but there are other verbs we can use to report what people have said. Put in the simple past tense of the verbs *admit, agree, answer, complain, explain, invite, offer, ~~suggest~~*.

➡ Bill suggested that Paul should fly to New Mexico.
1 Bill … to Paul that he hadn't yet started work on the program.
2 Paul … all Ed's questions about the software.
3 Bill and Paul … that they would start their own software company together.
4 Bill … that people were copying the software and not paying for it.
5 The company … its customers a free browser if they bought its software.
6 The company had to … to the government the reasons for its actions.
7 Bill … a group of top business people to stay at his house.

EXERCISE 20

Talking about jobs

Work with a partner.

Partner **B**: Please look at page 96.

Partner **A**: You are at the Job Centre, and you have just seen an advertisement for a job in telesales. You know that your English friend is looking for a job like that and might be interested. Ring your friend with news of the job. Answer his / her questions about it.

EXERCISE 19

I don't know, but I can find out.
Can you turn on the radio, please?
I'm searching for websites that tell you about job opportunities.
How do you get on with your new colleagues?

Put in the verbs *~~click on~~, concentrate on, ~~drop out of~~, ~~hurry up~~, ~~look for~~, look forward to, ~~pick up~~, ~~print out~~, ~~set up~~, ~~switch off~~, ~~wake up~~*. Use the correct form.

➡ I'm sure I switched off the computer before I left the house.
➡ There's a disk on the floor. I'll just pick it up.
1 The two young men agreed to … a computer software company.
2 I was having a very strange dream about the internet when I … this morning.
3 I'm … the CD. I can't find it anywhere.
4 I'm really … using the new operating system. I can't wait to try it.
5 This information I've got on the screen looks useful. Maybe I can … it … .
6 Let's hope this software will … and download a bit quicker.
7 Now you … the word 'OK' with the mouse.
8 Bill … college so that he could … his work for the new company.

AN OPPORTUNITY IN TELESALES

FONEBIZ

Fonebiz would like to invite you to join our team of busy telesales people at our modern offices in Milchester.

You will sell mobile phones and phone cards to personal and business users. This is a good opportunity to do exciting and interesting work and to earn good money. This job could start you on a great career path.

Good communication skills are important. Experience would be an advantage, but training is available. The main thing is that you must want to succeed. You will have to work some Saturdays and evenings.

Call Tony on Milchester 372504 for an interview.

Opinions

21

Simon I think we should have computers instead of teachers. We don't need teachers. We don't need classrooms either. We could learn at home.

Gemma I agree. Computers know more than teachers.

Jamie Exactly. Look at our business studies teacher. She couldn't answer my question today.

Louise Well, I think it's a bad idea. I like being at school with my friends. And I like having Mr Khan for maths. He's much nicer than a computer.

Expressing an opinion
- I think / I believe Germany will win the next World Cup.
- I don't think England will win.
- In my opinion testing products on animals is wrong.

Agreeing
- Yes, we should. / Yes, that's right. / Yes, I agree with you.
- Exactly. / Absolutely.

Disagreeing

– very direct
- No, we shouldn't. It's a stupid idea.
- Oh, rubbish. You don't know what you're talking about.
- I don't agree. My experience has been very different.

– more polite
- But don't you think there are some advantages?
- Well, I think it's a great show.
- On the other hand people shouldn't break the law, should they?
- Well, that's a matter of opinion, isn't it?

EXERCISE 21

You have read about globalization in Text 2. Now look at these arguments for and against globalization.

Yes to globalization	No to globalization
Globalization is making people better off. Living standards are improving.	Globalization means that a few people get very rich, but poor people stay poor.
Free trade worldwide is good for all of us. We can sell to other countries and enjoy their products.	Rich countries like those in the EU have set up trade barriers so that poor countries can't compete.
The big global companies are the successful ones. They can produce things efficiently.	There is too much power in the hands of big companies. They can move their factories to places where people will work for very little money.
The world is getting smaller. The internet is bringing us all together. Communication is a good thing.	The internet is an American toy. Communication is not truly worldwide. Half the people of Africa have never even made a single phone call in their lives.

Now say if these sentences are true, false or a matter of opinion.

1 The world is becoming a better place.
2 Trade between two countries can be good for both of them.
3 There are no more poor people in the world today.
4 International companies can sometimes move their offices from one country to another.
5 Big companies are more efficient than small ones.
6 On the internet or telephone you can communicate quickly with someone a long distance away.
7 Most Africans phone their friends every day.

EXERCISE 22

Work with a partner. Look at the arguments about globalization and write four sentences giving your own opinions. Then express each of these opinions to your partner and see if he / she disagrees.

The internet

A computer from the early 1960s

The internet became popular in the 1990s, but the story began thirty years before that, back in the days of the Cold War between the United States and the Soviet Union.

The internet grew out of the work of US universities on government military projects. Scientists in different parts of the country were working on these projects on their huge computers. They could talk to each other on the telephone and post information to each other, but this wasn't very efficient. Someone realized that it might be possible to connect the computers over the phone line so that information could be sent quickly from one computer to another. In 1969 the first ever computer network was set up between two universities in California – Stanford University and the University of California in Los Angeles. Soon scientists in other places wanted to join the network, and they were able to share information much more easily than before. They also started using the network to send messages to each other, something that was soon known as e-mail.

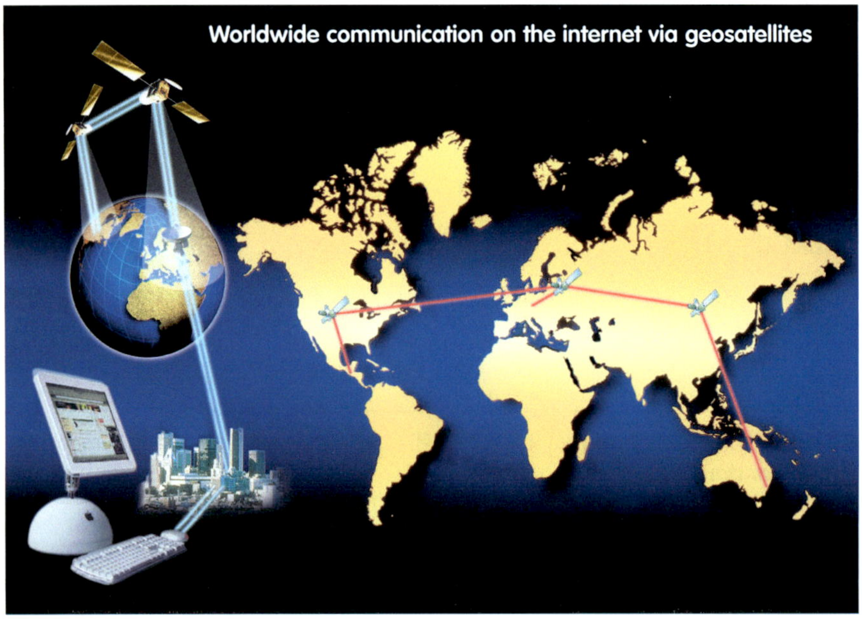

Worldwide communication on the internet via geosatellites

There were more developments. The network grew, and other networks were formed. Then they were joined together in a network of networks – the internet. The personal computer arrived. The worldwide web was invented in 1991, so now information could be put on websites and read by computer users. New software was produced to make the internet easier to use. Now everyone could use the internet. You could send e-mails to friends and colleagues, visit chat rooms, play games or look round a huge electronic library of words, pictures and sounds. You could also buy things on the internet, and internet sales became big business.

We can use the internet in all kinds of ways. It's true that hackers or criminals can sometimes find a way into other people's computers and destroy their files or steal money. But the internet can also be used to communicate and to do business, for information and education, and for entertainment.

1 Decide if each statement is true or false. If it is false, correct it.

1 The internet was developed in the Soviet Union.
2 The scientists who first used computer networks were working on business projects.
3 The main advantage of a computer network was that information could be sent more quickly.
4 The worldwide web came before e-mail.
5 A lot of things are bought and sold on the internet.
6 Criminals can always get into your computer.

2 Complete this paragraph. Use the words in brackets in their correct form and put in the right words.

The internet is a wonderful thing. It can save you a … of time and trouble. … example, you can buy things … (quick) and … (easy). You can even book a holiday on the internet. An English couple … Michael and Kate did this a year or two … . It was really easy, and it was … (cheap) than doing it in the … (tradition) way. They chose … (go) to Gerona in Spain. Some weeks later they … (fly) there from England. Being in Gerona was a strange experience for them. The local people all seemed … (speak) Italian instead … Spanish, and … were Italian flags everywhere. Michael and Kate soon realized that they were … fact in Genoa in Italy. The mistake they … made was to click the … box when they booked the holiday.

3 Look at these explanations and find the word in the text.

1 liked by many people
2 fighting between two countries
3 a group of people who run the country
4 a place where books are kept
5 producing and selling things
6 a person who does something which is against the law
7 learning things in school or college

4 Imagine you are applying for a job in computers. You will have to translate computer books from English into German. As a test, you have to translate these sentences.

1 Use the mouse to move around the screen and click on things.
2 There are several different ways you can open a file.
3 You can make a window bigger or smaller, and you can open more than one window at a time.
4 It is a good idea to organize your files so that they are easier to work with.
5 You might want to know how much memory the computer is using for the different jobs you ask it to do.
6 A website has a number of pages. The home page shows you what there is on the site.
7 You can download software from the web and use it on your computer.
8 If you are connected to a network, you can use programs from another computer.

2-23

5 Chloe and Tessa are talking on their way to school. Listen to the conversation.

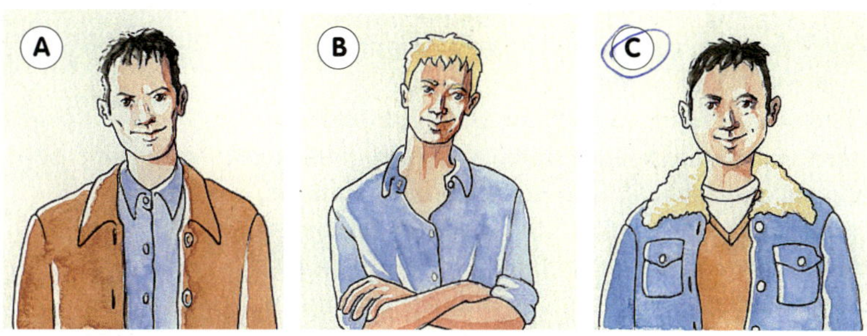

Part 1 (22)

Tessa tells Chloe about a website she has been looking at. Give the information.

1 the reason why Chloe couldn't get Tessa on her mobile
2 the month when the film about Robbie Williams will be on at the cinema
3 what the film is about
4 the place where Robbie Williams gave a concert last month
5 the title of the video of the concert
6 the day when the concert will be on TV
7 the time and the channel

Part 2 (23)

Chloe tells Tessa about someone she has been been sending e-mails to. Answer the questions.

1 Where is the picture of Chloe's friend?
a) on her desk b) in her bag c) in her computer
2 Who is Jake: A, B or C?
3 Which sentence best describes Tessa's attitude?
a) She thinks Chloe would be crazy to meet the guy.
b) She wants to meet Jake herself.
c) She thinks Jake will be just right for Chloe.

High flier

Helen Rose is a young high flier with a difference. Her business is saving lives as a helicopter paramedic with the Air Ambulance Service – and she loves it. At 25, she already has six years experience in the service and an old head on her young shoulders. She is friendly and easy to get on with. She smiles a lot, but she freely admits that she has sometimes cried during a difficult rescue.

The Essex air ambulance station is an old US Airforce control tower in the middle of an airfield near Chelmsford in Essex. A pilot and two paramedics (out of a team of 16) are on standby every day. Helen, the youngest of them by nine years, has brown hair with blonde highlights and is known as The Baby or Rosie. There is plenty of laughing and teasing, but Helen gives as good as she gets. 'I'm very direct. I'm not a girlie girl.' This seems to be a key to Helen's success as one of the team.

In her uniform of boots and orange jumpsuit, she looks ready for anything. Helen is the only woman on the team 'I'm only 1 metre 62, but I can do what I'm asked to do in difficult situations,' she says. 'I'm strong enough to do the job. And that's all that matters.'

Every day they wait for the phone to ring. They usually have three or four missions each day. The team can be on the scene in under ten minutes. Helen explains the importance of the 'golden hour'. 'If a patient is in the hospital inside 60 minutes, the chances for survival are greatly increased.' She remembers a bright, cold day in February. A man was riding a motorbike on a country lane. He went too fast round a bend and crashed into an oncoming car. 'He had face and neck injuries, but I also noticed his stomach was bloated. It looked like an internal rupture which can be fatal if you don't act quickly. Helen did and the biker lived. 'That feels good,' she says.

Helen sees plenty of serious injuries, but that's part of the job. There's one thing she's always afraid of, and that's when children are injured. 'When a child is in pain and doesn't understand what's happening, it's really awful,' she says.

Helen didn't really have any ambitions. When she left school, she didn't know what she wanted to do next. Her mother suggested the ambulance service, and Helen thought 'Why not?' She got a qualification as a medical technician and learned to drive an ambulance, and she applied for the Essex job. 'We did exams in map-reading and physiology as well as a physical test,' she says. 'I felt I'd achieved something.'

Since then Helen has achieved even more. She won a fire service award for her part in the rescue of a woman trapped in a house fire. 'We could see through the windows, but there was just black smoke,' she says. 'My partner kicked the door down, and I crawled in on my hands and knees to have a look.' Luckily fire officers arrived before Helen pushed herself too far.

Home life is very different. She is single 'at the moment' and lives with her brother Bob, his wife Viv and their two children. And the best part of the job? 'Getting home at the end of the day. I might be so tired I can hardly stand and I won't have time to eat, but I'll think, "Wow, we did all that, we made a difference." There's not one day when I haven't looked forward to coming to work.'

adapted from *AA Magazine*

UNIT 3

HIGH TECH, LOW TECH

MUSEUM GUIDE

Fifth floor
- The Science and Art of Medicine

Fourth floor
- Glimpses of Medical History

Third floor
- Heat and Temperature
- Photography and the Cinema
- Radio and Sound Studio
- In Future (Wellcome Wing)
- Flight

Second floor
- The Chemistry of Everyday Life
- Printing and Paper
- Weighing and Measuring
- Nuclear Physics and Power
- Light
- Computers
- Ships

First floor
- Materials
- Telecommunications
- Farming
- Maps
- Clocks
- The Weather
- Who am I? (Wellcome Wing)
- Food

Ground floor
- Engines
- Industry
- Space
- Virtual Voyages (Wellcome Wing)
- Making the Modern World

Basement
- The Garden (3-6 year-olds)
- Things (7-11 year-olds)
- The Secret Life of the Home

The Science Museum in London

An Early Phonograph

The Apollo 10 Space Capsule

An 18th Century Globe

The Difference Engine

24

WORDS AND PICTURES

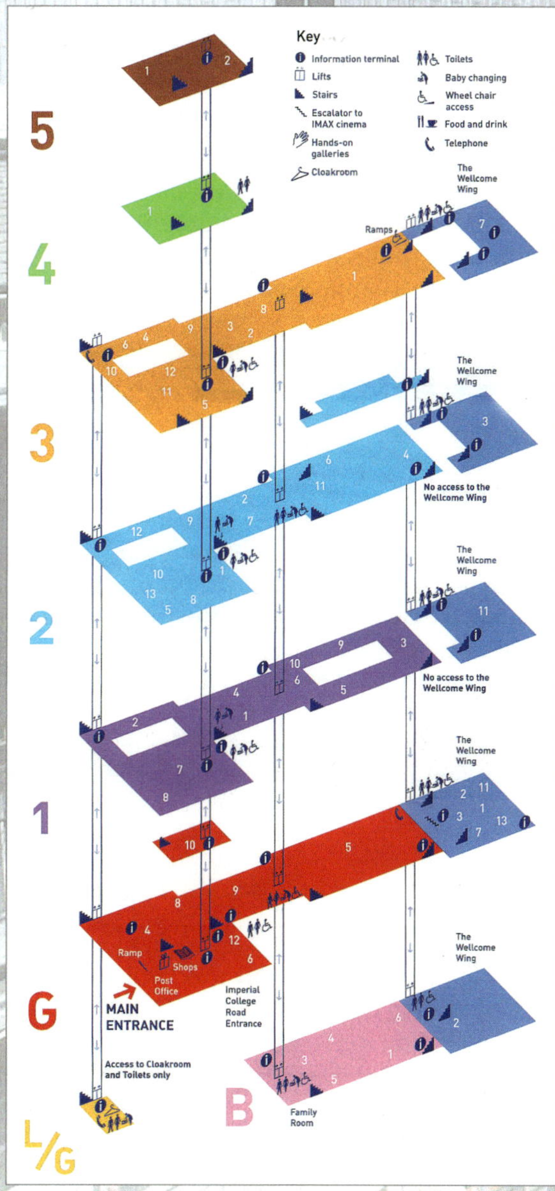

The Science Museum in London is a fascinating place. Here you can learn what science and technology have achieved. There's everything from satellites to model ships and from steam engines to scientific experiments.

SITUATION 1

25

A satellite is something that orbits a planet. The moon is a satellite of the earth. The earth has only one moon, but the planet Jupiter has sixteen moons, maybe more.

There are also artificial satellites. The first one, Sputnik One, was launched by the Russians in 1957. A few years later they launched a space probe which sent back photos of the surface of the moon. The far side of the moon had never been seen before.

Since then many more satellites have been sent into space. They are used for different purposes. TV pictures and phone calls can be sent around the world by satellite. Satellites can also be used to forecast the weather, to study the earth or other planets or to spy on other countries.

EXERCISE 1

	Active	Passive
Simple present	use	are used
	…	…

→ page 106

Look at the passive sentence and complete the active version.

➡ Satellites are used for different purposes.
We use satellites for different purposes.

1. Sputnik One was launched by the Russians in 1957.
   The Russians … in 1957.
2. Since then many more satellites have been launched into space.
   Since then the Russians and the Americans … .
3. The far side of the moon had never been seen before.
   No one … before.
4. Satellites can be used to forecast the weather.
   Experts … the weather.
5. An orbit of the earth will be completed every ten hours.
   The satellite … every ten hours.

Write a table in your exercise book and put in the verb forms from sentences 1–5.

EXERCISE 2

Put in the correct active or passive form of the verbs.

On 16 July 1969, Apollo XI was launched (launch) from Cape Kennedy, Florida. The spacecraft carried (carry) three Americans. It … (orbit) the earth and then the moon. A lunar module with two astronauts … (bring) down safely onto the moon, and they … (get) out and … (walk) around. Some experiments … (set) up and a US flag … (put) in the ground. The astronauts … (take) lots of photos.
All this … (could / see) live on TV and … (watch) by perhaps 600 million people. It … (remember) today as a great moment of history. Only twelve years before then, the Americans … (give) a shock when the Soviet Union … (become) the first country to launch a satellite into space. The next day, 21 July, the astronauts … (leave) the moon in the lunar module and … (return) to the spacecraft. Three days later Apollo XI … (pull) out of the Pacific Ocean near Hawaii. Since then many more spaceships … (launch), and more astronauts … (walk) on the moon, but the excitement of that first landing … (never / repeat). Perhaps more attention … (give) to the space adventure in the future, when astronauts land on Mars.

SITUATION 2

26

Nicola I haven't seen this game before.
Raymond It's good. It's called Astronaut.
Nicola What do you have to do?
Raymond Blast off in a spacecraft and dock with a space station. Then you have to build a laboratory.
Nicola But what's happening now?
Raymond I'm being attacked by an enemy spacecraft. It's already shot off one of my solar panels.
Nicola You're in trouble then.
Raymond Oh, I'll get out of it. Five minutes ago I was being pulled off course by a huge asteroid.

The passive progressive	Active	Passive	→ page 107
Present progressive	An enemy spacecraft is attacking the station.	The station is being attacked by an enemy spacecraft.	
Past progressive	An asteroid was pulling the spacecraft off course.	The spacecraft was being pulled off course by an asteroid.	

EXERCISE 3

A German woman wants to speak to an attendant at the Science Museum in London. Can you interpret for her? Complete the dialogue.

Woman *Kannst du ihn bitte fragen, wo das Benz-Auto ist?*
You Excuse me, this lady … know … is.
Attendant Well, it's normally here, but I'm afraid it's been moved.
You …
Woman *Und wo ist es jetzt?*
You …
Attendant Everything in this area is being changed around. So you can't see it at the moment. But it'll be back in two weeks.
You …
Woman *Ich war letztes Jahr hier und damals war das Auto auch nicht hier.*
You She says … last year, and … then either.
Attendant I expect it was being cleaned. Yes, it was. I remember now. I'm sorry she can't see it.
You *Er sagt …*

Space tourist

27

How would you like a holiday in space? A week on the moon? Two weeks on a space station? This isn't science fiction because people have already had holidays in space. The first was 60-year-old Dennis Tito, an American businessman from California. At the end of April 2001, Mr Tito and two Russian cosmonauts blasted off in a Russian Soyuz rocket and travelled to the International Space Station, 230 miles from the earth. His return ticket cost $20 million, including food and accommodation. It was hardly a last-minute bargain, but Mr Tito thought it was worth it. 'It was great,' he said when he returned to earth on 6 May. 'I just came back from paradise. I spent 60 years on earth and eight days in space, and it was two separate lives.'

Not everything has gone as well as it could have with the ISS project. There have been computer problems and lots of delays. There was a disaster in 2003 when seven astronauts were killed over Texas. There have also been arguments between the US and Russia about money. The project is so expensive, it could cost $100 billion. Some people said the money was being wasted and could be better spent on smaller projects on earth. But Dennis Tito isn't one of them.

The International Space Station (ISS) is the largest international space project ever. A number of countries are taking part. They include the US, Russia, Canada, Japan, Brazil, Germany and nine other European countries. Work began on building the ISS in November 1998, and in May 1999, a space shuttle docked there for the first time. In the first year there were 79 visitors from six different countries. In November 2000 a Russian spacecraft took the first long-term residents to the space station. There were three members of the crew on 'Expedition One'. The commander was Nasa astronaut Bill Shepherd, and with him were two Russian cosmonauts, Yuri Gidzenko and Sergei Krikalev.

The ISS orbits the earth every 90 minutes. It is about the size of a football field and has huge solar panels which use the power of the sun to run its computers and other systems. The place is partly a hotel and partly a scientific laboratory. A number of experiments are being carried out there which can only be done in conditions of weightlessness. Research is being done which could help to fight diseases on earth. And scientists hope to find out more about the effect on humans of life in space.

Mr Tito used to work for Nasa as a rocket engineer, so he already knew something about space. But he still had to do several months of tough training at Star City, the cosmonaut training centre near Moscow, before he was ready for the trip. He wasn't able to take a lot of luggage, but he packed a camera, a tape recorder to record his thoughts and a CD player. His eight CDs included opera and The Beatles. At the ISS he took a lot of photos of the marvellous views, but he had to do it through the windows because, of course, he wasn't allowed to open them. Outside the temperature varied from plus 120 to minus 157 degrees. He didn't have to worry about whether he should take a pair of shorts or not – he had to wear a grey spacesuit the whole time.

The Americans weren't very pleased when the Russians told them that Mr Tito would travel to the space station. The Americans didn't think he had the right qualifications; he would get in the way; it would be too dangerous; the ISS was a serious project, and tourists should be kept away. The Russians didn't agree, and anyway they needed the money. So after a lot of arguments the trip went ahead. Mr Tito was only the first space tourist. The Americans changed their minds when they saw how the idea of space tourism was increasing public interest in the project. We know that space travel is dangerous, but it is likely that there will be more opportunities for those who want a very special experience – and for only a few million dollars.

EXERCISE 4

Give the following information from the text.

➡ the distance from the ISS to the earth – 230 miles
1 the time it takes the ISS to orbit the earth - 90 minutes
2 the purpose of the experiments
3 the start date for work on the ISS N
4 a few details about the world's first space tourist
5 three things he had in his luggage
6 the price of the first space holiday
7 one reason for space tourism
8 one reason against it

EXERCISE 5

For each paragraph of the text or info box, choose one of these headings.

- Getting ready for space 5
- A new kind of holiday 1
- An international project 3
- Space tourism – yes or no? 6
- The ISS in trouble 2
- Why a space station? 4

EXERCISE 6

Look at this sentence from the text.

Mr Tito is an American **businessman**.

We can put two words together to make a new word.
business (*Geschäft*) + man (*Mann*) = businessman (*Geschäftsmann*)

sky + line = skyline

Complete the sentences. Find two words from the box and put them together.

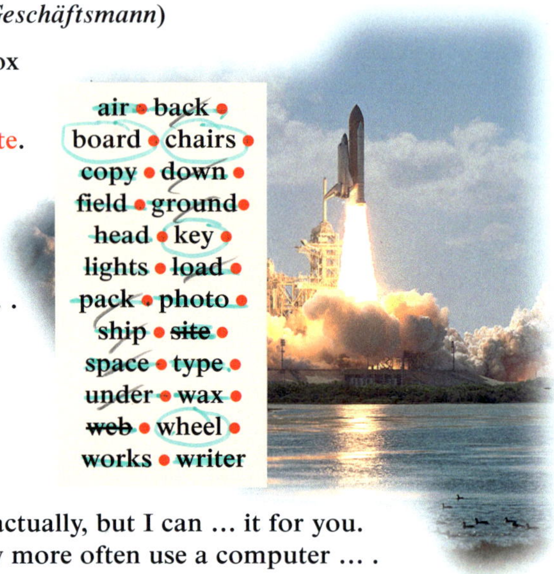

air • back • board • chairs • copy • down • field • ground • head • key • lights • load • pack • photo • ship • site • space • type • under • wax • web • wheel • works • writer

➡ You'll find all the details on our company **website**.

1 The … blasted off from Cape Kennedy.
2 The car … lit up the road in front of us.
3 They call it the subway in New York, but in London it's the tube or the … .
4 It's easier to carry all your camping stuff in a … .
5 We can … the information from the internet.
6 The helicopter landed on a small … .
7 At Madame Tussaud's we saw some … of famous scientists.
8 There is a special entrance for disabled people who arrive in … .
9 Can I have this page of notes? – Well, I need it actually, but I can … it for you.
10 People used to type letters on a …, but now they more often use a computer … .

EXERCISE 7

28-30

Listening

There's a news report on the radio about a trip to Mars. Listen to the report.

Part 1 (28)

Answer each question in a single word or phrase.

1 When is the space shuttle going to be launched?
2 What is the name of the shuttle?
3 How many people will be in the spacecraft?
4 What is the name of the commander?

Part 2 (29)

Write down the missing numbers.

1 The space shuttle is leaving on a journey of … million miles.
2 The crew will dock with the space station … months from now.
3 The space station started orbiting Mars … years ago.
4 It has … residents.
5 The station is … miles from Mars.

Part 3 (30)

In each sentence one word gives incorrect information. Write down the four correct words.

The crew will be the second group in history to walk on the planet Mars. They will stay there for ten weeks. They will take samples, do some experiments and explore one of the mountains. Although this is still quite a long time ahead, there is great interest in some parts of the world.

EXERCISE 8

Look at these sentences.

> I've bought some trousers. (eine Hose) → page 131
> These trousers are expensive. (Diese Hose ist …)

Words like *trousers* and *scissors* are called pair nouns. Pair nouns are plural and take a plural verb. We use the plural even when we mean only one pair.

We can say *a pair of …*, *two pairs of …* etc.

> Mr Tito didn't take a pair of shorts with him.
> There are two pairs of jeans in the washing machine.

Write a sentence about each picture.

➽ These trousers are dirty.
➽ This shirt costs £20.

EXERCISE 9

Look at these sentences.

> The crew was ready for the flight.
> The team has played well. → page 131

Crew and *team* both mean 'groups of people'. They are group nouns. In American English a singular group noun takes a singular verb such as *was* or *has*.

> The crew was / were ready for the flight.

In British English a singular group noun can take a singular or a plural verb.

Put in the words *army, audience, band, class, company, family, government, tribe*.

1 The … are doing a history test today.
2 The … are really enjoying the show.
3 The … lives in a flat in Birmingham.
4 The … was playing very loudly.
5 The … hasn't got enough weapons to fight a war.
6 The … makes plastic bottles at its factory in Ireland.
7 An Indian … was driven off the land it had lived on for centuries.
8 The … have brought in a new tax on newspapers.

Which of the sentences are correct only in British English?

EXERCISE 10

Look at this sentence from the text.

> Mr Tito used to work for Nasa as a rocket engineer. → page 130

This means that Mr Tito worked for Nasa in the past but does not work for them now.

Complete the sentences with *used to* and one of these verbs: *believe, burn, light, take, tell, travel, write*.

➽ Before there were clocks, people used to tell the time by the sun.
1 Before we had computers, people … everything with a pen or use a typewriter.
2 In the time before modern telecommunications, news … much more slowly.
3 Before central heating, people … wood or coal on an open fire to keep warm.
4 Centuries ago, some people … that the sun orbited the earth.
5 Before the motor car was invented, journeys … much longer than they do now.
6 Before the invention of the electric light, people … their homes with candles, oil lamps or gas lights.

SITUATION 3

31

Many electrical devices that we now regard as a normal part of everyday life were invented by an American around a hundred years ago. His name was Thomas Alva Edison. Edison invented a device for recording sound and a machine that showed movies. He also invented a new kind of battery. Perhaps his most famous invention was the light bulb.

Altogether Edison invented over a thousand different products and set up his own laboratory. He is often said to be the greatest inventor of all time, although some of his inventions were in fact developed by people who worked for him. Necessity is said to be the mother of invention, but in Edison's case the desire to make money also played a big part.

Thomas Alva Edison
1847–1931

be said to → page 107

Edison **is said to** be the greatest inventor of all time.
Edison **soll** der größte Erfinder aller Zeiten **sein.**

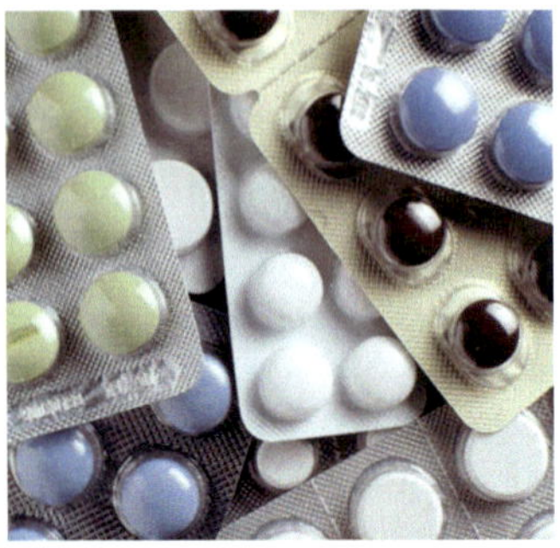

New products people are talking about

EXERCISE 11

Here are some details about new products and inventions that people are talking about.

➡ batteries that are said to have a much longer life
1 new cars that are said to use very little petrol
2 a new drug which is said to keep you free of all diseases
3 running shoes that are said to make you run faster
4 a computer operating system which is said to be very easy to use
5 a robot that is said to be able to do all your housework

Write sentences about each product.
Begin with *They say* … *People say* … or *I've heard* … .

➡ They say the new batteries have a much longer life.
1 I've heard that the new cars …

EXERCISE 12

'Necessity is the mother of invention' is an English proverb. It means that if you need to do something, then you will find a way to do it.

Find the proverbs and give the German version. If there isn't a German version, say what you think the proverb means.

Actions speak	is worth two in the bush.
All's well	the mice will play.
When the cat's away,	shouldn't throw stones.
People who live in glass houses	till you come to it.
One man's meat	than never.
A bird in the hand	louder than words.
Better late	that ends well.
Don't cross a bridge	is another man's poison.

➡ Actions speak louder than words. *Taten sagen mehr als Worte.*

SITUATION 4

32

Interviewer Gemma, you've won the British Young Inventor of the Year competition. Many congratulations.

Gemma Thank you.

Interviewer Tell us about your invention.

Gemma It's a bicycle brake light.

Interviewer Like on a car?

Gemma That's right. When a car driver uses the brake, you see the brake light. I've invented something similar for a bicycle. The movement of the brake triggers the light and warns people behind that you're slowing down or stopping.

Interviewer That's a great invention, Gemma. I think we should all have one fitted to our bikes.

Gemma I'd love to have it produced and sold. I think it could reduce the number of accidents.

Interviewer Gemma, what do you need to be a good inventor?

Gemma You need to recognize that there's a problem, and then you need to solve the problem. You have to find a good practical solution. And that usually means a lot of work.

	have	something	done
We've	had	our house	painted.
Did you	have	a new key	cut?
Would you like to	have	the computer	delivered?
You need to	have	the old battery	replaced.
We're	having	the dining-room	decorated.

→ page 108

EXERCISE 13

Read about each situation and then find a sentence with *having something done* or *had something done*. Use the verbs ~~*build*~~, *clean, cut, deliver,* ~~*fit*~~, *repair, take.*

- Mark didn't have any lights on his bike, but he thought he might need them when the evenings got darker, so now he's bought some. The man in the bike shop put them on for him. Mark has had some lights fitted.
- Our neighbours haven't got a garage to put their car in, and they've decided they would like one. Two men are putting it up at the moment. Our neighbours are having a garage built.

1 Nick needs a photo for his passport. He's smiling at the camera.
2 The Johnsons' old television refused to work any more, so they've bought a new one. Someone is on his way to their house now and is bringing the television in a van.
3 Sophie got some dirt on her coat, so two days ago she took it to 'Good as New Again' in the High Street. Today she's brought it home, and it really is as good as new with the dirt all gone.
4 Yesterday Jamie's mum told him his hair was getting too long. He's been to the hairdresser today.
5 Mr and Mrs Kelsey's washing-machine isn't working properly. An engineer has come to look at it, and he's working on it at the moment.

EXERCISE 14

Translate the sentences into good German.

- You could have the program produced by a software company. *Du könntest das Programm von einer Softwarefirma produzieren lassen.*

1 The school is going to have all its computers replaced with new ones.
2 We've had an alarm fitted to the computer room.
3 When I'm on holiday, I have my e-mails sent to my Hotmail address.
4 I'll have to have my computer repaired.
5 The computer company is having some new offices built here at the moment.
6 You can phone and have the new system explained to you.

33 Young inventors

THE CAST COOLER

Krysta Morlan from Vacaville, California, shows how a negative experience – like having a serious disease – can have a positive side too. Krysta has cerebral palsy, and she finds it difficult to walk. When she was still a student at Vacaville High School she had an operation on her legs. The operation was successful, but Krysta had to wear a full cast on both legs for a whole year. In the heat of late summer, she quickly found out how a cast makes the skin itch. Unfortunately, you can't scratch when you are wearing a cast. Krysta didn't want to spend a year in such a situation, so she decided to do something about the problem herself. She saw that the solution was to ventilate the area that was covered by the cast. With some help from her father, a mechanic, she found a way to do just that. She ran a narrow, plastic tube between the cast and her skin and then attached the tube to a small, light air pump. The pump is powered by a 9-volt battery. It takes in air and sends it through the tube to the surface of the skin. Krysta then solved the final problem when she attached the device to the cast with Velcro so that it would lie flat and would hardly be noticed.

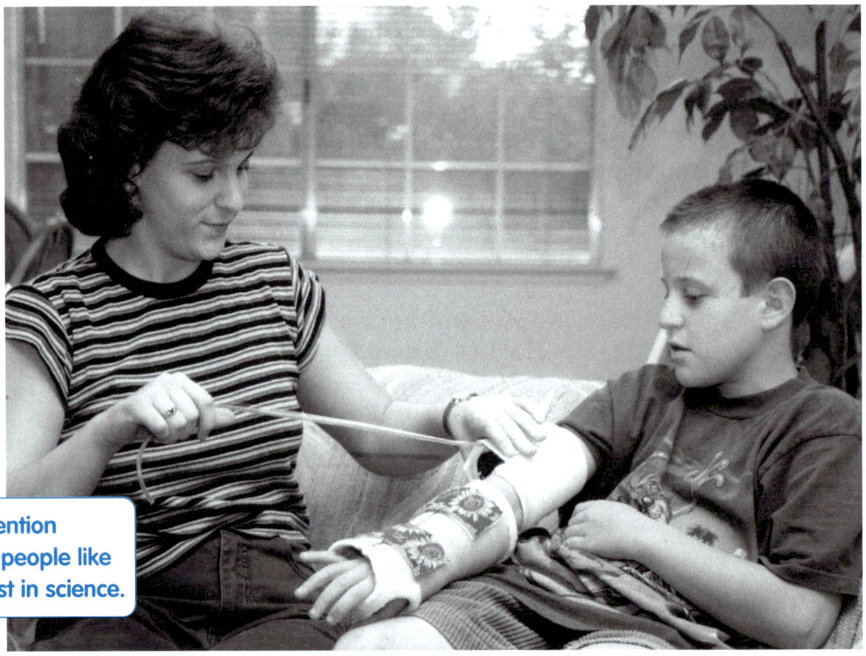

Krysta's Cast Cooler worked perfectly, and her skin stopped itching. Now she wants to share her invention with the thousands of children and adults who are in the same situation as she was in when she had the cast on.

The Lemelson-MIT Invention Apprenticeship encourages people like Krysta to develop their interest in science.

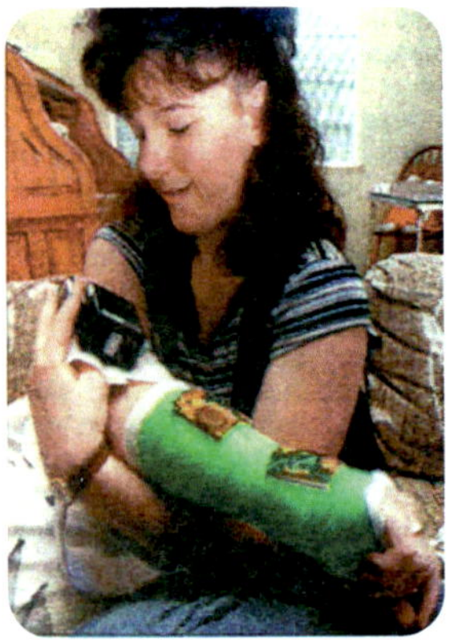

Krysta's invention won a prize. Her prize was an apprenticeship. It is called the Lemelson-MIT Invention Apprenticeship. The inventor Jerome H. Lemelson and his wife Dorothy set up the Lemelson-MIT program. It is run by the Massachusetts Institute of Technology. The program encourages young Americans to develop their inventions. People like Krysta are being helped to work on their ideas.

Krysta's next idea was a water bike, a machine that you can ride in the water, whether for physical therapy or just for fun. 'Everyone has ideas,' says Krysta. 'You just need a chance to act on them.' She wants to continue to invent products that will help disabled people or those who need therapy.

SLEEP SAFE

A young inventor at Bristol Grammar School has won a major prize in the Young Engineers for Britain competition. Jonathan Love (16), from the Sneyd Park area of Bristol, won £500 for his Sleep Safe invention, a device which is designed to reduce the number of cases of cot death. 'Cot death' is when a healthy baby dies in its sleep. It usually happens when the baby is lying face down.

Jonathan was able to have his device tested on a real baby, and it worked well. 'He has found a solution to something that all parents worry about,' said Paul Whitehouse, Director of Technology at the school. 'My wife and I were pleased to test it on our nine-week-old son Joe.'

The small device is worn in a tiny garment which gives out a radio signal if the baby rolls onto its front. This triggers an alarm unit that can be heard as far as 50 metres from the cot.

'Cot death is said to be a danger for young babies,' said Joe's mother Isobel Whitehouse. 'But Jonathan's invention will help parents to relax when their new-born babies are asleep, so they'll sleep better themselves.'

'My aunt was having a baby, and I wanted to reassure her,' said Jonathan. 'I decided to study cot death for my GCSE technology project, and it took a year to design and build Sleep Safe. The main idea was that the baby would be completely comfortable. I feel very happy that, after so much work, I've invented something that might save lives.'

Jonathan plans to spend some of the prize money on further development of his invention. His ambition is to go into computer engineering.

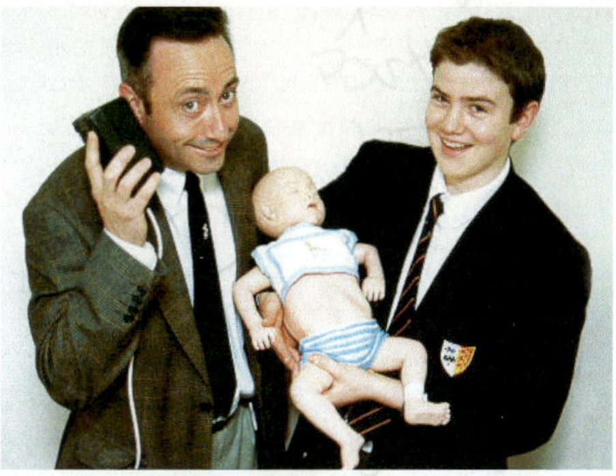

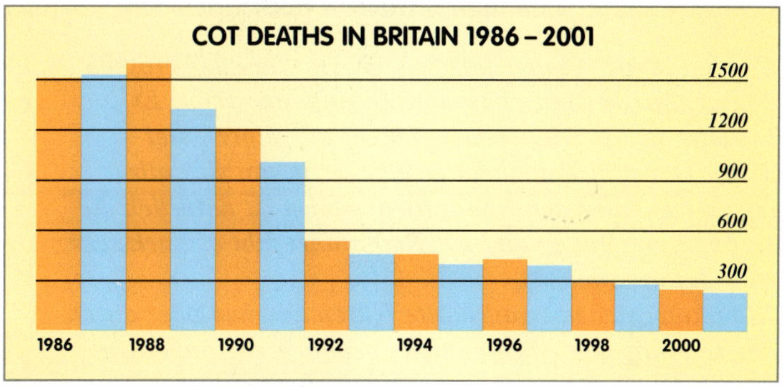

EXERCISE 15

Complete this paragraph about the Cast Cooler. Find a single word for each space. (Some of the words are in the text but not all of them.)

Krysta Morlan is … Vacaville, California. She has cerebral palsy, so she doesn't find walking very … . After an … on both legs, she had to wear a cast. Her skin itched, especially in the … weather. So Krysta … a cast cooler. This is how the cooler … . A pump sends … through a plastic … to the skin. The pump gets its power from a … . The cooler is fixed to the … with a piece of velcro. It was a simple idea, and it … the problem. Krysta hopes that thousands of other people can … the device. With the … of a Lemelson-MIT Invention Apprenticeship, she … on some of her other ideas. One of these was a bicycle that you can ride in the … .

EXERCISE 16

Answer the questions about Sleep Safe.

1 Which city does Jonathan live in?
2 What competition did he win?
3 What was his prize?
4 What is Jonathan's invention designed to do?
5 How did he test his invention?
6 What does Sleep Safe do if the baby rolls onto its front?
7 What do you think would happen after the alarm sounded?
8 What will the invention mean to parents?
9 Why did Jonathan first become interested in cot death?
10 What are his career plans?

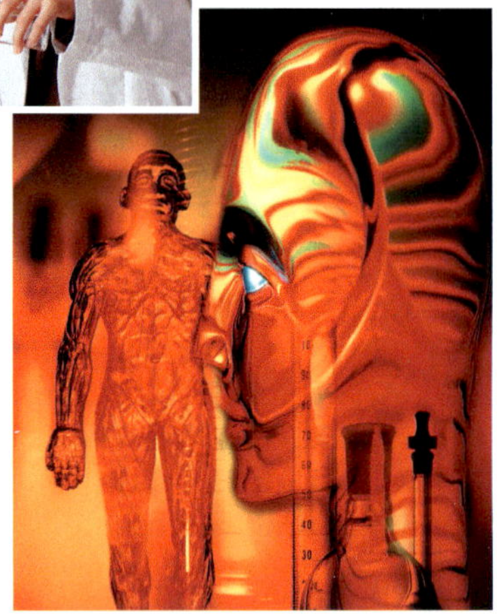

EXERCISE 17

Which of the two expressions fits the sentence?
You have seen all the correct words in this unit.

➡ The astronauts made / took lots of photos.
The astronauts took lots of photos.

1 The young inventor finally achieved / solved the problem.
2 Jonathan learned / studied cot death for his technology project.
3 Space tourism has increased / lifted public interest in the ISS.
4 Krysta attached / put the tube to a pump.
5 A number of experiments are being carried out / put through.
6 The rocket was pulled off course / way by an asteroid.
7 Krysta now has a chance to continue / develop the invention.
8 The radio signal causes / triggers an alarm.
9 The satellite was launched / thrown into space.
10 The power of the sun is used to drive / run the computers.

EXERCISE 18

Translate this information into English for visitors to Munich. These words will help you.

science • island • enough • travel • telescope • sky • replica • coal mine • sailing ship • daily

Das berühmte Deutsche Museum ist eines der größten Museen für Wissenschaft und Technik der Welt. Es befindet sich in München und steht auf einer Insel in der Isar. Ein Tag allein genügt nicht, um sich alles anzusehen. Eine der Hauptattraktionen ist natürlich die Computerabteilung und zur Raumfahrt gibt es auch sehr viele Informationen.
Man kann sich aber auch alte Uhren ansehen oder durch ein Teleskop den Abendhimmel beobachten. Außerdem kann man ein rekonstruiertes Kohlenbergwerk besuchen. Sehr interessant sind die Flugzeuge aus unterschiedlichen Jahrhunderten, z.B. die Rekonstruktion der Rumpler Taube, die 1910 von Edmund Rumpler in Berlin gebaut wurde. Der größte Gegenstand im ganzen Museum ist ein Segelschiff aus dem 19. Jahrhundert.
Das Museum ist täglich von 9–17 Uhr geöffnet.

Don't translate the name of the museum.
Here English speakers would say 'in the world' not 'of the world'.
For *genügen* use 'be enough'.

Say *Edmund Rumpler's ...*

Say *... is a 19th ...*
Use am and pm.

The famous Rumpler Taube

Soyuz space capsule

Beginning and ending a conversation

34

Beginning a conversation

- Hi. / Hello. How are you?
- Have you heard the news?
- Guess what. We're going on a class trip next week.
- Here you are. I've been looking for you. I need to ask you ...
- Hello. Do you mind if I join you?
- Excuse me. Do you know where the railway station is, please?
- Excuse me. Do you sell batteries? (in a shop)

Ending a conversation

- Sorry, but I have to go now. It's my piano lesson.
- I must dash, or I'll be late for my tea.
- It's been nice talking to you. / Nice to see you.

Oliver Hey, guess what!
Harriet What?
Oliver I've just been interviewed by a TV reporter.
Harriet Interviewed? What about?

* * *

Oliver They said it's going to be on the local news at six thirty tonight.
Harriet OK, I'll watch it. I must dash, Oliver. I'm playing basketball. See you!
Oliver Bye!

EXERCISE 19

1 Look at the way Oliver begins the conversation. Why does he say 'Guess what'? And to end the conversation, Harriet makes an excuse. What is her excuse? Why does she need one?

2 Work with a partner. You have some important news for your friend. Perhaps you did paragliding for the first time at the weekend. But your friend is in a hurry and finds an excuse to end the conversation.

Then change roles and practise another conversation with different news and a different excuse.

3 How might you begin a conversation in these situations?

a) At last you've found your friend.
b) You need to ask the way to the post office.
c) You are looking for sports magazines in a shop.
d) At lunchtime you see someone you know in the cafeteria, and you want to sit next to them.

EXERCISE 20

Asking for information

Work with a partner. Partner **B**: Please look at page 96.

Partner **A**: You and your English penfriend are at the Science Museum in London. There are a few things that you need to look at because they are important for your school work. This is what you are looking for.

- a lamp that was invented by Edison
- an old tractor
- some information about medical operations
- some old machines that were used in the first factories
- some recording equipment

Find out what floor you need to go to. Ask your friend to look at his museum guide. You can say:

Where can we find ...?, I'd like to see ... , What about ...?, What floor is that on?

When you have got the answers, go to the museum guide on page 37 and answer your partner's questions.

First Lady of the air

The early years of the last century were the pioneer years of flying. The first aeroplane flight was by Orville Wright in North Carolina in 1903. The aircraft climbed three metres above the ground, and the flight was ten seconds long. Less than 16 years later, two British pilots, John Alcock and Arthur Brown, made the world's first non-stop flight across the Atlantic, from Canada to Ireland.

These pioneers of flight were all men. But there were also women who wanted to break into this world. One of them was Amelia Earhart.

Amelia was born in Kansas in 1897 into a family of German origin. When an American pilot called Frank Hawks took her up into the air for the first time, she was immediately bitten by the bug. She regarded flying as a kind of freedom – for her personally and for all women. Amelia took flying lessons, and in 1921 she made her first solo flight. In the following year she spent all her money on her first aeroplane.

In June 1928 Amelia Earhart became the first woman to cross the Atlantic in an aeroplane. The pilot was an American called Wilmer Stultz. Amelia was only a passenger, but this flight made her a household name. One newspaper called her 'the First Lady of the air'. The early machines were very primitive, and flying was still a dangerous adventure.

Amelia Earhart 1897–1937

In 1932, after her solo flight across the Atlantic, Amelia Earhart was given the National Geographic gold medal by President Herbert Hoover.

Amelia was admired for her courage and skill. In 1932 she made the first solo flight across the Atlantic by a woman. In 1935 she flew solo from Hawaii to California.

Then on June 1 1937, she left Miami in a twin-engine Lockheed Electra on a flight around the world. With her was navigator Fred Noonan. For a month they flew east. On July 2, in the middle of the Pacific Ocean, they disappeared. US ships and aircraft searched the area, but nothing was ever found. Some people think she might have survived and lived on an island – or even returned secretly to the US – but the most likely explanation is that the aircraft came down in the sea and the pilot and navigator were both killed.

1 Correct the sentences.

1 The first flight in an aircraft was only ten minutes long.
2 Alcock and Wright flew non-stop across the Pacific.
3 During her first flight, Amelia slowly realized that she loved flying.
4 In 1922 she borrowed an aeroplane.
5 Amelia became famous after she had been the pilot on a flight across America.
6 In 1932 she flew across the Atlantic with only a navigator.
7 In 1937 she tried to fly around the world in a plane with a single engine.
8 Amelia and her navigator turned back over the Pacific.

2 Complete these two paragraphs. Use the words in brackets in their correct form and put in the right words.

In the early days, flying was quite a … (danger) thing to do, and pilots … (regard) as heroes. One … these heroes was … American called Charles Lindbergh. In 1927 he … (make) the first non-stop solo … (fly) across the Atlantic. A prize of $25,000 had … offered to the first person to do this. Lindbergh … (fly) from New York City to Paris in 33 hours 32 minutes. Perhaps his … (difficult) problem was to stay … all this time. If he … (fall) asleep, he … (die) in a terrible crash. When he … (land) at Le Bourget airport, … (he / give) a big welcome. He became a … (house) name in Europe and America.

Another hero was Amy Johnson. Amy wanted to show people that … (woman) could do things … well as men. Amy learned … fly at the London Aeroplane Club. She … (great / admire) in Britain because … her solo flight from London to Darwin, Australia in 1930. The journey of 9,960 miles … nineteen days. Amy Johnson … (break) many flying records. One day in 1941 she … (fly) over the mouth of the Thames when her aircraft … (appear).

Amy Johnson 1903–1941

3 Find the missing words.

1 down – drop, up – ???
2 sea – voyage, air – ???
3 car – driver, aeroplane – ???
4 slow – late, fast – ???
5 eat – eaten, bite – ???
6 go in – enter, go back – ???
7 argue – argument, explain – ???
8 independent – independence, free – ???
9 classroom – pupils, bus – ???
10 lesson – teacher, route – ???

4 Put in a form of *be*, *have* or *do*.

1 Amelia Earhart … remembered today as a great pioneer of flying.
2 When she flew across the Atlantic, no other woman … ever done that before.
3 The early pilots … admired for their courage.
4 When Amelia arrived at the airfield, a newspaper reporter … waiting for her.
5 How long … it take today to fly to the US?
6 Flying … been made much safer since those early days.
7 When a pilot flew solo, she … to do everything.
8 Amelia … want to do anything other than fly planes.
9 No one … ever found the aircraft, and probably no one ever will.
10 The pilot felt very worried because the aircraft … being blown off course.
11 We decided to try to land and … the engine repaired.

5 Lauren and her husband Nick have just been to Greece on holiday. Lauren is telling her friend Richard about it. Listen to the conversation.

35-36

Part 1 (35)

Which of these things happened on the flight out to Greece?

a) The flight was very late.
b) One of the engines failed during the flight.
c) One of the pilots refused to fly the plane.
d) The weather conditions were very bad.
e) They had to land at a different airport than they had expected.
f) When they arrived, one piece of luggage was missing.

Part 2 (36)

Answer the questions about the flight home.

1 How late was the flight?
2 Why was it late?
3 Where did they land?
4 How did Lauren and Nick get back to Birmingham?
5 How did they feel when they got home?

Great failures of technology

Technology is a wonderful thing. Here are some strange but true stories from the world of technology.

About forty years ago an Englishman called Arthur Pedrick set up his own 'research laboratory'. He invented more than 150 devices, but he never managed to have any of them actually produced. One of his big ideas was a series of pipelines that would take snow from the Antarctic to irrigate the Australian desert. He also invented a horse-powered car, with the car in front and the horse behind. The horse's food is in a box in front of it. When the driver puts his foot down, this changes the position of the box, and the horse has to go faster to reach the food.

******

Mr Pedrick had a rival in Mr Yasujiro Kikowo of Tokyo. He had already invented motorized ice-skates when he began work on his greatest project, the toilet bicycle. He worked on it for ten years. Instead of a saddle, the bicycle has a funnel through which human waste passes on its way to a container down below. The inventor has also created a plastic skirt which protects the toilet cyclist from a cold wind and also from the view of other road users. Sales have been slow, but Mr Kikowo thinks his invention is 'the way forward'.

******

An Englishman went on holiday to what was then Yugoslavia. He took 24 photos. When the film was developed, he had 24 photos of his left ear. He admitted that he didn't know much about photography.

******

Way back in 1962 the US launched the Mariner I space probe to Venus. It was a wonder of technology. The plan was that it would fly for 100 days and then orbit the planet Venus. However, Mariner I went way off course only four minutes after it had blasted off and had to be destroyed. It was found later that a minus sign had been left out of the program. 'It was human error,' a spokesman said. This minus sign cost $18 million, and that was even more money then than it is today.

Manchester United fan Tony Smart collapsed as he was watching his team and was taken to hospital. An X-ray showed that he had a 7.5 centimetre nail in his head. Ten days earlier someone at the factory where Tony works had accidentally dropped a nail gun on his head. It didn't hurt much, so he didn't think any more of it. Doctors pulled the nail out, and after two weeks in hospital Mr Smart went home. He was perfectly OK, but he didn't remember anything about the match.

******

When Mr Harold Senby of Leeds began to have problems with his hearing, he went to hospital and had a hearing aid fitted. It didn't seem to help, but Mr Senby supposed that nothing could be done about it. Twenty years later the hospital discovered that the aid had been fitted to the wrong ear.

******

George Plumpton of New York created a huge firework which he thought would be the most spectacular ever. It weighed 720 pounds, and it was designed to make a display over half a mile high. Crowds watched excitedly as Mr Plumpton lit the firework. Unfortunately there were no pretty lights. He just had time to get out of the way before the firework exploded and blew a three-metre deep hole in the ground.

******

At a sports club in the north of England, things were always being stolen from the men's changing room. To catch the thief, the police set up a secret camera. When the film was played back, the only person it showed was a naked policeman walking around the room as he was looking for his clothes. They had been stolen by the thief.

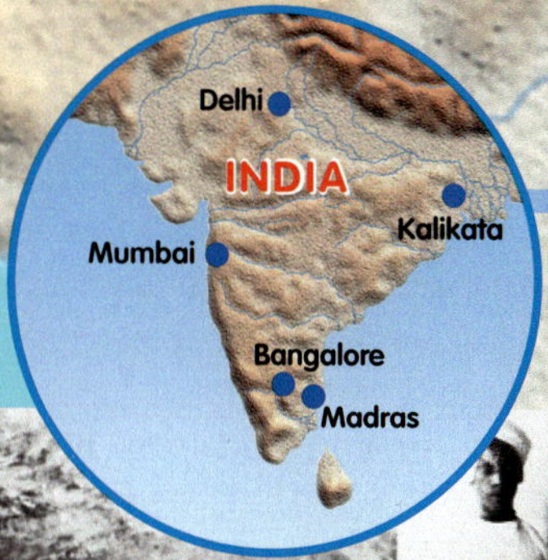

UNIT 4

AFTER THE EMPIRE

WORDS AND PICTURES

37

A British army major relaxing in 1870

A hundred years ago Britain had the largest empire the world had ever seen. It included Canada, Australia, New Zealand, India and parts of Africa.

India was at the heart of the British Empire. It had been a trading centre since the 16th century and had been ruled by the East India Company until the British government took direct control. A relatively small number of British soldiers and officials were able to control the whole country. In the photo you can see a British official and his Indian servant.

The old quarter in Delhi

India has been an independent nation since 1947. Today it is the world's largest democracy, with a population of about one billion. The largest cities are Mumbai (Bombay), Kalikata (Calcutta) and Delhi. India has a lot of industries such as textiles and machinery.

Most Indians live in villages and work on the land. Many people are poor, so some of them move to the cities, where they hope to earn a better living. Indian cities are very crowded. Poor people live in slums or on the streets, and well-off people live in apartment blocks, or they own big houses with gardens, and they have servants.

Information technology is big in India, and there are lots of IT experts. Bangalore is the country's Silicon Valley. But only well-off people can afford to buy a computer.

India has the largest number of young people in the world, but half of them live in poverty. Of the 220 million school-age children, about 100 million do not go to school. Many of them will never learn to read. Their parents do not send them to school because children are needed to help in the home or in the fields. Some children do other jobs to earn money for the family, and some of them work long hours in dangerous jobs.

The main language of India is Hindi, but English is also an official language. Although English is spoken by only about four per cent of the population, it is important in higher education, science and technology, and it can be the passport to a good job.

Computer training in Delhi

SITUATION 1

38

A street scene in Madras

Vikram Pandit, 17, lives in Madras. He is being interviewed by a reporter from a magazine called *Indian Youth*.

Verb + to-infinitive → page 109

I'm sure I can **manage to get** a job.
Vikram **hopes to go** into software development.

Verb + ing-form → page 110

He **enjoys working** with computers.
Won't you **mind leaving** India?

Verb + to-infinitive / ing-form

Many Indians **like to watch / like watching** cricket.
Vikram **loves to solve / loves solving** problems.

Reporter Vikram, I'd like to find out what the dream job would be for young people in India today.

Vikram For me it would be a job with a software company. I enjoy working with computers, and I love solving problems. So that's what I hope to do in my career. And I think that's true of many young people I know. Software development is a real hot job.

Reporter And what about a qualification?

Vikram Well, I'm going to study at the Institute of Technology here. Then I want to go to the United States and work in California. I'm sure I can manage to get a job in software there.

Reporter So you won't mind leaving India?

Vikram Well, I'll come back after a few years and maybe set up my own company.

Reporter You could do that here in Madras. We have our own IT Park now.

Vikram Yes, but really I'd prefer to have my company in Bangalore.

Reporter Tell me, Vikram, do you have any other hobbies, or do you spend all your time in front of a computer?

Vikram Almost all my time, but I like playing cricket, too.

View over Delhi

EXERCISE 1

Complete these sentences about India. Put in the *to*-infinitive or *ing*-form of the verb in brackets.

➡ In the days of the Empire the Indians had to do (do) what the British told them.

1 India has managed … (build) up some hi-tech industries.
2 Lots of Indians enjoy … (watch) Bollywood movies.
3 Some boys were practising … (throw) a cricket ball.
4 Most people in country areas seem … (be) quite poor.
5 The government has tried … (improve) the standard of living.
6 The wet season finishes in September, when it stops … (rain).
7 Don't forget … (take) off your shoes when you enter a temple.
8 My friend suggested … (visit) the Taj Mahal.

SITUATION 2

39

Indira Chandra is 14 years old and lives in Uttar Pradesh in the north of India. She has just started school for the first time. Indira is following a ten-month primary education programme at the Udaan Training Camp. This project is run by CARE-India, an organization which helps poor families to improve their lives.

Before she came to the camp, Indira worked in the village where she lived. She helped her mother, and she looked after her younger brothers and sisters. Sometimes she fetched water for the family, and sometimes she took the cattle into the fields. Now a new world has opened up for Indira, and she is learning to read and write. 'Udaan' means 'flight', and the project will enable Indira and other girls to 'fly high on the wings of education'.

Learning to read and write

'We never sent Indira to school before,' says her mother. 'In our village people would laugh at the idea of education for girls. They expect girls to do housework and become a good wife. Then we heard about the project. It wasn't difficult to persuade Indira to try it. She loves it. I want her to study higher classes, too. I'm not going to force her to marry too soon and be stuck in the village for the rest of her life.'

Verb + object + to-infinitive → page 109

Indira's mother **wants her to study** higher classes.
The project will **enable the girls to get** an education.
Some parents **force their daughters to marry** at a young age.

EXERCISE 2

Mr Baker is a teacher. He is taking a group of English pupils on a trip to India. They are visiting an Indian school. Combine each pair of sentences. Use a verb + object + *to*-infinitive.

➡ The pupils should write a diary of the trip. Mr Baker is encouraging them.
Mr Baker is encouraging the pupils to write a diary of the trip.

1. The pupils are visiting a local temple. One of the teachers has invited them.
2. They have to take off their shoes. Mr Baker is reminding them.
3. The girls are wearing long trousers. He has persuaded them.
4. Some of the pupils are learning Hindi. An Indian teacher is helping them.
5. The Indian pupils can speak English so well. The visitors didn't expect that.
6. The pupils have gone off with their Indian friends. Mr Baker has allowed it.
7. The pupils mustn't be back late. He has warned them.

EXERCISE 3

Look at these ways a teacher might tell you to do something.

- Look at page 45, please.
- Can you look at page 45, please?
- I want you to / I'd like you to look at page 45, please.

What might a teacher say in these situations?

➡ when you aren't listening
I want you to listen, please.

1. when your homework is so bad that you ought to do it again
I'd …
2. when everyone is making too much noise
Can …
3. when the pupils aren't sitting in their proper places
I'd …
4. when the teacher thinks it's time for all the class to start thinking about their project
I want …
5. when it's hot and none of the windows are open
Can …

Great Soul

40

A young man from India was travelling by train from Durban to Pretoria. During the journey a white passenger complained about having to sit near someone with brown skin. Although he had a ticket, the Indian was thrown off the train by a policeman and had to spend the night in a very cold waiting room. The young man's name was Mohandas Gandhi. It was 1893, and he had just arrived in South Africa to start a new job as a lawyer.

At that time South Africa was a British colony. The Indians, like the blacks, were badly treated by the whites. Most Indians did the worst jobs, the ones that no one else wanted to do. The Indians worked very hard, and most of them lived in poverty. They did not have the right to own land or to travel freely. Gandhi's experience on the train made him realize how the Indians were being treated. He decided to do something about it – to lead a campaign for equal rights for Indians.

Gandhi grew up at Porbandar on the west coast of India. He was a shy boy who liked being on his own. When he was 13, he married a local girl called Kasturba. The marriage had been arranged when they were small children. Kasturba stayed in India while her husband studied in London and then went to South Africa. In 1896 she and her two sons joined Mohandas in Durban. Gandhi was a successful lawyer and had become quite rich. But soon he decided to give up his money and all his nice clothes. He even tried to give away Kasturba's jewels.

As a result of Gandhi's campaign, a new law was passed in South Africa which gave the Indians more rights, although they still didn't have as many rights as white people. When in 1915 Gandhi returned to India with Kasturba and their four sons, he was given a hero's welcome.

At that time India was also a British colony. But the Indians wanted the chance to rule themselves instead of always doing what British officials told them. Gandhi led a campaign against British rule. It was a non-violent campaign, because Gandhi didn't believe in violence. He wanted people to stop obeying British laws and to stop paying taxes. But he told his followers not to fight back even if the police attacked them.

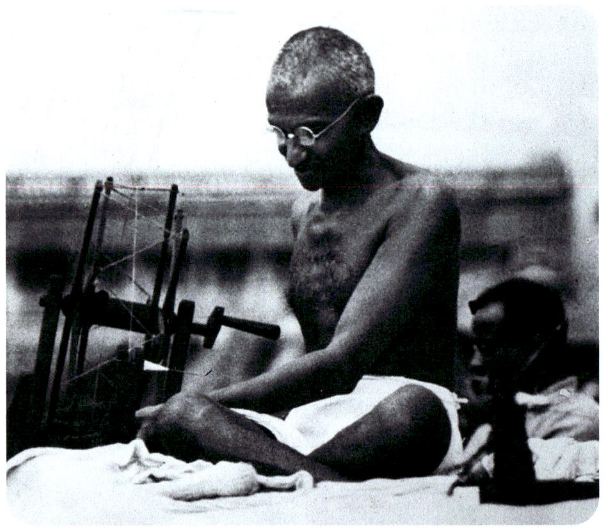

Gandhi was a Hindu. He believed in living a simple life. He didn't kill animals, and he didn't eat meat either. He believed we should love other people and not hurt them. He felt sympathy for people of other religions – Muslims and Christians, for example – and he didn't regard them as his enemies. Gandhi wanted to end the caste system. He didn't believe that the lowest caste, the 'untouchables', were worse than other people. He called them 'children of God'.

Gandhi believed that Indians were poor because the factories had taken work away from the village people. The factories were owned by the British. Gandhi told Indians they should spin their own cloth instead of buying it, and he himself always wore a simple cloth. He established communities where people tried to follow these ideas.

There was also a campaign against the salt tax. People used to boil sea water to make salt. But the British introduced a law which said that people were not allowed to do this. The law forced the Indians to buy salt and pay tax on it. Gandhi led a 240-mile protest march to the sea. The marchers were attacked and beaten by police, but they refused to resist. Hundreds were injured. Gandhi was arrested and put in prison. But he never minded going to prison.

Finally, on 15 August 1947, India became independent. Unfortunately Gandhi had failed to bring Hindus and Muslims together. The country had to be divided, and parts of the old India became the new Muslim state of Pakistan. On 30 January 1948, Gandhi was shot dead by a Hindu who didn't like his friendly attitude to Muslims.

Gandhi helped the Indian people to find ways of resisting the British and to achieve their independence. He is greatly admired and is regarded as the 'Father of the Indian nation'. Gandhi's example has encouraged other people to use non-violent methods. One of these people was Martin Luther King, the leader of the civil rights campaign in the US until his death in 1968. But today many people feel that in modern India it is impossible to lead the simple life that Gandhi believed in.

Gandhi was given the name Mahatma. This name means 'great soul'.

EXERCISE 4

Complete each sentence. Use the word *because*.

➡ Gandhi was thrown off the train because a white passenger complained about having to sit near him.

1 He decided to fight a campaign for the Indians in South Africa ...
2 Gandhi married Kasturba ...
3 He became quite rich in South Africa ...
4 When Gandhi returned to India, he got a hero's welcome ...
5 The Indians couldn't decide things for themselves ...
6 Gandhi never fought back ...
7 He called people of the lowest caste 'children of God' ...
8 People weren't allowed to make their own salt ...
9 Someone shot Gandhi ...
10 Gandhi is regarded as the Father of the Nation ...

EXERCISE 5

Find the words in the text for these explanations.

1 someone who can speak for you in court
2 being poor, not having enough money
3 to understand
4 nervous and afraid to speak to other people
5 using your strength to destroy something or to hurt someone
6 to do what you are told to do
7 a friendly feeling towards others
8 someone who doesn't like you and might want to hurt you
9 a group of people who live together
10 money that you have to pay to the government

EXERCISE 6

Put in a noun which is formed from the verb in italics. Sometimes the noun has the same form as the verb.

➽ Mohandas *married* Kasturba. The marriage had been arranged by their parents.
1 How did it *feel* to be in a Hindu temple? – It was a very strange …
2 The family *stayed* in South Africa for a long time. They returned to India after a … of 21 years.
3 Don't *argue* with the officials. You mustn't get into an … .
4 The family *arrived* back in India. Their … created a lot of excitement.
5 Gandhi's followers *discussed* his ideas. They had a very long … .
6 I can *explain* his methods. The … is really very simple.
7 Non-violent methods *succeeded*. They finally brought … to the movement.
8 Salt *cost* money, and the … weighed heavily on ordinary Indians.
9 My brother has *applied* for a job in India. He sent in his … today.
10 Gandhi *died* after he was shot. His … was a great shock to the nation.
11 What does Mahatma *mean*? Does the name have a …?
12 The Air India flight was *advertised*. We saw an … in the newspaper.

Make a table and write each noun and verb pair in one of these groups.

Nouns which

- end in …ion,
  ➽ invite – invitation
- end in …ment,
  ➽ develop – development
- end in …ing,
  ➽ begin – beginning
- end in …al,
  ➽ survive – survival
- have the same form as verbs,
  ➽ walk – walk

Be careful. Two pairs are different. Put them in a group called 'other'.

Scene from the 1982 film Gandhi

EXERCISE 7

Read this short text and then say if you think Gandhi was right in his opinions. Give your own opinion in about 60 words.

Gandhi believed in living a simple life, and he was against all violence. In the spring of 1919 at Amritsar in northern India, British soldiers fired into a crowd of men, women and children. Over 300 people were killed and many more injured. Even then, Gandhi was against any violent attacks on British soldiers or officials. But he now believed for the first time that India should become independent.

EXERCISE 8

Talk about these two photos. What is similar about them and what is different? Explain the background to each photo.

Martin Luther King, Washington, 1963

Bradford, England, 2001

Soldiers protect a Hindu temple from Muslim attack

Read this text about religion in India.

About eight out of ten Indians are Hindus. Hindus worship at a temple. There are many different groups with different beliefs. Hindus are divided into four castes. Most believe that their soul survives after the body dies. People who lead a good life can be born again into a higher caste. Another Hindu belief is that the cow is a holy animal, and they believe in treating it well. There are also many Hindu festivals such as Diwali. One of the most popular is Dussehra, in September or October. This festival celebrates the victory of the god Rama over the evil king, Ravana. Huge models of Ravana are burned.

About one tenth of the Indian population are Muslims. Muslims believe in one God, called Allah, and they worship at a mosque. There are strict rules about praying at different times of the day. There are also rules about how Muslims should behave in everyday life. For example, they are not allowed to drink alcohol. Muslims must also visit the holy places at Mecca at least once in their lives. This visit is a way of celebrating their beliefs.

Although most Indians are Hindus, the country has no official religion. The Indian flag has three colours: orange for Hindus, green for Muslims and white for the hope of peace between them. Unfortunately India has not always succeeded in achieving real peace between Hindus and Muslims. In 1992 in the holy Hindu city of Ayodhya, a mosque was destroyed by a group of Hindus who were angry at seeing such a Muslim building in the birthplace of their god, Rama. In the violence that followed, over a thousand people were killed.

Hindus attack Muslim houses and shops

EXERCISE 9

Look at these sentences.

We can use an *ing*-form after a phrase with a preposition such as *believe in, angry at, way of.*

Hindus **believe in treating** the cow as a holy animal.

One group was **angry at seeing** a mosque in a holy Hindu city.

A visit to Mecca is a **way of celebrating** Muslim beliefs.

→ page 111

Complete each sentence with a preposition and the *ing*-form of the verb in brackets.

Varanasi, a holy place for Hindus

➡ Gandhi did not succeed ... (bring) Hindus and Muslims together.
Gandhi did not succeed in bringing Hindus and Muslims together.

1 Muslims believe ... (obey) God at all times.
2 Indians never seem to get tired ... (take) part in festivals.
3 People here are proud ... (live) in a holy city.
4 The tourists were interested ... (visit) a temple.
5 They are thinking ... (visit) Ayodha.
6 I was worried ... (leave) my shoes outside the temple.
7 Thank you ... (show) us around.
8 I didn't take any photos because I was afraid ... (do) something that someone might find offensive.
9 Dussehra is a way ... (celebrate) the victory of good over evil.
10 The reason ... (burn) Ravana is that he is defeated by Rama.

SITUATION 3

41

On 22 June 1948, a ship called the Empire Windrush arrived at Tilbury, east of London, with 492 passengers, most of them men from Jamaica. It wasn't easy to find work in Jamaica, and some of the passengers thought their chances would be better in England. They were all answering a call for help. Britain needed more workers to help it get back on its feet after World War II – to sweep the streets, to drive the buses and to work in the hospitals and factories. The problem was where to find them. The government's solution was to invite workers from Jamaica to come and do these jobs.

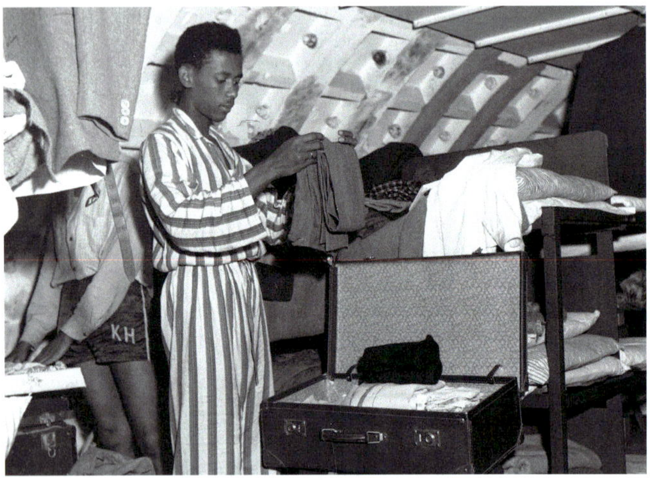

Jamaica was still part of the British Empire, and the immigrants regarded Britain as the 'mother country'. They didn't know exactly what to expect, but they knew Britain was a wonderful place because that's what they had learned in school. Unfortunately it wasn't as wonderful as they thought, and they were not always made welcome. The new Britons couldn't easily find places to live. For many blacks the only rooms available were in slums. They had to learn how to cope with discrimination and racism. Some of them even wondered whether to give up and go home.

Question word + to-infinitive → page 108

The problem was **where to find** workers to do all the jobs.
The immigrants weren't sure **what to expect**.
They had to learn **how to cope** with discrimination.
Some of them wondered **whether to go** home.

EXERCISE 10

A group of refugees have arrived in a foreign country. These are the questions they are asking themselves.

Look at their questions and complete this paragraph. Use a question word or *whether* and a *to*-infinitive.

The refugees don't know what to do next. They have no idea …[1] in this new country. They're wondering …[2]. Their first problem is …[3] somewhere to live, because they need a roof over their heads. They can't decide …[4] for an empty building. And they don't know …[5] for help. They don't speak the language, so they don't know …[6] with people. They must earn some money soon, but they don't know …[7] for work. They're wondering …[8] to the police, but they're worried they might be thrown out of the country if they do.

SITUATION 4

42

The Notting Hill Carnival takes place in London at the end of August. This annual festival began in 1964 and was started by immigrants from Trinidad in the West Indies. The idea was to bring together the people of the area where only a few years earlier there had been race riots on the streets. Most of the residents suffered from poor housing and from racism and needed something to celebrate.

At first the carnival was a small parade, but today it is a huge event. There are two million visitors for the two days of the carnival. The crowds have become so big that 7,500 police officers and 200 first aid workers are needed. There are usually more than 60 costume bands, and there are also steel bands and calypso singers. The parade goes on for at least six hours. It is said to be the largest carnival outside Rio. The costumes are spectacular. The crowds of visitors drown in the bright colours and the loud music. There's 'soca' (a mixture of soul and calypso), reggae, hip hop, garage, jungle and more.

EXERCISE 11

The word *soca* is formed from two other words, *soul* and *calypso*.
It is a mixture of two words: *soul* + *calypso* = *soca*.

Answer the following questions about similar words.

1 If you stayed at a *motel*, what kind of place would that be?
2 What kind of person is an *Amerindian*?
3 What can land at a *heliport*, and what does the word mean?
4 What time of day would you eat *brunch*, do you think?
5 What does *Eurovision* mean?
6 What is *telebanking*?
7 Who are *Interpol*?
8 If you were watching a *sitcom* on TV, what kind of programme would that be?

EXERCISE 12

Make a mind map about music. Find as many words as you can.

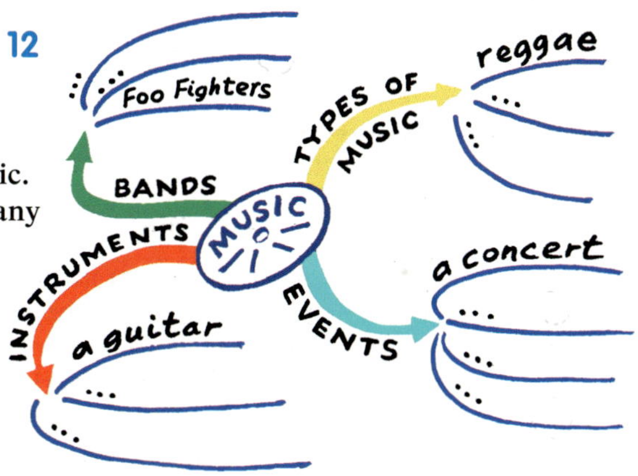

43

Black and British

Lloyd Harris is a radio chat show presenter. Today on his show he's talking with a group of young black people whose parents or grandparents came to Britain from the Caribbean. Kizzy (15), and Aaron (16) are still at school. Olivia (17) is at college. Jordan (17) is unemployed.

Lloyd … So tell me, what is it like to be black and British? Is it possible? Can you be both?

Olivia Yes, of course you can. What else are we? Just because two of my grandparents came here from Jamaica – that doesn't mean I'm not British. I grew up here. I don't want to go and live in Jamaica. Anyway, I like a cup of tea and a biscuit in the morning, so I must be British.

Lloyd But what about racism? Is that a problem for you?

Olivia No, not really. Not very often. People sometimes tell me to go back where I came from, but they're just ignorant. This is where I come from. I'm a Londoner. I wouldn't know where else to go.

Kizzy Yes, but it's more serious than that, isn't it? What about job discrimination? My sister, she's been to university, and she's really clever, and she's going to be a lawyer. And she says that white people with the same qualifications have got jobs much quicker than her. It takes a black person twice as long to get a job.

Jordan That's right. Look at the number of black people who haven't got a job at all. Me included.

Aaron Yeah, it's like they want you to stay in your place – at the bottom.

Olivia Yes, but it isn't as bad as it used to be at one time. My grandad talks a lot about the Empire Windrush –

Jordan Yeah, we've all heard about that.

Olivia – and how he came to the Mother Country with big hopes for the future, and what a shock it was when people were so unfriendly. How at first he had to live in a hostel. And when he was looking for a place to live, he saw signs in the windows that said 'No dogs and no niggers', and he didn't know what to do.

Lloyd But things have changed, haven't they? That would be illegal today.

Aaron And it would start a riot.

Jordan Yes, but in those days black people just accepted that kind of thing. We wouldn't take that kind of shit, would we?

Kizzy My dad saw the Brixton riots. He says it was the fault of the police. They used to treat every black person as a criminal.

Aaron They still do, don't they?

Jordan What about Stephen Lawrence? He was minding his own business, waiting for a bus, and he was attacked by some white boys and killed. And guess what? Those killers are still walking the streets, even though everyone knows who they are.

Aaron Just because Stephen was black, the police didn't take it seriously. They don't care about black people.

Olivia Well, maybe they've learned a lesson.

Aaron I doubt it.

Lloyd Do you think white people are less prejudiced, less ignorant about us than they used to be?

Kizzy Well, young people are OK, most of them anyway.

Lloyd Do you have white friends at school?

Kizzy Yes, of course.

Aaron But at school we have our own gangs, don't we? The white kids, the Asians, the blacks.

Olivia That's true. But it's different at college. It's really great. You're just treated as an individual person. There's no problem with racism at all.

Kizzy Like I said, it'll be different when you start looking for a job. That's when the problems start. I mean, how many top people in industry or politics are black, people with real power?

Aaron There are black footballers, but I haven't noticed any black prime ministers …

BLACKS IN BRITAIN

- *The first blacks in Britain arrived 2,000 years ago, centuries before the Anglo-Saxons. They were African soldiers in the Roman army.*
- *From about 1500 there were black servants from Africa. Britain grew rich from the slave trade with America and the Caribbean.*
- *In the 20th century many black people in British colonies such as Jamaica fought for the Mother Country in two world wars.*
- *In 1948 the arrival of the Empire Windrush was the start of a new wave of immigration.*
- *In the 1960s and 1970s laws were introduced to make race discrimination illegal.*
- *In 1981 there were riots in Brixton in south London and in other cities where black people felt they were being badly treated by the police.*
- *In 1993 18-year-old Stephen Lawrence was attacked and killed by four young white men as he waited at a bus stop in south-east London. The police failed to investigate properly, and later an official report described them as racist.*
- *In the same year, Paul Ince of Manchester United became the first black captain of the England football team.*
- *In 2002 Britain had its first black cabinet minister.*

Paul Boateng, Britain's first black cabinet minister, 2002

EXERCISE 13

Look at these statements and say which of the young people they are about. Find the place in Text 2 which shows that your answer is correct.

➡ One of the young people hasn't experienced much racism.
That's Olivia. Lloyd asks if racism is a problem for her, and she says, 'Not very often.'

1 One of them is unemployed.
2 Someone's grandfather experienced discrimination when he was looking for accommodation.
3 Someone thinks the police are more interested in protecting whites than in protecting blacks.
4 One of them thinks young blacks today will resist racism. Their parents and grandparents accepted it too easily.
5 One of the young people explains how it is more difficult for blacks to find work.
6 One person feels much more British than Jamaican.
7 Two of the young people say that there aren't many blacks in really important jobs.

EXERCISE 14

Look at the information in the green box above and then make sentences from this table.

The first black people in Britain	was that the police didn't do their job properly.
Laws against discrimination	served Britain in two world wars.
A lot of blacks in the colonies	came with the Roman army.
The slave trade	were introduced in the 1960s and 1970s.
The reason no one was arrested for the murder of Stephen Lawrence	were the first of many who have come since 1948.
The immigrants on the Empire Windrush	happened because the blacks were angry at the police.
The riots in British cities	made lots of money for Britain.

➡ The first black people in Britain came with the Roman army.

EXERCISE 15

Some words have more than one meaning.

> We're all members of the human race. (race = *Rasse*)
> I'm running in the 100 metres race. (race = *Rennen*)

Put in the missing words. Use each of these words twice: *bank, letter, lie, light, mean, ~~run~~, still.* Sometimes you need to put an ending on the word.

- We had to run to catch the bus.
- What does your dad do? – He runs a taxi company.

1 There are 26 … in the alphabet.
2 Melanie is working at a … in Dublin.
3 I don't feel very well. I'm going to … down.
4 It's … raining. When is it going to stop?
5 What does this word … ?
6 It was … of you not to buy your sister an ice-cream.
7 Edison invented the electric … bulb.
8 I send lots of e-mails, but I don't write many … .
9 Tell me the truth. I don't want to hear any … .
10 The bag is heavy, but the case is quite … .
11 If I'm going to paint a picture of you, you'll have to keep … .
12 Some people were standing on the … of the river.

Give two different German translations of each word. You can use your dictionary.

- run = *laufen / leiten* 1 letter = …

EXERCISE 17

44-45

Listening

Vincent Bailey is talking about how he came from the West Indies to live in England. Listen to his story.

Part 1 (44)

Choose the right answer.

1 Has Vincent experienced any racist attitudes in Britain?
a) Yes, all the time. b) Yes, mainly in the early years.
c) No, never.
2 How did Vincent learn about jobs in England?
a) From a relative who lived there.
b) From an English friend. c) He saw an advertisement.
3 Why did he leave Jamaica?
a) He had no job. b) He didn't like it there.
c) He wanted to earn more money.
4 Which of these describes Vincent on the Empire Windrush?
a) a young man on his own b) a man with his wife
c) a man with his two brothers

EXERCISE 16

Arthur Harris is of West Indian origin. He is talking about coming to England and about young people today and their attitudes. Find the right verb and put in a *to*-infinitive or an *ing*-form.

'I came to England over 50 years ago, when I was a young man. I'd tried to find a job in Jamaica, but I couldn't. So I decided … to England. I lived in a hostel with other Jamaicans for a few weeks. The first thing was to get work. I soon succeeded in … a job as a hospital cleaner. They expected me … long hours. It was hard work too, but I've never minded … hard. Not like today. Young people don't seem … much work at all, do they? As far as I can see, they just enjoy … out to night clubs. People today allow their kids … just what they want. Rose and I weren't interested in … to night clubs. We wanted … our own house. Rose persuaded me … it, and I'm glad she did. We managed … enough money from what we earned. We worked hard and we didn't complain. I don't believe in … about everything. I think you should keep your head down and do your job. I've been good at … my head down. I don't believe in riots. I don't do things like that. That's just not my way of … things. I've had no trouble. And we've been very happy.'

Part 2 (45)

Listen and take notes. Note down the information you hear about the following.

- where Vincent stayed at first
- his first job
- his second job
- the members of his family
- what his children do now
- his third job

46

Hope, doubt and interest

Expressing hope
- I hope you get that job you've applied for.

Expressing doubt
- The film will be in English. – Are you sure?
- Do you think you'll win the prize? – I doubt it. / I don't think so.
- I doubt if there's a performance on Sundays.

Expressing interest
- We're all going on a trip to India. – Really? / Are you really? / Oh, that's interesting.
- This looks interesting. / That sounds fascinating.

Hector I'm looking forward to *Bombay Dreams*. I hope we can get tickets.
Keesha Well, I doubt it actually. These West End musicals are very popular. But we can try. Remind me what the story is about.
Hector It's about a poor boy from the slums who dreams of becoming a Bollywood movie star.
Keesha It sounds interesting. I'd certainly like to see it.

EXERCISE 18

Work with a partner. Write a short dialogue and act it out.

Partner **A** *Sage, dass du nächste Woche zum Popfestival in Glastonbury gehst.*
Partner **B** Zeige Interesse und sage, dass du noch nie da warst.
Partner **A** *Sage, dass du auch noch nie da warst und dass du dich wirklich darauf freust.*
Partner **B** Äußere deine Hoffnung, dass das Wetter trocken bleibt.
Partner **A** *Sage, dass du das auch hoffst, aber dass du es bezweifelst. Man hat für nächste Woche Regen vorhergesagt.*

EXERCISE 19

Writing about places

Work with a partner.

Partner **B:** Please look at page 96.
Partner **A:** Read this information about Jamaica.

Jamaica is an island in the Caribbean south of Cuba. It is 146 miles long and about 50 miles wide. It has a population of 2.6 million, mainly of African origin. The capital is Kingston. Other important towns are Montego Bay and Spanish Town. Exports include sugar, coffee and bananas. The official language is English, although many people speak a Jamaican dialect. Jamaica was a Spanish colony until 1655, when Britain took control. The island became independent in 1962.

Partner **B** has some similar information about Trinidad and Tobago. Ask partner **B** for the same kind of information as you have in your text.
You can start like this:
Where are Trinidad and Tobago? How big are the islands?
Then use the answers to write a similar text about Trinidad and Tobago.

Township Soweto

Soweto

No one knows exactly how many people live in Soweto, but it's probably about four million. Soweto is a crowded black township near Johannesburg in South Africa – the name means 'South Western Township' – and it covers a huge area. There are some well-off people who live there in brick houses, but most of the residents live in camps in one-room shacks they have built from pieces of old metal. The conditions are awful. Each toilet and water tap is shared by dozens of people.

In Kumale Street, in a part of Soweto called Orlando West, is the Hector Petersen Museum. Back in 1976, in the time of apartheid – when the races were kept separate – students were marching to protest against the way they were treated by the white government. A couple of blocks from here, twelve-year-old Hector was shot dead by the police. He was the first of over 500 who were killed in the uprising. The events in Soweto helped to turn world opinion against the apartheid system. A movement called the 'African National Congress' (ANC) led the fight against apartheid. The system finally came to an end in 1994 when Nelson Mandela became president of the new South Africa.

Things are changing for black South Africans, but very slowly. The government is building houses in Soweto, but the shacks have not disappeared. When people move out of a shack and into a new house, there are always other people ready to move in and take their place. There are many problems – unemployment, crime, drugs and especially AIDS. About ten per cent of the population has AIDS.

Under the old apartheid government, young people had ideas about changing the system. Many of them supported the ANC because they wanted to win their freedom from white rule. But these days there is much less interest in politics. The ANC has won power, but many young people believe that politicians are corrupt and not interested in solving the country's problems or improving the lives of ordinary people. Young people now are more likely to be interested in new cars, clothes, money and a career – if they're lucky enough to have one. Many unemployed young blacks turn to crime. Guns are widely available, and gun violence is increasing. Schools are doing their best to keep guns out of the classroom.

There is a long hard road to travel before the people of Soweto can enjoy true peace and freedom.

The bridge across the main street to Soweto

1 Decide if each statement is true or false. If it is false, correct it.

1 There are poor people and well-off people in the township of Soweto near Johannesburg.
2 Hector Petersen is famous because he was the only person who died in the Soweto uprising.
3 Apartheid began in 1994 when Nelson Mandela became president.
4 Because the government isn't doing anything, some people in Soweto are still living in metal shacks.
5 The fight against apartheid made many young people think about how things could be different.
6 Today young people spend more time worrying about everyday things like what they should wear.

The African National Congress (ANC) logo

2 Correct the sentences. Replace each word in italics with its opposite.

1 Soweto is a *tiny* area.
2 The conditions are *excellent*.
3 Hector Petersen is *alive*.
4 Things are changing *fast*.
5 The ANC *lost* their fight against apartheid.
6 The country needs a period of *war*.

3 Explain the meaning of these words from the text.

1 most of the *residents* (line 9)
2 a toilet is *shared* (line 12)
3 the *events* in Soweto (line 17)
4 world *opinion* (line 17)
5 the shacks have not *disappeared* (line 21)
6 not interested in *improving* their lives (line 29)
7 *unemployed* young blacks (line 33)

4 Complete these paragraphs about Nelson Mandela. Use the words in brackets in their correct form and put in the right words.

Nelson Mandela was … in 1918 in a village in South Africa. He attended school, and he also helped to look … the family's cattle. When he was 22, he went to Johannesburg. He lived in a … (crowd) black … (town) called Soweto. He saw that blacks … (not earn) much money and that whites lived in large houses with swimming … in their gardens. Mandela worked as a … (law). Some of South Africa's laws were very … (race). Mandela … (hate) the evil apartheid system, so he joined the ANC and organized a campaign … segregation.

Mandela's campaigns did not succeed in … (change) the system. The police were looking … him, so he had … go underground. Then he … (catch) by the police and sent to prison for life.

In 1990, 71-year-old Nelson Mandela experienced his first moment of … (free) for 27 years. Four years … (late), he … (become) president of his country.

Nelson Mandela, President of South Africa, in 1994

The long years in prison had not … (break) Mandela. He was ready to build the new South Africa. Even … the whites had … him so badly, he did not want revenge. He always thought it was worth … (listen) to what other people had to say. His aim was still that blacks and whites should have … opportunities.

7-49

5 Antoinette Sithole is Hector Petersen's older sister. She is telling the story of what happened on the day her brother died. Listen to what she says.

Part 1 (47)

Complete the sentences. Put one word in each space.

1 The day Hector died, Antoinette was … years old.
2 The students of Soweto wanted to use their own … in school.
3 Everyone ran out of the way when they heard the … .
4 Antoinette hid behind a … .

Part 2 (48)

1 Antoinette recognized Hector's … .
a) face b) shirt c) shoe
2 Hector was carried away by a … .
a) reporter b) student c) teacher
3 He was driven to the hospital by a … .
a) policeman b) reporter c) teacher
4 He had been injured in the … .
a) arm b) leg c) neck

Part 3 (49)

Answer the questions.

1 Who told Antoinette's mother about Hector's death?
2 What was Hector very good at?
3 How did Antoinette's sister die?
4 Why don't the family have any photos of Hector?

Anita and me

Meera Syal

'Anita and Me' is a novel about a nine-year-old girl called Meena whose parents came to England from India. Meena grows up in a village in the English Midlands in the 1960s. She makes friends with an older white girl called Anita.

One day near the end of the summer holidays, I saw Anita in the park. She was sitting alone on the swings, and from a distance she looked like a little old lady. She was in her school uniform of green sweater, grey skirt, white blouse, grey and green tie and long white socks, but the socks were the only things that fitted her. Her sleeves were much too long, and the skirt came below her knees, even though she was sitting down on the swing. I called out to her, but she hardly looked at me. At first I thought she was in one of her moods, and I began wondering what I had done wrong the last time we met. I had said sorry about her dog dying, hadn't I? But as I got closer, I saw that her eyes were red.

'What's up?'
She tried to smile
'Nothing. Got me new uniform today.'
I nodded stupidly.
'Me mom's gone,' Anita said calmly.
'Oh,' I said. 'Where?'
'Dunno. She left a note for dad. She's gone off with a butcher. Dad says good riddance.'

I did not know what to say. I knew if mama had run away and left a note, I would now be rolling around and pulling my hair out, the way they did in the Indian films. Then I would have followed the butcher in a car and stabbed him with his own knife while his back was turned. I would have emptied mama's wardrobe and set fire to all her clothes and danced round the burning saris. I would not have sat calmly on a swing.

'These came this morning,' Anita went on in that same voice. She was talking about her uniform. 'I expect she ordered them ages ago. She knew she was going.' Anita held her huge sleeve. 'And look, the silly cow still don't know my size.'

I then did something I had never done before. I put my arm around Anita and kissed her and whispered,
'Sorry, Nita, I really am.'
'Whassup with you?' Anita shouted, wiping her cheek furiously.
'Am yow a lezzie?'
'What's a lezzie?' I asked.
Anita rolled her eyes. 'Yow don't know nothing, do ya? I bet yow don't know what a virgin is neither!'
'Yes, I do!' I said. At least I knew that the mother of Jesus was one.
'So am yow then?'
'What?' I said.
'Am yow a virgin then?'
Anita gave me a dangerous look.

I tried furiously to think of what I and Mary, mother of the King of Kings, might have in common. Like me, she was not from England, but then she was much older than me. She rode a donkey, she was married – no real connection there. I tried to remember how Anita had said 'virgin' – did it sound like something you wanted to become, or a terrible disease you wouldn't want to have? I had to decide; Mary was the mother of someone pretty important, so virgins could not be so bad. 'Yeah, I am one actually,' I said confidently.

'Me too,' said Anita. 'But not for long, eh?' She winked at me and laughed. I laughed back knowingly and decided to ask papa about it when I got home.

(adapted from *Anita and me* by Meera Syal)

50

Island in the sun

JAMAICA – THE HOME OF REGGAE

Jamaica with its white beaches, magnificent rain forests and beautiful waterfalls has a sad past. Columbus visited this tourist paradise on his second voyage in 1494 and the island came under Spanish rule. The English captured the Caribbean island in 1655 and it remained a British colony until 1962. The earliest inhabitants of the island were the Taino people. However, after the arrival of the Europeans many Tainos died, some because they were badly treated by the white men and others from European diseases such as smallpox. Under the English, the sugar trade grew and slaves were brought from Africa to work on the sugar plantations. Almost a million slaves were brought to Jamaica before the slave trade was stopped in 1807, and today more than 90% of Jamaica's population is black. The longing of the slaves for freedom can still be heard in today's reggae songs. Reggae developed in the 1960s and was a mixture of different styles, such as North American rhythm and blues and Jamaican ska. It gave black people a voice to express how they felt about their oppression. The reggae singer Bob Marley had top hits all around the world. He was the first superstar from a developing country. Since his death in 1981, reggae has remained popular and still influences the music of today. In hip hop, for example, you can find DJing and rhyming simple language.

THE RASTAFARIAN RELIGION

Emperor Haile Selassie 1892-1975

The Rastafarian religion is both a faith and a way of life. It has its origin in Africa. Rastafarians worship Haile Selassie. He was called Ras Tafari until he became the Emperor of Ethiopia in 1930. Rastas believe that blacks are the chosen people and that they will return to Africa. They believe in the dignity of black people and are proud of their history. They protest against the oppression of black people at the hands of the white man. To stress their black identity and their Rasta beliefs, they grow their black hair like wool in dreadlocks. True Rasta men eat only natural food. This food is called 'ital'. They don't eat meat or salt or anything from cans, and they don't drink alcohol. They have had a big influence on Caribbean society and have produced lots of reggae stars. However, drugs are a serious problem in Jamaica because the Rastafarians smoke marijuana ('ganja'), both for religious reasons and as a way of protesting against society.

COOL RUNNINGS

51

The main thing you need for bobsledding is ice. Lots of ice. However, Jamaica, where it never snows, has an Olympic bobsled team. In the 1980s four Jamaicans were captured by Olympic fever. They won the world's attention and the audience's hearts when they took part in the bobsled competition at the 1988 Calgary Winter Olympics – although they had never touched a real bobsled before.

Back in Jamaica, three sprinters and a reggae singer practised in a cart on dirt tracks and beautiful beaches. Although they had tried to get used to freezing temperatures in an ice-cream truck, the weather was still a shock to them when they arrived in Calgary where it was minus 25°C with strong winds. At first everything went wrong and they couldn't even find a sponsor to help them buy some equipment. In the end they bought an old bobsled. The audience cheered them when they raced. Everyone wanted to see them win a medal. Even teams from other countries helped them – although some members of European teams made racist comments and told them to go back where they came from. In the last race, they had a crash at 80 mph but they got up on their feet and pushed their old bobsled across the finishing line. Since then Devon Harris, Patrick Robinson and their team have taken part in more Winter Olympics, and the Jamaican team has enjoyed a lot of success. Their biggest problem is that people can't help smiling when they hear the words 'Jamaican Bobsled Team'.

Maybe you have seen the film *Cool Runnings*, a comedy with a lot of slapstick situations and great action scenes. But the film also shows that the Jamaicans needed courage to take part in such a dangerous sport. What people like about the film is that the new boys tackle the high-tech world of the Olympic games and manage to win everyone's respect – and that the story is true. However, the film does not deal with any of the problems of Jamaican society such as poverty, violence or drugs. The title *Cool Runnings* is a Caribbean expression which means 'peaceful journey' – and that's what the film is about. It makes you feel good. The message is: Do your best! Live your dreams!

Scene from the film Cool Runnings

EXERCISE 1

Here are some dates from Jamaica's history. What happened in these years?

1494 • 1930 • 1962 • 1981 • 1988

EXERCISE 2

Answer the questions about *Cool Runnings*.

1 What is so strange about having a Jamaican bobsled team?
2 How did the team prepare for the Olympic race? Mention two things they did.
3 How did the other teams react?
4 What is the Jamaican team's biggest problem today?
5 Why do people like the film *Cool Runnings*?

Jamaican 2-men bobsled, Winter Olympics, Salt Lake City 2002

EXERCISE 3

Search the internet for news about the Jamaican bobsled team. You can also print out their flag and some photos.

EXERCISE 4

Complete these sentences about Jamaica. You can look again at pages 100–101 for information on the three main types of *if*-clause.

1 If Europeans … (not settle) in Jamaica, the Tainos … (not catch) European diseases.
2 Marijuana … (not be) such a big problem on Jamaica today if the Rastafarians … (not smoke) it as part of their religion.
3 If the sugar plantations … (not need) so many workers, the slave trade … (be) less important.
4 If Bob Marley … (not be) a big star, reggae … (not become) so popular all around the world.
5 People who watch *Cool Runnings* … (not laugh) so much if the film … (tell) us more about poverty.
6 The message of the film is that if you … (follow) your dreams and … (stay) true to yourself, you … (be) successful in the end.

EXERCISE 5

Four Jamaicans tried a new sport and got as far as the Olympic Games. Could you do the same? Complete the sentences.
Use a *to*-infinitive or an *ing*-form of the verbs in brackets.

1 If you hope … (do) well at your sport, it's a good idea … (join) a sports club.
2 You'll have … (practise) every day and concentrate on … (get) better.
3 Don't think about … (give up), even if things go wrong sometimes. It's always worth … (do) your best.
4 Someone might want … (sponsor) you if you succeed in … (win) your local championships.
5 We look forward to … (see) you at the Olympic Games – if you manage … (get) there!

SONG

52

Get Up, Stand Up
by Bob Marley and Peter Tosh

Get up, stand up, stand
up for your right (3 times)
Get up, stand up, don't give up the fight

Preacher man don't tell me heaven is
under the earth
I know you don't know what life is really
worth
Is not all that glitters in gold and
Half the story has never been told
So now you see the light, aay
Stand up for your right. Come on.

Get up, stand up, stand up for your right
Get up, stand up, don't give up the fight
(Repeat)

Most people think great God will come
from the sky
Take away ev'rything, and make ev'rybody
feel high
But if you know what life is worth
You would look for yours on earth
And now you see the light
You stand up for your right, yeah!

Get up, stand up, stand up for your right
Get up, stand up, don't give up the fight
Get up, stand up. Life is your right
So we can't give up the fight
Stand up for your right, Lord, Lord
Get up, stand up. Keep on struggling on
Don't give up the fight

We're sick and tired of your ism and skism
game
Die and go to heaven in Jesus' name, Lord
We know when we understand
Almighty God is a living man
You can fool some people sometimes
But you can't fool all the people all the time
So now we see the light
We gonna stand up for our right

So you'd better get up, stand up, stand up
for your right
Get up, stand up, don't give up the fight
Get up, stand up, stand up for your right
Get up, stand up, don't give up the fight

Counting trees

53

Young people sometimes take time out after they leave school and before they start a permanent job. Have you ever thought of doing that? You can travel around, see new places and meet new people.

Some people do voluntary work abroad. There's lots of information on the internet about several organizations that arrange this kind of work. They can tell you how old you have to be, what kind of qualifications you need and the sort of projects you can work on. They'll also tell you the places you can go to and how to apply. The photos on both these pages are from students working abroad.

Let's visit a chat room for people who have done voluntary work or who want to find out about it. At the moment Declan, Melissa and Helen are in the chat room.

Declan what did u do melissa
Melissa teaching in thailand

Claude enters the room.

Declan everyone does teaching
Claude hi room
Melissa not everyone
Helen hi claude

Declan well i did teaching in india
Claude what else can u do
Melissa after thailand i travelled around se asia with a friend

Tom enters the room.

Tom hi
Helen u can do a conservation project like i did in namibia, i measured and counted trees

Claude with a boy or girl melissa
Melissa mind your own business
Declan counting trees sounds boring

Tom some1 talk2 me
Helen also i helped to build a school, it was great
Tom wheres namibia

Angelika enters the room.

Helen it's the experience of working with people different from you, learning to respect them
Declan yeah right

Angelika hello im angelika
Melissa why count trees
Tom i said wheres namibia
Claude sw africa of course
Declan tom ur soooooo ignorant

Helen it was one particular kind of tree, giraffes eat the leaves of it
Melissa OIC

Helen i had to study the wildlife too
Angelika do you always need to speak english in these countries
Claude how do people get the money to travel

Tom in ecuador u speak spanish on the project, u have to do a spanish course first

Melissa u have to earn the money claude, how else, i was a waitress for 3 months
Angelika it would be interesting to learn a new language

Claude i h8 work
Helen where r u from angelika
Angelika germany
Claude what are the conditions like
Declan in india i lived in a hut with 4 other people
Helen i had to camp some of the time

Declan u have to be prepared for primitive conditions, its part of the experience
Helen it teaches u about yourself and what u can do

Angelika how old were u when u did that declan
Tom its good to do something useful for other people
Declan 19, between school and uni
Helen what r u going to do angelika
Angelika im thinking about it, maybe improve my english
Melissa in thailand i was in a pretty remote place and i was a kind of celebrity
Helen i no what u mean

Melissa people used to turn round and look at me
Claude nice, all those girls looking at me, cant wait
Tom ur english is good angelika
Angelika so does everyone think voluntary work is a good idea

Declan claude ur an idiot
Melissa go away claude
Claude ok bye

Claude leaves the room.

Angelika thx tom
Helen voluntary work looks good when you apply for a job
Declan i learned more from the kids than they learned from me, it really changed me

Melissa u should do it while u have the chance
Angelika i think i will

EXERCISE 1

When people are talking in a chat room, they don't always use punctuation or capital letters, and they often use abbreviations that save time: *u* for 'you' and *any1* for 'anyone'.

Write the full sentences.

➜ what did u do
What did you do?
1 some1 talk 2 me
2 I no what u mean
3 ur english is good
4 OIC
5 I h8 work
6 ur an idiot
7 thx tom
8 where r u from

EXERCISE 2

Look closely at the conversation and give a reason why people say these things.

➜ *Claude* hi room
Claude says 'Hi, room' because he has just entered the chat room and is saying hello to everyone.
1 *Melissa* mind your own business
2 *Tom* some1 talk 2 me
3 *Declan* yeah right
4 *Declan* tom ur soooooo ignorant
5 *Melissa* go away claude

EXERCISE 3

Answer the questions.

1 Why does the conversation in the chat room look strange when you read it? Why are some questions not answered immediately?

2 Have you ever visited a chat room? What did you talk about? Find out if any of your classmates have taken part in one of these conversations. If you and your partner were in a chat room, what would you talk about?

3 Do you think chat rooms are a good idea? What are the advantages and disadvantages?

EXERCISE 4

When Helen got home after she finished her voluntary project, a reporter from the local newspaper interviewed her. Complete the interview.

1 *Reporter* Where did you do your project, Helen?
Helen In … .
2 *Reporter* And what kind of project was it? What did you have to do?
Helen …
3 *Reporter* And why are the trees important?
Helen …
4 *Reporter* And I believe you built something, too.
Helen …
5 *Reporter* Did you enjoy the work?
Helen …
6 *Reporter* And were you paid for the work?
Helen …
7 *Reporter* What did you learn from the experience?
Helen …
8 *Reporter* And do you think the experience will help you in your career?
Helen …

EXERCISE 5

Here are some abbreviations and symbols that you can use in chat rooms or in e-mails or text messages on your mobile. Match each one with the correct words. It might help if you read the abbreviations out loud.

1	IMHO	a) I'm bored
2	2L8	b) (do you) want to?
3	Cusoon	c) happy
4	zzzz	d) too late
5	:-)	e) not tonight
6	HAND	f) start at the beginning
7	S@TB	g) in my humble opinion
8	12?	h) very very happy
9	X	i) no!
10	:-)))	j) today
11	NT2NITE	k) have a nice day
12	2d	l) a kiss
13	9!	m) see you soon

➜ 1g) IMHO means 'in my humble opinion'.

And what do you think these mean?

1 CU2moro
2 RUOK?
3 B4Ugo
4 gotNE£££?
5 CUL8R
6 LO
7 :-(
8 ILUVU
9 UR2good24get

Why English?

54

GLOBAL ENGLISH

About 5,000 different languages are spoken around the world, but English has become the main language of communication. What makes it the world language? There are certainly more native speakers of Spanish and Chinese. But English is the main foreign language in over a hundred countries – one fifth of the world's population can speak English. And language teachers say that its grammar is easier than other languages because there aren't any difficult endings on words, such as there are on German words, for example.

However, the most important reason why English is the most widely spoken language is that it has always been the language of power, politics and business – in the past because of the British Empire and today because of the United States. It is spoken on every continent – you can find English advertisements and signs for tourists everywhere. Presidents and ministers argue in English and you surf the internet in English. Business people from Norway and Italy can travel to France to discuss matters of trade with partners from South Africa – in English, of course. And international pop singers enjoy rhyming English words (love – above, you – true, maybe – baby). The British usually feel proud that English has become the world language, but they sometimes need to realize that not everyone in the world speaks British English. There are many other varieties of English, too.

THE LANGUAGE OF FREEDOM

When Nelson Mandela became South Africa's first black president in 1994, eleven official languages were recognized, nine African languages, Afrikaans and English. South African hip hop uses all of these languages. To many black South Africans, however, English is the language of freedom. It is the language which brings them international attention in the media and which offers them education and a better future. Afrikaans is the language of the Dutch settlers who invaded the country, made it a colony and organized the slave trade there in the 17th century. The first English settlers arrived in 1820. Today, English is the second language for millions of Africans and it has also influenced their native languages. Africans call someone who has visited Europe a 'been-to', for example.

BINGLISH AND HINGLISH

South Asia is another area where English is used as a second language. Over the centuries the British have explored this region and traded with its people. India was 'the Jewel in the Crown' of the British Empire until it obtained its independence in 1947. In New Delhi you'll find that English is widely used as the language of government and education. It has even replaced the native Hindi on many of India's street signs, in shops and on the internet. Many Indians work for British companies and feel close to the European way of life even though India has been independent for more than 50 years now. Sometimes Indian forms of English create new words, for example a female cousin is called a 'cousin-sister' and a sister-in-law a 'co-sister'. Boys who tease girls are said to be 'eve-teasing'. A lot of people use a mixture of Bengali, Hindi and English and create new languages called Binglish and Hinglish which are often used in the media and in advertisements.

SPANGLISH

Today more than 26 million people in the US are of Hispanic origin and millions of families speak Spanish at home. The Spanish language has influenced the south of the United States for centuries. Many places in this region have Spanish names, such as the states of Florida and Colorado and cities like Los Angeles, El Paso and Santa Fe. Using Spanish words allows Hispanics to hold on to some of their own culture. But life in America means that they also need English words to talk about everyday things as well as to express American ideas. Instead of always having to decide which language they should use, the Hispanic population in the US has created a way of speaking called Spanglish – a mixture of Spanish and American English words and grammar.

In British English most words are not written the way they are spoken. The spelling sometimes shows how the words were pronounced hundreds of years ago. In Spanglish, English words are pronounced in a 'Spanish style', for example by dropping final consonants and replacing 'Vs' with 'Bs'. A Hispanic would use a 'bacuncliner' instead of a 'vacuum cleaner'. Other words are sometimes given Spanish endings. For example 'shootiar' means 'to shoot'. In this way new words are invented, and that might be a reason why Spanglish has become very popular with Hispanic rappers as well as with writers. It is mainly a spoken language, but Hispanics also write the words as they hear and speak them. They use 'wan' for 'one' and 'faiv' for 'five'. Can you guess what 'hu', 'wer', 'wat' and 'wai' mean?

EXERCISE 1

Answer the questions.

1 Why has English become the global language? Give three reasons.
2 Why do black South Africans prefer English to Afrikaans?
3 Explain two ways in which English words are changed in Spanglish.
4 Which new 'English' words have been created by people whose first language isn't English? Give two examples and explain them.

EXERCISE 2

In the text 'Spanglish', what do the place names in lines 3–4 mean in English? You might need to look in a dictionary or on the internet for help. Your teacher will help you to find internet addresses.

EXERCISE 3

Translate the first paragraph (page 75 lines 1–11) into good German. There may be some words that you don't know or don't remember.
Try to work out their meaning from the context in which they are used.

EXERCISE 4

Use the words in brackets in their correct form or find a word from the same family.

1 Of all the … (Europe) languages, English has become the … (important).
2 The best … (argue) for learning English is that it's the language of … (busy) and worldwide … (communicate).
3 You might be … (worry) if you saw a … (friend) sign which … (say): 'Here you can become a marvellous schnitzel!'
4 A few years ago, when some … (France) ministers felt that they had to protect … (they) language against English influences, they tried to reduce the number of British and … (America) songs on radio programmes.
5 But they had to … (real) that no radio station could survive without playing … (population) music from Britain or America.
6 In some countries English words are used but are given new … (mean). Germans, for example, phone their friends on a 'Handy' – but they can't believe that this word isn't … (useful) in the same way in English. It's … (actual) a 'mobile phone' or a 'cellphone'.
7 It is … (interest) that Germans even give some English words German … (end). They go 'joggen' instead of 'jogging' in the evenings.
8 As a … (globe) language English has … (success) in changing Russian words, too. When young people in Moscow do sport, they wear 'shoozy' on their … (foot).

British tourists often find mistakes on English signs when they go abroad. How many can you find in this photo?

EXERCISE 5

Complete the second sentence so that it has the same meaning as the first.

➜ Some African languages have been influenced by English.
English has influenced some African languages.
1 India obtained its independence in 1947.
India became …
2 You can find English advertisements everywhere.
English advertisements …
3 English words don't have as many forms as German words.
German words …
4 Not everyone speaks English.
There are some people …
5 The British Empire was the reason why English was used so widely.
English was used so widely …
6 English has replaced Hindi on many street signs.
Many street signs are now …

Mutiny on the Bounty

55

In the 18th century, crossing the ocean on a sailing ship was extremely dangerous, and conditions were terrible. Sailors were always wet, cold and hungry but they had to work really hard, day and night. Life on board a ship was dangerous because of accidents and heavy storms. Some voyages across the seas took almost three years. The Empire's breadfruit ships sailed from England to Tahiti in the South Pacific, loaded young breadfruit plants, took them to Jamaica where they were used to grow food for the British slaves on the sugar plantations – and sailed back to England again. Altogether such a voyage was about 30,000 kilometres on the open seas. The HMS Bounty, a small and uncomfortable ship, never returned from this nightmare.

In 1787, the Bounty left England with her captain William Bligh, first officer Fletcher Christian and a crew of 43 men, all aged between 15 and 40. This was the beginning of one of the most famous sea stories of all times. Bligh's plan was to sail to Tahiti westward around Cape Horn, at the tip of South America, but because of heavy storms the Bounty had to travel eastward and take the longer route around the Cape of Good Hope, at the south-east corner of Africa. Bligh was an expert sailor but difficult to get on with, and his exhausted crew often complained and refused to obey him. The crew themselves were no angels. One day Bligh accused Christian of stealing food for the officers. The atmosphere on the ship was extremely tense. So when they had arrived at Tahiti to load the breadfruit plants, they decided to stay there and relax for a time. In fact they stayed for five months. The crew really enjoyed the blue skies, the good food, the beautiful girls, ... Most of them wanted to stay. Travelling back to England would mean giving up this paradise for another twelve dangerous months on board. But Bligh forced them onto the ship and sailed off.

Scenes from the film Mutiny on the Bounty with Mel Gibson as mutineer Fletcher Christian and Anthony Hopkins as Captain Bligh

The crew then started to whisper among each other: Why don't we stay a little longer? Why not go back and enjoy Tahiti, its wonderful weather and the friendly people? Why can't the captain go back to England on his own? Why don't we give him the small boat and say goodbye to him? Of course these were just dreams. Mutiny would mean certain death because the Royal Navy would do everything in its power to capture and kill them. They would never be able to return to England ever again. Forget it, they thought. But three weeks later, Fletcher Christian, John Adams and a few crew members were talking quietly in their beds. They reached a decision. On the morning of April 28, 1789, the mutineers took their swords and guns and pushed Bligh and 18 sailors into a small open boat just seven metres long. They threw down food and fresh water for a week or two. That day the Bounty was thousands of kilometres away from land. So they sent Bligh and his men to their certain deaths.

The 'Bounty bastard breadfruit Bligh', as the mutineers shouted after him, now had a real problem. His hungry, wet and tired sailors started to give up hope. Captain Bligh, however, became a legend. His courage saved their lives.

They managed to survive a seven-week voyage of 7,000 kilometres and reached the island of Timor on their crowded little boat. Then Bligh returned to England on a Dutch ship with news of the mutiny.

But back to the mutineers on the Bounty. The soldiers of the Royal Navy would soon come to kill them. Where could they hide? They went back to Tahiti, where 14 mutineers left the ship to stay with their new Tahitian wives. A few months later, these men were captured and hanged in Britain. Fletcher Christian and eight other mutineers took their Tahitian wives and some friends on board and sailed away on the Bounty. They were never seen again. After three months, the Royal Navy gave up looking for them.

It wasn't until 19 years later that the world found out what had happened to them. An American captain, Mayhew Folger, discovered a strange English-speaking community on the remote island of Pitcairn. Their fathers had been the mutineers and had burned the Bounty after their arrival on the island. Only John Adams was still alive, and he was able to tell Folger what had happened. The English mutineers had planned to take the whole island for themselves and to use the people from Tahiti as slaves. There had been several years of fighting, and all the men had died or been killed – except John Adams. Folger found him on the island with nine women and 23 children.

EXERCISE 1

For each paragraph of the text, choose one of these headings.

- Life on the ocean
- The mutiny
- What happened on Pitcairn Island?
- Back to Tahiti
- The Bounty's voyage to Tahiti
- Captain Bligh survives

EXERCISE 2

Who could have said this?

1 Men in our job have to work very hard, and we never get enough to eat.
2 I know it was you who took the food!
3 Let's put them in the small boat and give them a bit of food and water.
4 It's no good. We're in the middle of the ocean. We're going to die.
5 We can't find them anywhere.
6 I'm the only one on the island who has survived.
7 You wouldn't believe it – everybody here speaks English.

EXERCISE 3

Why? Complete these sentences on the text.

1 The British Empire needed breadfruit plants because ...
2 The crew didn't like Bligh because ...
3 The mutineers had to forget about going home to England because ...
4 Christian's mutineers burned the Bounty because ...
5 The Tahitians fought the mutineers because ...

Breadfruit plant

EXERCISE 4

In his famous diary Bligh wrote about the mutiny. But what about the other side of the story? Choose one of the following people. What do you think were their thoughts or feelings about the mutiny and the mutineers? Write at least 80 words that the person might have written in his or her diary.

- a girl from Tahiti who met the mutineers
- the young midshipman Peter Heywood (15 years old)
- Fletcher Christian
- John Adams
- Mayhew Folger

56-57

EXERCISE 5

Listening

Somewhere on a remote island two men are having a conversation. Listen to what they say.

Part 1 (56)

Choose the right answer.

1 The conversation takes place on ... .
a) Tahiti b) Pitcairn c) the Falklands
2 The islander was named after ... .
a) his birthday
b) the date of the mutiny
c) the king's birthday
3 When Fletcher Christian talked about England, he mentioned ... .
a) wet weather b) good food
c) his mother
4 John Adams is the island's ... .
a) captain b) leader c) guide

Part 2 (57)

Read the following questions. Note down the answers to the questions as you listen.

1 Why doesn't Thursday go back to England? (Two reasons.)
2 Who is the visitor?
3 What does 'Kah Wah' mean and which language does it come from?
4 Why does the visitor gladly accept the invitation? (Two reasons.)

Untitled (Michael Rosen)

58

I was going to buy my sister a box
of chocolates, but she's on a diet.
It's a seafood diet.
If she sees food, she eats it.

Untitled (Michael Rosen)

59

Mississippi said to Missouri,
'If I put on my New Jersey
What will Delaware?'
Virginia said 'Alaska'.

60

John Bun

Here lies John Bun,
He was killed by a gun,
His name is not Bun,
But Wood,
But Wood would not
Rhyme with gun,
But Bun would.

from a gravestone
in Southampton

Sipping Cider (Anonymous)

61

The sweetest girl I ever saw
Sat sipping cider through a straw.
I said to her 'My dear, what for
Do you sip cider through a straw?'
She said 'My dear, why don't you know
That sipping cider's all the go.'
So cheek by cheek and jaw by jaw
We both sipped cider through a straw.
That's how I got my ma-in-law,
Through sipping cider through a straw.
And now I've got ten kids or more
Through sipping cider through a straw.

Tall story

62

The sole survivor of an atomic war
(Who was also a bit of a joker)
Arrived in a land where everything
Had forgotten what it was.

He said to an old tree
'Repeat after me,"I am a bomb".'
'I am a bomb', said the old tree,
And promptly exploded.

This goes to show
You can never be too careful if
You are
The sole survivor.

Brian Patten

Where is the forest?

63

Where is the forest?
  cried the animals.
Where are the trees?
We needed the wood,
  said the people.
Wood to make fires.
Wood to build houses.
We cut it down.

Where is the forest?
  cried the animals.
Where are the trees?
We needed the land,
  said the people.
Land for our cattle.
Land for our roads.
We cut it down.

Where is the forest?
  cried the animals.
Where is our home?
Gone, whispered
  the wind.
Gone. Gone. Gone.

John Foster

Luka

64

My name is Luka
I live on the second floor
I live upstairs from you
Yes I think you've seen me before

If you hear something late at night
Some kind of trouble, some kind of fight
Just don't ask me what it was
Just don't ask me what it was
Just don't ask me what it was

I think it's because I'm clumsy
I try not to talk too loud
Maybe it's because I'm crazy
I try not to act too proud

They only hit until you cry
And after that you don't ask why
You just don't argue anymore
You just don't argue anymore
You just don't argue anymore

Yes I think I'm OK
I walked into the door again
Well, if you ask that's what I'll say
And it's not your business anyway

I guess I'd like to be alone
With nothing broken, nothing thrown
Just don't ask me how I am
Just don't ask me how I am
Just don't ask me how I am

Suzanne Vega

1 A great film

A There are a number of films about young Indian people that are comedies. They show the struggle in people's daily lives between the old and the new Indian culture. The result is often a lot of funny situations. Read the text and then answer the questions.

Bend It Like Beckham

The story is about an Indian girl in Britain who is struggling against her parents' traditional views. Jess likes to kick a football just like Beckham. But her parents would be furious if they knew. They want her to marry and live the traditional way. Jess, however, is determined to have it her way. There are lots of funny scenes in this film. It all gets a little dramatic at the wedding of her sister Pinky …

- Who is Beckham?
- How do girls / women in India live when they don't adopt the modern western lifestyle?
- Is the actress Parminder Nagra much like Jess in her private life?
- Have you seen the film? Do you remember any funny scenes? Which ones?

If there's a follow-up movie one day, it might be called … and the new story about Jess might go like this …

Think of a title and plot you would like. Then write a short film review like the one above.

B Collect information on Bollywood films: where they are filmed, what the topics are, how much they cost, how many people watch them, how many new ones there are each year …

Make a transparency or a poster or give a short report of about 15 minutes to your class. Maybe you can put the information on your school website.

2 The job interview

Imagine you're knocking on a door behind which your future lies. Well, this sounds a bit dramatic, but that's how it'll be with most of your job interviews in the coming months. What are you going to say and do when you enter the room? Ask your business studies teacher for some useful tips and create a radio play for your class. In groups, write down a job interview from start to finish and record it as a radio play. It's up to you to decide which qualifications are necessary and if there's a happy ending and the candidate gets the job.

3 Rastafarian culture

1 **Ganja** Who knows more about this? Find out why there are different opinions about it and how the topic of ganja is related to reggae artists.
2 **Reggae** Are you interested in this style of music? Find out more about the musicians, some of their songs and the meaning of their song lyrics.
3 **Rastafarians** Find out about their way of life. Where do most of them live? What do they believe in? Where did their religion come from? Who was Haile Selassie and what does 'Babylon' stand for in their religion?
4 **Fashion** Find out more about how reggae musicians wear their hair and the colours they like. Where did it all come from? Why red, gold and green?

Use the questions in 1–4 to collect information on each topic. When you've collected enough information, work in groups and make a domino puzzle for your class. There should be 20 cards with a question at the bottom of each and the answer on the top of another card. So you must find 19 questions and answers to make and work out the puzzle. This is how you could start.

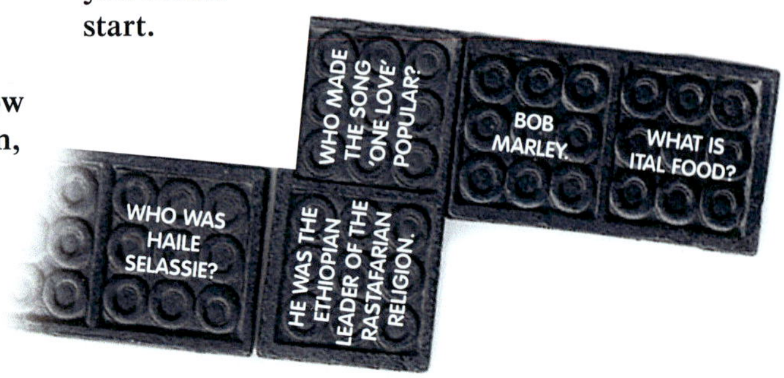

4 Aspects of South Africa

A Find e-mail partners for your class in South Africa. Use a search engine to look for schools and then send them an e-mail. Ask if any pupils would be interested in getting in touch with you. You could ask them about

- their age
- their family
- their hobbies
- the area where they live (sights, famous people, places they like, nature, wildlife, entertainment, ...)
- their school (how they get there, their school system, favourite subjects, ...)

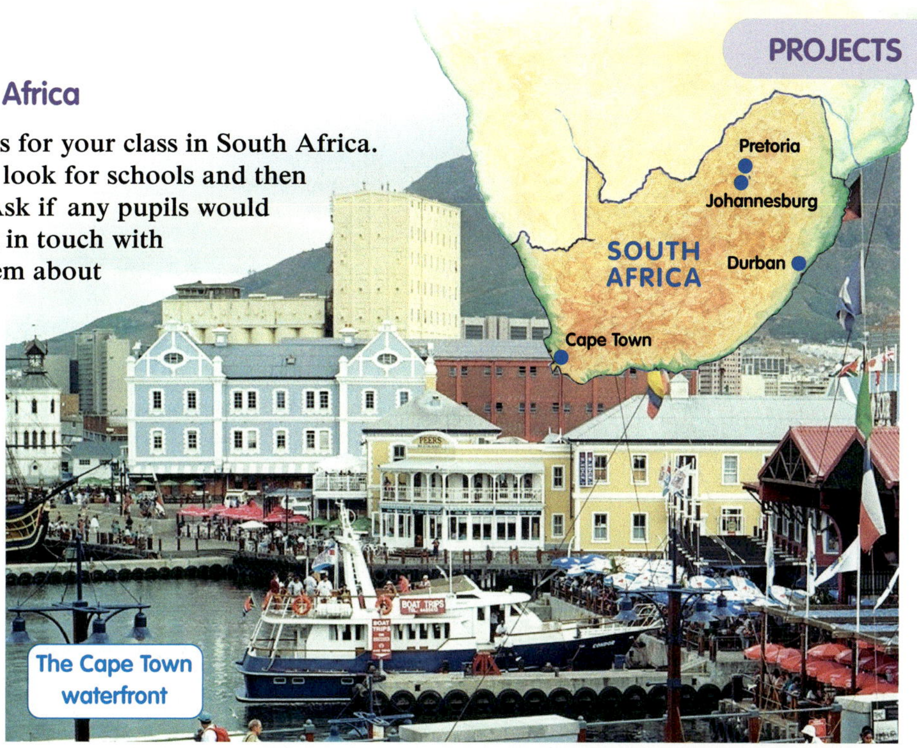

The Cape Town waterfront

B 'Howzit? Let's meet at the robot, oke, or give me a tinkle.' Most South Africans can speak English but this doesn't really mean that you will understand them. 'Frikkadel, platteland, lekker, kaalvoet' – well, some Afrikaans words that they use in their English may seem familiar to you. Try to find out more about their language! Make a little dictionary for the other pupils. For example, the sentence above means 'How are you? Let's meet at the traffic lights, fellow, or call me.'

Penguins at Cape Town

A typical South African landscape

Waterfall in the Eastern Transvaal Mountains

Nkosi Johnson

C He was born with Aids and woke up a nation. Who was Nkosi Johnson? Do some research on the internet. Why did he get the The World's Children's Prize? Tell your class more about his life and show them some photos.

EXERCISE 1

The people of Oldthorpe want to go on a protest march against plans for a chemical factory. Look at the map and choose the correct prepositions.

at • up • onto • into • under • from • to • around • over • down • through • in

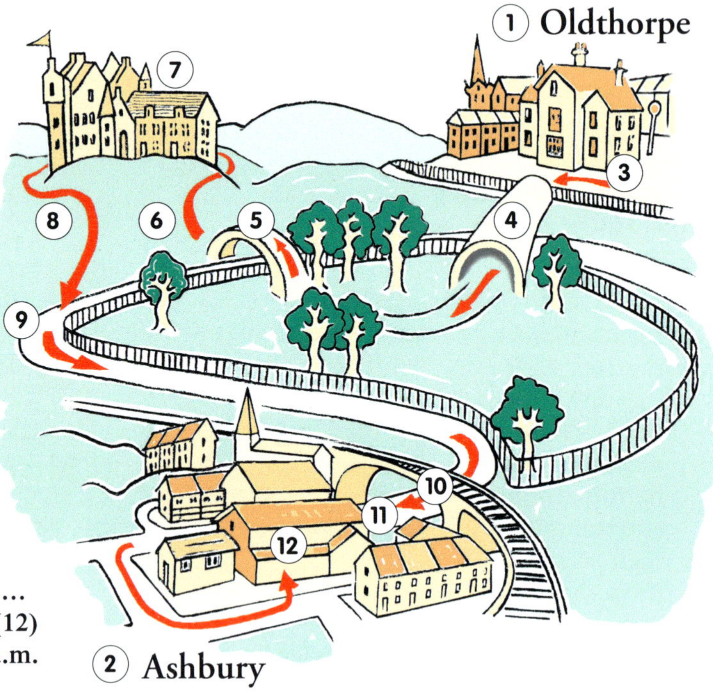

Our march will go … (1) Oldthorpe … (2) Ashbury. We'll meet … (3) the police station at 9.30 a.m. The route is as follows: Go … (4) the tunnel and then … (5) the bridge, … (6) the hill, … (7) the castle and then … (8) the hill again … (9) the main road to Ashbury. Then it's … (10) the railway bridge and … (11) Ashbury. Our march will finish … (12) the Community Centre at about 11.30 a.m.

EXERCISE 2

Linda is talking to Mr White, the boss of a computer company. Put in the correct prepositions. Be careful. Sometimes you don't need a preposition.

Mr White Hello, Linda. You've been working for us … a year now, haven't you?

Linda Yes, I've been here … last summer.

Mr White Oh, yes, I remember. You joined the design department … July, didn't you?

Linda That's right. I remember the date because it was the day before my birthday, so I had to do all the shopping … my party … work.

Mr White You're doing a great job. Would you like to go to the CeBIT trade fair next week? I can't go myself. I've got meetings here … Wednesday and Thursday.

Linda Oh, that would be just wonderful. When is it exactly?

Mr White It starts … 12th March and goes on … a week, … 19th March. As it's in Hanover, Germany, you could be back … 20th March.

Linda Of course, I'd like to go, thank you.

Mr White … Thursday morning 13th March there's a talk on Internet crime. It's … 9.30 a.m. I'd like you to take some notes … the talk. Then, … the fair when you're back you can tell me about it.

Linda I'd better find out about travel and accommodation then.

Mr White That's no problem. There's a flight to Hanover … every morning … 6.45 a.m. My secretary can book a flight for you … this morning.

EXERCISE 3

Here is a TV report from the British International Motor Show in Birmingham. Put the adjectives in brackets into their correct form.

Welcome to the British International Motor Show here in Birmingham. Today I've been looking at the … (late) car models. Among the attractions is the new CLK GTR, the … (expensive) production car ever made. It can go from 0 to 100 in about 3.8 seconds: That's … (fast) than most of the other cars on show. As you can see it's a little … (small) than many other cars here, but inside it's … (large) than it looks and it's one of the … (comfortable) cars I've ever seen. Although it's not the … (fast) car in this show, it's probably the … (safe). It's got … (good), … (efficient) brakes and it's … (easy) to drive. And it's … (economical) than most cars here. For me it's the … (good) car in this year's motor show.

EXERCISE 4

Look at this table and then complete the dialogues below.

my	mine	myself
your	yours	yourself
his	his	himself
her	hers	herself
our	ours	ourselves
your	yours	yourselves
their	theirs	themselves

1 *Frank* Hello, Linda. I'm phoning because I found a blue umbrella in my car. Is it ...?
Linda Well, maybe. But Gerry's umbrella looks the same. Has it got a yellow label?
Frank Wait a minute. No, it has a green one.
Linda Then it must be Gerry's because ... has a yellow label.
Frank Oh, I see.
Linda You know, Gerry and I bought ... two blue umbrellas on ... visit to London. ... umbrella is blue with a green label. So the umbrella in your car must be ... .

2 *Mum* I'm off now. Please do ... homework now. Grandma is here this afternoon. If you need ... help, you can always ask her. But I think you can do it by ... .
Angie Well, I think I can do it by ... too.
Mum You and Grandma can make ... some tea or coffee if you like.

3 *Jane* Let's hope Susan gives ... enough time to get to the airport.
Ryan Don't worry. She'll be all right.
Jane Remember the Smiths. They missed ... plane last summer. All the other planes were delayed but ... took off on time. Later they asked ... why they hadn't left a little earlier.
Ryan Well, you know, the Smiths have got a very old car. It broke down on the way to the airport.
Jane Is Susan's car OK?
Ryan Oh, there is no problem with ... .

4 *Hugh* Hi, Paul and Tony. Did you bring ... new computer games?
Tony Sorry, Hugh. We'll have to play Greg's new game because we left ... at home.
Hugh But I want to play ... . They must be really cool. Can you go and get them?

EXERCISE 5

Complete the following text with active or passive forms of the verbs in brackets.

Londoners sleeping on the Underground during the Blitz of 1940-41

The Second World War ... (start) in September 1939 when Poland ... (invade) by the German army. In the spring of 1940 Hitler's army ... (conquer) much of north-west Europe. Denmark, the Netherlands, Norway, and Belgium ... (fall) to the Germans in a few weeks.

In June 1940 France ... (defeat), and things ... (look) very bad for Britain because she was almost alone in Europe. Suddenly life in Britain ... (change) completely. Night after night German planes ... (drop) bombs on London and other towns. Lots of public buildings, factories, railways and private homes ... (destroy). More than 60,000 people ... (kill). In London people ... (sleep) in the Underground railway stations. Many children ... (send) away to spend the war in the safety of the countryside. People also ... (get) ready to fight a German invasion. Road signs ... (take) down and beaches ... (cover) with chain-link fences and barbed wire. Things ... (be) even worse at sea. German U-boats ... (hunt) ships filled with food from the United States and Canada. Each month, more and more ships ... (sink) by U-boats.

Then things ... (change) for Britain. After the Japanese attack on Pearl Harbor, Hawaii, the Americans ... (declare) war on Japan and Germany. In North Africa the Germans ... (beat) by the British army at El Alamein. The leaders in Britain then ... (start) planning a landing in France. On 6 June 1944 a large number of boats ... (carry) the invasion army to the beaches of Normandy. Other soldiers ... (land) with planes and parachutes.

After a few weeks France and Belgium ... (get back) their freedom. British soldiers ... (march) into Germany in early 1945. In the east the Nazis ... (drive) from Russia. Berlin ... (fall) in April and the war ... (end). The victory ... (celebrate) in Britain and all over Europe.

EXERCISE 6

Here is the database of a school library in Johannesburg. Make sentences and use passive forms.

	Title	Person	From	To
➠	*The Quiet American (Greene)*	Nigel	20 May	7 June
➠	*Harry Potter and the Chamber of Secrets (Rowling)*	Julie	15 May	–
➠	*The Lord of the Rings (Tolkien)*	Julie	15 May	–
1	*Animal Farm (Orwell)*	Lisa	17 May	14 June
2	*Three Men in a Boat (Jerome)*	Robin	16 May	10 June
3	*Braveheart (Wallace)*	Alex	17 May	–
4	*Nineteen Eighty-four (Orwell)*	Chris	01 June	7 June
5	*Timeline (Crichton)*	Jessica	21 May	–
	Jurassic Park (Crichton)	Jessica	21 May	–
6	*Gone with the Wind (Mitchell)*	Jane	02 June	–
7	*The Old Man and the Sea (Hemingway)*	Paul	25 May	30 May
	Huckleberry Finn (Twain)	Paul	25 May	30 May
8	*Oliver Twist (Dickens)*	Kevin	17 May	29 May

➠ *The Quiet American* was taken out by Nigel on 20 May. It was returned on 7 June.

➠ *Harry Potter* and *Lord of the Rings* were taken out by Julie. They haven't been returned yet.

EXERCISE 7

Complete this dialogue with the correct form of the verb in brackets (*ing*-form or *to*-infinitive). Sometimes you have to add a preposition.

Teacher I think I ought … (tell) you before I tell anyone else. I've decided … (leave) the school. I'm planning … (move) to Dublin next month.

Headmaster Thank you … (tell) me. But why do you want … (leave)? You've worked for this school for 17 years now. You can't say you are no longer interested … (work) here.

Teacher Oh no. I've really enjoyed … (be) here. But there is, mmh, a problem.

Headmaster Well, yes. What's wrong?

Teacher I don't like … (say) this, but I'm tired … (work) with Mrs Hillary, the head of the English department. I'm afraid I have to tell you, I simply don't look forward … (teach) the children any more.

Headmaster I see. What about … (tell) me about your problem?

Teacher Well, it's not only my problem. Most of my colleagues have started … (complain). I want … (be) fair to her. She's a young and ambitious person. But she's full of these new ideas. Instead … (concentrate) on real problems she tries … (change) things all the time.

Headmaster Shouldn't we take every chance … (improve) our school? We need … (introduce) a few changes from time to time. You seem … (be) afraid … (change) things.

Teacher But she's got so many stupid ideas. She's introduced more than 40 new lists and forms. We're good … (teach) children, you know, but we refuse … (complete) stupid forms.

Headmaster I'm beginning … (understand) your problem. But don't worry. Mrs Hillary has chosen … (leave) the school after the summer holidays anyway. Perhaps you'd like … (stay) with us now?

EXERCISE 8

Join the clauses 1–8 with a–h and put in *who, which, whose* or *where* only where necessary.

1 Some years ago a computer was something
2 In 1998 a group of Indian scientists had an idea
3 They developed the Simputer, a cheap and simple computer
4 The Simputer uses software
5 The team hopes to help the 35% of Indians
6 With this new device farmers can find new markets for the vegetables
7 If several people share one Simputer, they can buy cheap smartcards
8 The Simputer has attracted interest from countries in South America and Africa

a) they grow in their region.
b) most Indians couldn't afford.
c) cannot read.
d) could help India's poor people to join the information age.
e) can read web pages aloud in native Indian languages.
f) price is about $200.
g) chips store information about each person.
h) people can't afford expensive computers, either.

➡ 1b) Some years ago a computer was something most Indians couldn't afford.

EXERCISE 9

Find the questions you need to ask to get the answers 1–10 from the following text.

Woman gets ring back after 27 years

A woman has got back a gold ring which was found inside an apple, 27 years after she says she lost it. Twelve year-old Jamie-Louisa Arnold discovered the ring when … (1). The owner, Rosalind Pike, now 37, says she was given … (2) by her parents while on holiday. She lost it at a pool in … (3) when she went swimming with … (4) in 1975. Rosalind said: 'I couldn't believe it when I saw the ring because … (5). To see it inside an apple was very strange. I never thought I'd see it again. I knew it was mine because … (6). I left the ring on my towel at the side of the pool but … (7) I noticed it had gone. I just thought it had been lost. I just wish the ring could tell me exactly what has happened over the years.' … (8) from Cowlinge, Suffolk, bit on the ring while she was eating … (9) at a holiday park near Colchester. She said, 'I felt … (10) when I gave it back to Rosalind.'

1 she bit into an apple.
➡ When did she discover the ring?
2 the £5 ring
3 Colchester, Essex
4 primary school class
5 she lost it years ago
6 it had the same marks inside
7 when I came out of the water
8 Jamie-Louisa
9 an apple
10 very happy

EXERCISE 10

Complete this radio report with the right prepositions and put in the correct forms of the verbs in brackets.

Hello. This is Donna Kitchener. I … (speak) to you from the Dorchester Hotel … London. In a few minutes you … (hear) an interview … Sean Connery. He … (knight) … the Queen tomorrow morning. But first of all some facts about Mr Connery's life: Thomas Sean Connery … (be born) into a working class family in Edinburgh, Scotland … 25 August, 1930. His father … (work) as a truck driver. Sean and his younger brother … (grow up) in poverty. After he … (leave) school at the age of 13, Sean … (must / work) in many jobs … earn some money. At 16 he joined the Royal Navy … three years. The two tattoos which he … (have) since then read: 'Mum and Dad' and 'Scotland Forever'. In 1953 he … (take) part in the Mr Universe competition for Scotland and … (come) third. This … (lead) to a job in the theatre. After 1950 he … (appear) in a number … film roles. In 1962 people first … (hear) the famous words 'Bond, James Bond'. *Dr. No*, the first Bond film, … (make) him so popular that three more Bond films … (make) in the next five years. Sean … (play) many different roles in films over the years. In the 80s and 90s he … (star) in such films as *Highlander*, *The Name of the Rose*, *The Untouchables*, *The Hunt for Red October*. Connery … (always / love) his native country, Scotland, and he … (be) an active member of the Scottish National Party for many years.

A Very Short History of British Literature

The Anglo-Saxons who came to the British Isles had no written literature. But they brought with them a number of stories and war songs which were written down later when the Anglo-Saxons became Christians. The most important of these stories is the Old English poem *Beowulf* (8th century). It's an adventure story about a hero who helps the Danish king against a huge monster called Grendel.

Geoffrey Chaucer 1340-1400

After the battle of Hastings in 1066 two languages were used in England. The Norman rulers spoke French. English was used by the Anglo-Saxon farmers.

Around 1387 **Geoffrey Chaucer** began writing *The Canterbury Tales*. The book is about a group of pilgrims who are on their way to Canterbury. To pass the time more quickly, each pilgrim has to tell a story. As the pilgrims are from different social classes, the reader gets a complete picture of English society at that time. Chaucer used the English language at a time when most books were still written in French or Latin.

William Shakespeare 1564-1616

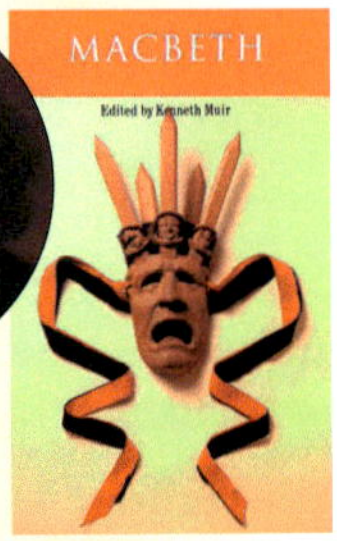

When Londoners wanted entertainment at the time of Queen Elizabeth I, they went to the theatre. Rich and poor people came to see the comedies and tragedies by the best writers of the age. The greatest of them was **William Shakespeare**. His most famous plays include the tragedies *Hamlet* and *Romeo and Juliet*, the history plays *Henry V* and *Richard III* and the comedies *Twelfth Night* and *A Midsummer Night's Dream*.

Jane Austen 1775-1817

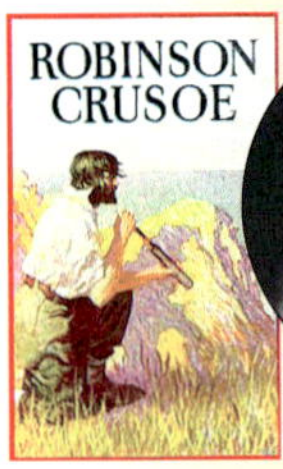

Daniel Defoe 1660-1731

In 1719 **Daniel Defoe** wrote the first English novel, *Robinson Crusoe*. The hero is left alone on an island after his ship has sunk. But he is able to survive there with the few things he has. He is helped by Man Friday, who becomes his servant after Crusoe saves him from death. The book is written in simple language and is based on a true story.

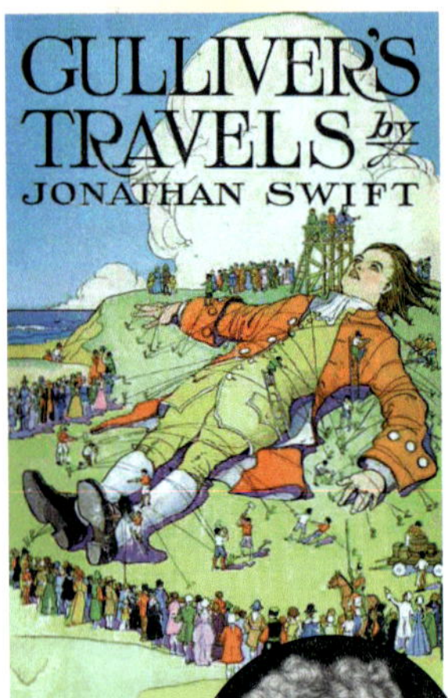

Jonathan Swift 1667-1747

At about the same time **Jonathan Swift**, an Irish writer, who spent much of his time in London, wrote *Gulliver's Travels*. He made fun of the way British people thought about religion, manners and science at that time. The English traveller Lemuel Gulliver visits Lilliput, where the people are all tiny, then he travels to a land where the people are giants and afterwards to a land where the horses are clever and the people stupid and cruel.

Emily Brontë 1818-1848

Personal relationships and everyday life play an important part in **Jane Austen's** novels. Her best-known books are *Emma*, *Pride and Prejudice* and *Mansfield Park*. Her *Sense and Sensibility* is a clever comedy about the English upper middle class where money and social position are very important.

Lewis Carroll
1832-1898

Sir Arthur Conan Doyle
1859-1930

Agatha Christie
1890-1976

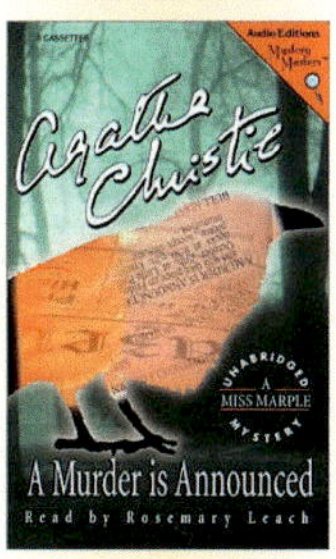

Charles Dickens was the most popular English author of the 19th century. His novels often describe the bad conditions in which poor people lived. Most of his books were first written in parts for magazines. His most famous novels are *David Copperfield* and *A Tale of Two Cities*.

Oliver Twist is a story about life in the workhouse, about thieves and pickpockets. *A Christmas Carol* is one of his most loved books. On the night before Christmas Ebenezer Scrooge, a mean old man sees the ghosts of Christmasses past, present and future. He realizes that he has been very nasty to everybody and sends presents to his poor employee Bob Cratchit.

The three sisters **Charlotte**, **Emily** and **Anne Brontë** lived most of their time in a village in Yorkshire. They began writing novels and poetry at a very early age but died before their books became really famous. Emily's *Wuthering Heights* is a story about the love-hate relationship between Catherine Earnshaw and Heathcliff.

Lewis Carroll who taught mathematics at Oxford University is best known for his children's book *Alice in Wonderland*. Alice, a young girl, dreams she follows a white rabbit down a hole and has a number of fantastic adventures.

Eric Arthur Blair, who was born in India and educated in England, wrote under the name of **George Orwell**. In 1944 he finished *Animal Farm*, a political fable based on the story of the Russian Revolution. In this book some farm animals take over a farm and set up a society where all animals are supposed to be equal. But eventually the pigs form a nasty dictatorship which is even worse than the farmer had been.

Iris Murdoch's novels show strange and complicated relationships among middle-class people in the 20th century. Her book *The Sea, The Sea* won the Booker Prize.

A popular type of fiction is the British detective story. **Arthur Conan Doyle** created the famous detective Sherlock Holmes and his friend Dr. Watson. His stories were followed by the thrillers of **Agatha Christie.** She created the detectives Hercule Poirot and Miss Marple. Her play *The Mousetrap* has been running in a London theatre since 1952. In the 1960s **Ian Fleming** became famous with his James Bond stories.

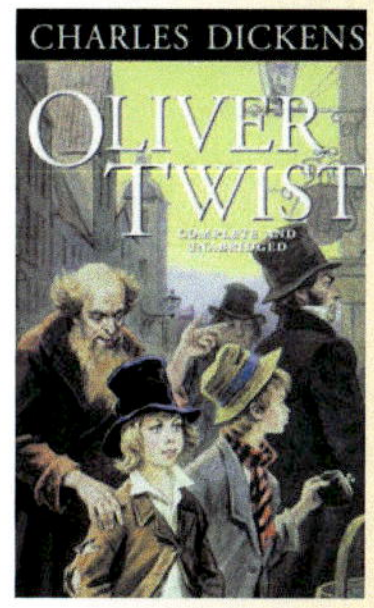

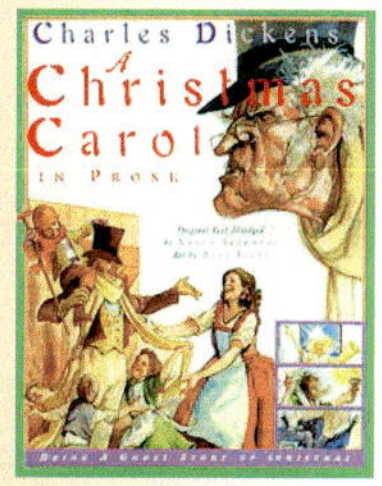

Charles Dickens
1812-1870

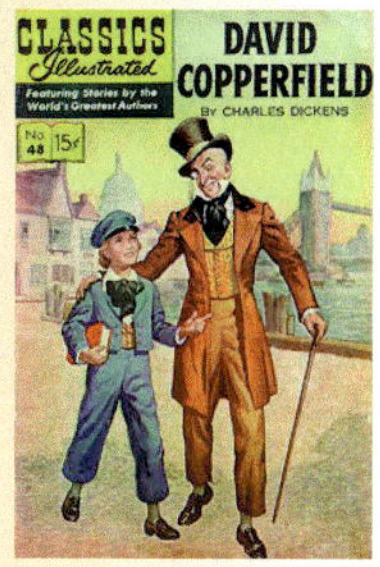

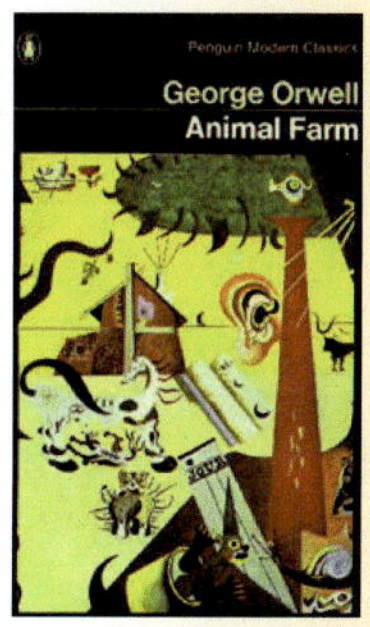

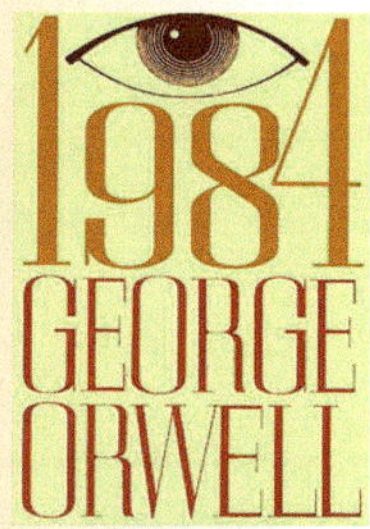

George Orwell
1903-1950

Iris Murdoch
1919-1999

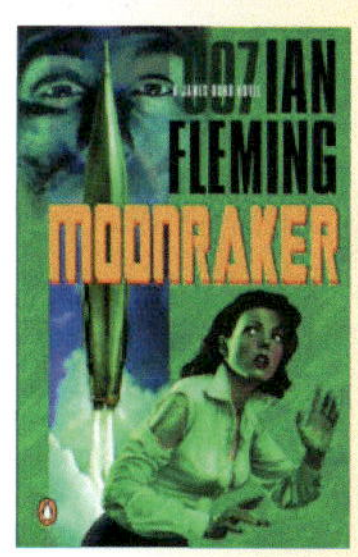

Ian Fleming
1908-1964

A GIVING INFORMATION ABOUT YOURSELF

The interviewer may ask you about what you're doing at the moment, what you've done in the past, or about your plans for the future.

TIPS

1. *Try to answer in about two or three sentences. Don't answer in just a single word or phrase and then wait for the next question.*
2. *Don't prepare a long speech. If you learn everything by heart, it will sound very unnatural.*

EXERCISE 1

Prepare six questions for your partner. Ask questions about

- your partner's address (Ask him / her to spell something, e.g. a street name or his / her family name)
- how your partner travelled to school today
- your partner's spare time activities
- your partner's plans for the holidays

EXERCISE 2

Partner **A**

Ask partner **B** some questions about social problems. Ask about the following topics.

- unemployment
- racism
- problems between young and old
- being rich or poor

➽ Lots of people are unemployed. What are their problems?
➽ Do you think there is ...?
➽ When you are ...

Partner **B**

Ask partner **A** about young people's problems. Ask about the following topics.

- problems with parents
- difficulties at school
- drugs or alcohol
- crime

➽ Why do you think so many teenagers have problems with their parents?
➽ Some young people ...
➽ Drinking alcohol ...

EXERCISE 3

Partner **A**

You bought a computer two months ago. Now it's broken. When you switch it on nothing happens. You want to have it repaired. You need it before next weekend.

Partner **B**

You work in a computer shop. Partner **A** is a customer who comes in to have a computer repaired.

A Can I help you?
B Yes, please. It's this computer ...
A ...

B REACTING TO PICTURE PROMPTS

The interviewer will give you pictures to talk about. First you talk about your own two pictures. Then you have to talk about your partner's pictures too. You will have 2–5 minutes to prepare. You can make notes if you like, but don't try to write complete sentences. Just try to make a list of things that you can mention.

TIPS

1. *Don't get nervous if you don't know all the words for the things in the picture.*
2. *Don't wait for the interviewer to ask questions. Just keep talking as long as you can.*

EXERCISE 4

Partner **A**

Talk about pictures **1** and **2** at the top of the next page for two minutes. Mention the main differences between the two pictures.

Partner **B**

Talk about partner **A**'s pictures at the top of the next page for about 30 seconds.

Partner **B**

Talk about pictures **3** and **4** at the bottom of the next page for two minutes. Mention the main differences between the two pictures.

Partner **A**

Talk about partner **B**'s pictures at the bottom of the next page for about 30 seconds.

Partner A **Pictures 1 and 2**

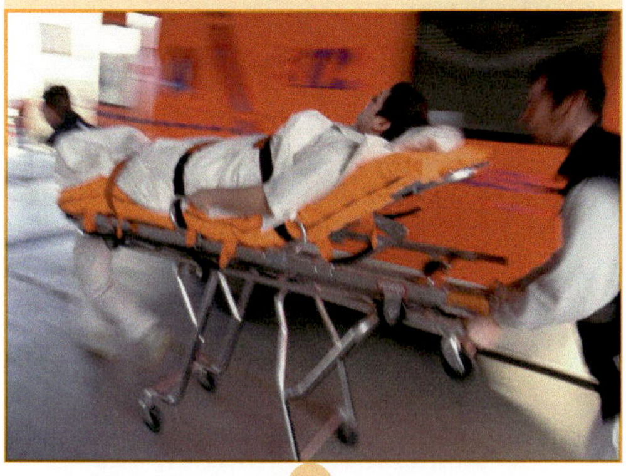

Partner B **Pictures 3 and 4**

C COMMUNICATING WITH A PARTNER

The interviewer will ask you to talk about a number of pictures with your partner.

TIPS

1. *Talk to your partner, not the interviewer. Listen to what your partner says and react.*
2. *Don't try to say everything yourself; give your partner a chance to speak too.*

EXERCISE 5

Look at some pictures showing different kinds of activities for an evening out. Imagine you want to spend the evening together. Decide which would be the best thing for you and your partner.

When you translate from English into German, make sure your translation is in good German. Follow these five steps and read the tips 1–7 before you start.

- If you want to translate an English text, first read the text from beginning to end.
- Then start writing a first rough translation.
- If you don't know a word, try to guess its meaning from the context.
- If you can't find the correct translation, use a dictionary.
- Now write down your final version.

HERE ARE SOME USEFUL TIPS

1 Yesterday we played basketball for half an hour.
Gestern spielten wir eine halbe Stunde lang Basketball.
- Be careful with the word order. It's often very different.

2 Do you think they'll come?
Glaubst du / Glaubt ihr / Glauben Sie, dass sie kommen (werden)?
Bist du / Seid ihr / Sind Sie der Meinung, dass ... ?
Meinst du / Meint ihr / Meinen Sie, dass ... ?
- There are often several correct translations, not only one.

3 My sister likes watching musicals.
Meine Schwester sieht sich gerne Musicals an.
- Sometimes you have to say things in a different way in German.

4 What's on TV tonight?
Was läuft heute Abend im Fernsehen?
- The preposition isn't always the same in German.

5 We've lived in Brighton since 1997.
Wir wohnen seit 1997 in Brighton.
- There is sometimes a different tense in German.

6 The body was lying on the kitchen floor. The flat was on the second floor.
Die Leiche lag auf dem Küchenboden. Die Wohnung war im zweiten Stock.
- Remember to translate the correct meaning. Think of false friends – floor means *Fußboden*, *Stockwerk*, not *Flur*.

7 We're meeting the day after tomorrow.
Wir treffen uns übermorgen / in zwei Tagen.
- You can't always translate phrases word for word.

After Unit 1

My name is Bond, James Bond

Ian Fleming, who created James Bond in the 1950s, led a life that was as adventurous as that of 007. During the Second World War, after working as a journalist and banker, Fleming directed secret spy missions for Britain. In the final year of the war, Fleming travelled to Jamaica for a conference. He fell in love with the island and built a home there, where he wrote all his Bond novels, starting with *Casino Royale* in 1953. Fleming once described Bond as 'an interesting man to whom strange things happen'. Bond shared his author's love of beautiful women, fine food and wines and fast cars. From 1953 to 1964, Fleming wrote 13 James Bond novels and one collection of short stories. Since Fleming's death on 12 August 1964, various authors have continued to write James Bond books.

You already know the noun 'adventure'.

A 'spy' tries to get secret information about another country.

'Novel' isn't German *Novelle*.

You already know the verb 'collect'.

'Various' means 'several different'.

TRANSLATION PRACTICE

After Unit 2

Applying for a job

HOW TO WRITE A LETTER OF APPLICATION

- You must write clearly. The manager sometimes reads hundreds of letters of application. Do not send any photocopied letters. But it's a good idea to write your letter on the computer.

> Don't use *du* in your translation.

- Make sure you haven't made any mistakes in spelling or grammar. Why not ask your teacher to check the letter for you?

> You must use a subject in German.

- Don't forget to mention your qualifications, things you're interested in and any work experience you have.
- The most successful letter is one that gives the reader all the necessary information about you and is short at the same time.

> Use a plural in your German translation.

HOW TO PREPARE FOR A JOB INTERVIEW

- Don't be late for your job interview and dress smartly.
- During the interview look at the interviewer, not at the computer on their desk.

> 'Their' means 'his' or 'her'.

- Try to relax and be yourself.
- Keep the conversation going. Don't just answer 'yes' or 'no'.
- Don't only talk about what you hope to get from your future employer. Explain what you can do for them, as well.
- Prepare some questions of your own about the job, the training, etc.

> Try to use only one adjective in German.

- At the end don't forget to thank the interviewer for seeing you.

After Unit 3

Modernizing London

In 1863 London's Metropolitan Railway was opened to the public. It was the world's first underground railway. Life wasn't very pleasant for the first Tube passengers. As locomotives were driven by steam, breathing was sometimes quite a problem, because it wasn't easy to get enough air into the tunnels. The underground was electrified in 1890.

> 'Pleasant' means 'nice'.
>
> There is a similar word in German.

The first petrol-driven motor cars appeared in 1885. The speed limit was four miles an hour in the country and two miles an hour in the towns. Until 1895 a person who carried a red flag had to walk in front of the car to keep its speed down and to warn others.

> 'Speed' means how fast something goes.

The telephone reached London in 1878. But at first there were only seven or eight people in London who were interested in this new invention. In 1891 people who had a telephone were able to speak to their friends in Paris as a cable had been laid on the bottom of the English Channel. The first red telephone boxes were put up in 1884.

A new safety bicycle was developed in 1885. Earlier cycles had been difficult to ride and dangerous. The new bicycle made cycling available to everyone.

> The opposite is 'danger'.

PAIR WORK

UNIT 1 Exercise 20

What's on TV tonight?

BBC 1	BBC 2	ITV	Channel 4	Channel 5
8.00 **EastEnders** *The soap continues*	8.00 **Golf** *US Masters live from Augusta*	8.00 ?????	8.00 **The Tower** *Series on the history of the Tower of London*	8.00 ?????
8.30 ?????	10.00 ?????	9.00 **Who Wants to Be a Millionaire?** *Quiz show*	9.00 ?????	10.00 **Film: Bridget Jones's Diary** *Comedy about a young woman's love life*
9.00 **Down to Earth** *Drama series about a family who have moved to the country*		9.30 ?????	10.00 **Friends** *Rachel tells the others about Barry and Mindy's divorce plans*	
10.00 ?????				

Partner **B**: Ask partner **A** what the missing programmes are.

- Find out when the news is on and what channel it's on.
- You don't want to watch the film on Channel 5. Ask if there's another film on.
- Find out if the golf on BBC 2 is the only sport on.
- Ask about comedy.
- Find out what else is on tonight and what kind of programmes they are.

UNIT 2 Exercise 20

Talking about jobs

Partner **B**: You are looking for a job in telesales, and your English friend is calling you about a job that you might be interested in. Try to find out the following information. Make notes.

Be sure to thank your friend when he / she has given you the information.

- what kind of job it is
- the name of the company (correctly spelled)
- what you would have to do
- what qualifications are needed
- how much the job pays
- where you would work
- if you have to work at weekends
- if there is a phone number you can ring

UNIT 3 Exercise 20

Asking for information

Partner **B**: You and your English penfriend are at the Science Museum in London. There are a few things that you need to look at because they are important for your school work. First look at the museum guide on page 37 and answer your friend's questions about things in the museum. For example, if your partner says 'I'd like to see some old telephones', you could answer 'That'll be telecommunications on the first floor'.

When you've answered the questions, it's your turn to ask for information. This is what you are looking for.

- some old cameras
- the different drugs that doctors use
- the module that landed on the moon
- some information about TV satellites
- some information about nuclear power

You can say *Where can we find …?, I'd like to see … , What about …?, What floor is that …?*

UNIT 4 Exercise 19

Writing about places

Partner **B**: Read this information about Trinidad and Tobago.

Trinidad and Tobago are islands in the Caribbean off the coast of Venezuela. Trinidad is the larger of the two and is about 30 miles across. The islands have a population of 1.3 million, mainly of African and Indian origin. The capital is Port-of-Spain. Other important towns are San Fernando and Arima. The main export is oil. The official language is English, although some people speak Spanish or Hindi. Trinidad and Tobago were Spanish colonies until 1802, when Britain took control. The islands became independent in 1962.

Partner **A** has some similar information about Jamaica. Ask him / her for the same kind of information as you have in your text. You can start like this.

- *Where is Jamaica?*
- *How big is the island?*

Then use the answers to write a similar text about Jamaica.

Grammatical terms Grammatikalische Fachausdrücke

active ['æktɪv]	Aktiv, Tatform	*We **bought** the new radio.*
adjective ['ædʒɪktɪv]	Eigenschaftswort, Adjektiv	*big, good, bad, dangerous, expensive, …*
adverb ['ædvɜːb]	Adverb	***very** big, **usually**, …*
adverb of frequency [ˌædvɜːb əv 'friːkwənsi]	Adverb der Häufigkeit	*always, often, never, …*
adverb of manner [ˌædvɜːb əv 'mænə]	Adverb der Art und Weise	*carefully, slowly, well, …*
article ['ɑːtɪkl]	Geschlechtswort, Artikel	*a, an, the*
auxiliary verb [ɔːɡˌzɪliəri 'vɜːb]	Hilfsverb	***don't** know, **is** swimming, **has** seen*
***by*-agent** ['baɪeɪdʒənt]	Urheber einer Handlung im Passivsatz	*The phone was invented **by Bell**.*
clause [klɔːz]	Teilsatz	***He was late** because he missed the last bus.*
comparative [kəm'pærətɪv]	Komparativ, erste Steigerungsform	***bigger**, **better**, **more** interesting, …*
comparison of adjectives [kəmˌpærɪsn əv 'ædʒɪktɪvz]	Steigerung der Adjektive	*big – **bigger** – **biggest**; **as** big **as**, **bigger than***
conditional [kən'dɪʃənl]	Konditional	*I **wouldn't** do that.*
conditional sentences [kənˌdɪʃənl 'sentənsɪz]	Bedingungssätze	*If you **went** to India, you **could** see Bollywood.*
conjunction [kən'dʒʌŋkʃn]	Bindewort, Konjunktion	*and, or, but, after, when, …*
consonant ['kɒnsənənt]	Mitlaut, Konsonant	*b, c, d, f, g, k, …*
contact clause ['kɒntækt klɔːz]	Satz ohne Relativpronomen	*The girl **he met** was Lisa.*
direct object [daɪˌrekt 'ɒbdʒɪkt]	direktes Objekt, Akkusativobjekt	*He drinks **milk**. She gave him **a present**.*
emphasizing pronoun [ˌemfəsaɪzɪŋ 'prəʊnaʊn]	verstärkendes Pronomen	*I saw the accident **myself**.*
future with *going to* ['fjuːtʃə]	Futur mit *going to*	***I'm going to leave** now.*
future with *will* ['fjuːtʃə]	Futur mit *will*	***I will come** tomorrow.*
***if*-clause** ['ɪfklɔːz]	*if*-Satz, Bedingungssatz	***If** you ask me, I'll tell you.*
imperative [ɪm'perətɪv]	Befehlsform, Imperativ	*Now **listen**. **Don't talk** to your neighbour.*
indirect object [ˌɪndaɪrekt 'ɒbdʒɪkt]	indirektes Objekt, Dativobjekt	*She gave **her father** a present.*
indirect speech [ˌɪndaɪrekt 'spiːtʃ]	indirekte Rede, nichtwörtliche Rede	*Kim said (that) she liked Westerns.*
infinitive [ɪn'fɪnətɪv]	Grundform, Infinitiv	***to** go, **to** see, **to** eat, **to** run, **to** work, …*
***ing*-form** ['ɪŋfɔːm]	-*ing*-Form	*singing, dancing, sitting, …*
irregular verb [ɪˌregjʊlə 'vɜːb]	unregelmäßiges Verb	*do – **did** – **done**, buy – **bought** – **bought**, …*
long form ['lɒŋ fɔːm]	Langform	*He **is** reading. She **does not** work.*
main clause ['meɪn klɔːz]	Hauptsatz	***Peter isn't at school** because he's ill.*
main verb ['meɪn vɜːb]	Vollverb	*work, dance, read, write, play, …*
modal auxiliary [ˌməʊdl ɔːɡ'zɪliəri]	Modalverb	*can, must, could, might, ought to*
negative question [ˌnegətɪv 'kwestʃn]	verneinter Fragesatz	***Don't** you **like** beans?*
negative statement [ˌnegətɪv 'steɪtmənt]	verneinter Aussagesatz	*Emily **doesn't like** tennis.*

Grammatikalische Fachausdrücke

noun [naʊn]	Nomen, Substantiv	*house, book, tea, plan, idea, …*
object ['ɒbdʒɪkt]	Satzergänzung, Objekt	*She likes* ***pop music.***
***of*-phrase** ['ɒvfreɪz]	Fügung mit *of*	*the name* ***of the game***
passive ['pæsɪv]	Passiv, Leideform	*The gangster* ***was caught*** *(by the police).*
past participle [,pɑ:st 'pɑ:tɪsɪpl]	Partizip Perfekt	*John has* ***called.*** *She hasn't* ***eaten*** *anything.*
past perfect [,pɑ:st 'pɜ:fɪkt]	*Past perfect* (Plusquamperfekt)	*I* ***had seen*** *the film before.*
past progressive [,pɑ:st prə'gresɪv]	Verlaufsform der Vergangenheit	*She* ***was reading.*** *We* ***were watching*** *TV.*
personal passive [,pɜ:sənl 'pæsɪv]	persönliches Passiv	*I* ***was offered*** *some sweets.*
personal pronoun [,pɜ:sənl 'prəʊnaʊn]	persönliches Fürwort, Personalpronomen	*I, you, she, … , me, us, them, …*
phrasal verb [,freɪzl 'vɜ:b]	Verbindung Verb–Adverb, Verb–Präposition	*to put* ***on****, to sit* ***down****, to take* ***away*** *…*
plural ['plʊərəl]	Mehrzahl, Plural	*book**s**, letter**s**, dog**s**, wom**e**n, child**ren**, f**ee**t*
positive ['pɒzətɪv]	Positiv, Grundform des Adjektivs	***good*** *– better – best,* ***interesting*** *– more interesting – most interesting*
positive statement [,pɒzətɪv 'steɪtmənt]	bejahter Aussagesatz, Erzählsatz	*I* ***speak*** *English and French.*
possessive adjective [pə,zesɪv 'ædʒɪktɪv]	adjektivisch gebrauchtes, besitzanzeigendes Fürwort, Possessivpronomen	*my, your, his, her, its, our, your, their*
possessive form [pə,zesɪv 'fɔ:m]	besitzanzeigende Form, *s*-Genitiv	*Adam**'s** computer, his friends**'** books*
possessive pronoun [pə,zesɪv 'prəʊnaʊn]	nominal gebrauchtes Possessivpronomen	*mine, yours, his, hers, ours, yours, theirs*
preposition [prepə'zɪʃn]	Verhältniswort, Präposition	*in, at, on, with, because of, …*
preposition of direction [prepə,zɪʃn əv də'rekʃn]	Präposition der Richtung	***to*** *school,* ***onto*** *the table,* ***into*** *the water, …*
preposition of place [prepə,zɪʃn əv 'pleɪs]	Präposition des Ortes	***at*** *the bus stop,* ***on*** *the wall,* ***in*** *the house, …*
preposition of time [prepə,zɪʃn əv 'taɪm]	Präposition der Zeit	***at*** *seven o'clock,* ***on*** *Sunday,* ***in*** *winter, …*
prepositional verb [prepə,zɪʃnl 'vɜ:b]	Präpositionalverb, Verbindung Verb-Präposition	*to look* ***after****, to listen* ***to***
present participle [,preznt 'pɑ:tɪsɪpl]	Partizip Präsens	*He is* ***going*** *home. It's* ***freezing*** *cold.*
present perfect [,preznt 'pɜ:fɪkt]	*Present perfect* (Perfekt)	*We* ***have finished*** *the lesson.*
present perfect progressive [,preznt pɜ:fɪkt prə'gresɪv]	Verlaufsform des *present perfect*	*We* ***have been reading*** *for two hours.*
present progressive [,preznt prə'gresɪv]	Verlaufsform des Präsens	*I* ***am watching*** *TV.*
pronoun ['prəʊnaʊn]	Fürwort, Pronomen	*I, me, himself, this, …*
proper noun [,prɒpe 'naʊn]	Eigenname	*Mr Smith, Munich, the Thames*
propword ['prɒpwɜ:d]	Stützwort	*Do you want the red* ***one*** *or the green* ***ones****?*
question ['kwestʃn]	Frage, Fragesatz	***Is Adam at school?*** *– No, he isn't. –* ***Where is Adam?***
question tag ['kwestʃn tæg]	Frageanhängsel	*It's cold today,* ***isn't it?***
question word ['kwestʃn wɜ:d]	Fragewort	*what, when, where, who, whose, why, which, how*

reflexive pronoun [rɪˌfleksɪv ˈprəʊnaʊn]	Reflexivpronomen, rückbezügliches Fürwort	*He hurt* ***himself.***
regular verb [ˌregjʊlə ˈvɜːb]	regelmäßiges Verb	*call – call**ed** – call**ed**, …*
relative clause [ˌrelətɪv ˈklɔːz]	Relativsatz	*The girl* ***who phoned*** *was Mary.*
relative pronoun [ˌrelətɪv ˈprəʊnaʊn]	Relativpronomen	*who, that, which, whose*
reported speech [rɪˌpɔːtɪd ˈspiːtʃ]	indirekte Rede, nichtwörtliche Rede	*Kim said (that) she liked Westerns.*
		Do you know if she is coming to our party?
sentence [ˈsentəns]	Satz, Satzgefüge	*I love Star Trek. Do you speak French?*
short answer [ˈʃɔːt ɑːnsə]	Kurzantwort	*Do you understand? –* ***Yes, I do.***
short form [ˈʃɔːt fɔːm]	Kurzform	***I've*** *got a rabbit. She**'s** over there. – I* ***can't*** *see her.*
simple past [ˌsɪmpl ˈpɑːst]	einfache Form der Vergangenheit	*I* ***called*** *Katie. She* ***bought*** *a new skirt.*
simple present [ˌsɪmpl ˈpreznt]	einfache Form des Präsens	*She* ***reads*** *love stories every day.*
singular [ˈsɪŋgjʊlə]	Einzahl, Singular	*book, letter, dog, woman, child, foot*
statement [ˈsteɪtmənt]	Aussage, Aussagesatz	*She likes cats. I don't like dinosaurs.*
subject [ˈsʌbdʒɪkt]	Satzgegenstand, Subjekt	***Jessica*** *likes maths.* ***The girl over there*** *is Sophie.*
subject question [ˈsʌbdʒɪkt kwestʃn]	Frage nach dem Subjekt	***Who*** *phoned you?*
superlative [suːˈpɜːlətɪv]	Superlativ, höchste Steigerungsform	***biggest, best, most*** *interesting, …*
tense [tens]	grammatische Zeit, Tempus	*present tense, past tense, …*
time [taɪm]	(wirkliche) Zeit	*past, present, future*
***to*-infinitive** [ˈtuːɪnˌfɪnətɪv]	Grundform mit *to*, *to*-Infinitiv	***to*** *go,* ***to*** *see,* ***to*** *eat,* ***to*** *run,* ***to*** *work, …*
verb [vɜːb]	a) Zeitwort, Verb	*be, love, play, get up, … ; can, will, do, …*
	b) Satzaussage, Prädikat	*She* ***likes*** *yoghurt. We* ***can play*** *cards.*
vowel [ˈvaʊəl]	Vokal, Selbstlaut	*a, e, i, o, u*
word order [ˈwɜːd ɔːdə]	Wortstellung	*subject – verb – object (S – V – O)*
***yes/no*-question** [jesˈnəʊ kwestʃən]	Entscheidungsfrage	***Is Adam at home?*** *– Yes, he is. / No, he isn't.*

GRAMMATIKANHANG

1 so, neither and nor

so, neither und nor

Chloe **is** from Cornwall, and **so is** Tim.
Mrs Kelsey **has** a German car. ~ **So has** my father.
I **can** speak French. ~ **So can** I.
Chloe **likes** gigs. ~ **So does** Jordan.
The Websters **live** in London. **So do** the Fosters.

Um einer bejahten Aussage zuzustimmen, verwendet man:

so + **Hilfsverb** + **Subjekt** (dt.: **auch**)

Steht im vorausgehenden Satz ein Hilfsverb (*is*, *has*, *can*, …), so wird dieses übernommen. Andernfalls steht für das Vollverb eine Form von *do*.

I **can** speak Italian. ~ **So can** I. / I **can, too**.
(*Ich auch.*)

Beachte: *too* in der Bedeutung „auch".

Tim **isn't** in Cornwall now. ~ **Neither is** Chloe. / **Nor is** Chloe.
I **haven't** been to Cornwall. ~ **Neither have** I.
Mrs Kelsey **can't** speak French. ~ **Nor can** I.
I **don't** work on Saturdays. ~ **Neither do** I.

Um verneinten Sätzen zuzustimmen, verwendet man:

neither/*nor* + **Hilfsverb** + **Subjekt** (dt.: **auch nicht**)

I **can't** swim. ~ **Neither can** I. / I **can't either**.
(*Ich auch nicht.*)

Beachte: *not … either* in der Bedeutung „auch nicht".

2 conditional sentences

Bedingungssätze

If you **feel** tired, we **won't** go out tonight.

Ein Bedingungssatz besteht aus zwei Teilen: einem Nebensatz mit *if* und einem Hauptsatz. Ein Bedingungssatz gibt die Bedingung an (**Wenn du müde bist**) unter der ein bestimmtes Ereignis (**wir gehen … nicht aus**) stattfindet.

a Open condition (type 1)

Offene, erfüllbare Bedingung – Typ 1

IF-CLAUSE	MAIN CLAUSE
If you **go** to Hollywood,	you**'ll** see the film studios.
If there**'s** a quiz on,	we **can** watch it.
If he **buys** the new CD,	he **must** bring it with him.
If you **don't understand**,	you **should** ask me.
If you **have** problems,	please **tell** me.

Wir verwenden im

IF-SATZ	HAUPTSATZ	
	will-future	
simple present	Modalverb *can*	+ Infinitiv
	Modalverb *must*	+ Infinitiv
	Modalverb *should*	+ Infinitiv
	Befehlsform	

- **Was ist, wenn …**
  Diese *if*-Sätze drücken aus, was unter bestimmten Bedingungen geschehen wird, kann oder soll.

b

Unwahrscheinliche, nicht erfüllbare Bedingung – Typ 2

Wir verwenden im

IF-SATZ	HAUPTSATZ
	Modalverb *would* + Infinitiv
simple past	Modalverb *could* + Infinitiv
	Modalverb *might* + Infinitiv

◆ **Was wäre, wenn …**
Diese *if*-Sätze drücken aus, dass es sich nur um eine **Annahme** handelt. Man sagt, was in Zukunft geschehen würde, **falls eine bestimmte Bedingung erfüllt würde**.

Beachte: die Redewendung *If I were you …* :
If I were you, I wouldn't tell her.
Ich an deiner Stelle würde …

unreal condition – type 2

IF-CLAUSE	MAIN CLAUSE
If I **knew** her name,	**I'd tell** you.
If I **had** my own car,	I **could drive** to school.
If you **asked** me,	I **might buy** you a drink.

c

Nicht mehr erfüllbare Bedingung – Typ 3

Wir verwenden im

IF-SATZ	HAUPTSATZ
	would have + *past participle*
past perfect	*could have* + *past participle*
	might have + *past participle*

◆ **Was wäre gewesen, wenn …**
Diese *if*-Sätze beziehen sich auf die Vergangenheit. Man überlegt, was passiert wäre, wenn eine bestimmte Bedingung erfüllt worden wäre. Die **Bedingung** wurde aber **nicht erfüllt, deshalb ist auch das Ereignis nicht eingetreten**.

imaginary past action – type 3

IF-CLAUSE	MAIN CLAUSE
If you **had worked** harder,	you**'d have passed** the test.
If he **had run** faster,	he **could have won** the race.
If I **hadn't been** so tired,	I **might have helped** you.

3 modal auxiliaries + have + past participle

Why did you throw the bottle out of the window?
You **could have hit** someone.
You **should have been** more careful.
I **would have come** with you but I had no time.

Modale Hilfsverben + have + Partizip Perfekt

Mit *could* / *should* / *would* + *have* + **Partizip Perfekt**

kann man ausdrücken, was **hätte geschehen können/sollen** oder was **eventuell passiert wäre**.

UNIT 2

1 reported speech

Darren **told** Mrs Taylor he wanted to work with computers.
Susan **mentioned** that she had never worked with animals.
Sue **said (that)** she wanted to be a web designer.
(*... sagte, dass sie ...*)

Die indirekte Rede

Was jemand gesagt hat, kann man auf zwei Arten wiedergeben:

- Die **direkte Rede** (*direct speech*) gibt wieder, was jemand **tatsächlich gesprochen** hat. Direkte Rede steht meist in Anführungszeichen:
  Englisch: '...' / "..."   Deutsch: „..."
- In der **indirekten Rede** (*reported/indirect speech*) **berichtet** man, was jemand gesagt hat. Man verzichtet dabei auf den genauen Wortlaut des Sprechers/der Sprecherin.

Die indirekte Rede wird durch bestimmte Verben eingeleitet, die über die Aussage berichten:
say, *tell*, *add*, *answer*, *mention*, *report*, *write*, ...
Auf diese Verben kann **that** folgen. Meist wird es jedoch weggelassen. Im Englischen steht, im Gegensatz zum Deutschen, kein Komma vor der indirekten Rede.

Beachte: *tell* wird verwendet, um auszudrücken, **zu wem** etwas gesagt wurde. Wir verwenden *say*, wenn die Person nicht genannt wird:
*She **told me** she wanted to find another job.*
*She **said** she wanted to find another job.*

Aussagesätze in der indirekten Rede

reported statements

2

In der indirekten Rede gibt es sowohl **Veränderungen** der **Zeitformen**, als auch der **Pronomen** und der **Orts-** und **Zeitangaben**.

'	**I'm**	meeting	**you**	**here**	**tomorrow**	.'
	↓		↓	↓	↓	
He said	**he was**	meeting	**me**	**there**	**the next day**	.

Veränderung der Zeitformen

tense changes

a

Steht das einleitende Verb im *simple present* oder im *present perfect*, so bleibt die Zeitform wie in der direkten Rede. Die Form des Verbs kann sich aber durch die Verschiebung der Person verändern: *I play* → *he plays*.

Bill: 'I often **work** on Saturdays.'
Bill **says** he often **works** on Saturdays.
Bill **has said** he often **works** on Saturdays.

Steht jedoch das **einleitende Verb** im *simple past*, so werden die Zeitformen der direkten Rede meist um **eine Zeitstufe in die Vergangenheit gesetzt**.

Mona: 'I **like** modern languages.'
→ Mona **said** she **liked** modern languages.

Das Verb in der Aussage verändert sich vom
- *present* → *past*

Besteht die Verbform aus mehreren Wörtern, so verändert sich das erste Wort:
am enjoying → *was enjoying*
have been → *had been*

Jane: '**I'm thinking** about my future.'
→ Jane **said** she **was thinking** about her future.

Peter: '**I've** never **done** any practical work.'
→ Peter **said** he **had** never **done** any practical work.

Steht das Verb in der Vergangenheit, so ändert es sich zu *past perfect* oder es bleibt unverändert.
- *past* → *past perfect* oder *past*

Rick: 'Mrs Taylor **gave** me a lot of advice.'
→ Rick said she **had given** him a lot of advice.
→ Rick said she **gave** him a lot of advice.

Modalverben ändern sich in der Regel:
- *will* → *would* *can* → *could*
  may → *might* *must/have to* → *had to*

Paul: '**I'll** go on holiday next week.'
→ Paul said he **would** go on holiday next week.

Folgende Modalverben bleiben unverändert:
- *would*, *could*, *should*, *might*, *ought to*

Mike: 'I **would** like to have a different job.'
→ Mike said he **would** like to have a different job.

b Changes of person, time and place

Janet (to her mother): **I'd** like to go to Greece for **my** holiday.
Janet's mother (to her husband): Janet said **she'd** like to go to Greece for **her** holiday.

MONDAY, 14 JUNE, 3 PM

Janet: 'We're going on holiday **tomorrow**, Luke.'

MONDAY, 14 JUNE, 5 PM

Luke: Janet phoned and said they were going on holiday **tomorrow**.

TUESDAY, 15 JUNE

Kim: Janet phoned yesterday and said they were going on holiday **today**.

FRIDAY, 18 JUNE

Kim: Janet phoned on Monday and said they were going on holiday **the next day / on Tuesday**.

Änderungen von Personen, Zeit und Ort

In der indirekten Rede werden die **Personal-** oder **Possessivpronomen** immer **aus der Sicht des Sprechers / der Sprecherin** gewählt.

Zeitangaben hängen häufig vom Zeitpunkt ab, zu dem etwas berichtet wird. Die Veränderungen werden **aus der Sicht des Sprechers / der Sprecherin** gewählt.
Wird noch am selben Tag berichtet, so bleibt die Zeitangabe unverändert. Erfolgt der Bericht einen Tag oder mehrere Tage später, so ändern sich die Zeitangaben.

Mögliche Änderungen:
now → *then, at that time*
today → *(on) that day, yesterday, last (Tuesday), …*
yesterday → *the day before, last (Tuesday), …*
tomorrow → *the next day, the following day, today, on Tuesday, …*
last week → *the week before*
next year → *the following year*

Beachte: Diese Veränderungen können nicht schematisch durchgeführt werden!

Die Veränderung der **Ortsangaben** hängt vom jeweiligen Standort des Sprechers/der Sprecherin ab.

Mögliche Änderungen:
here → *at his/her/their house, flat, there, …*

Fragen in der indirekten Rede — reported questions 3

werden durch Verben wie *ask*, *want to know*, *wonder* eingeleitet. Stehen diese Verben im *simple past*, so erfolgt die **Zeitverschiebung** wie bei Aussagesätzen.

Hugh: 'When **will** the boss arrive?'
→ Hugh **asked** when the boss **would** arrive.

Bei **Fragen ohne Fragewort** wird die indirekte Rede mit *if* oder *whether* (= ob) eingeleitet.

Nick: '**Have** you **seen** my CV, Sheila?'
→ Nick **asked** Sheila **if/whether** she **had** seen his CV.

Bei **Fragen mit Fragewörtern** (*how*, *what*, *when*, *where*, *why*, …) werden diese in den indirekten Fragesatz übernommen.

Nick: '**How did** you **like** the job interview?'
→ Nick **wanted to know how** she **(had) liked** the job interview.

Die Wortstellung des indirekten Fragesatzes verändert sich nicht. Sie entspricht der **Wortstellung von Aussagesätzen** (Subjekt – Verb). Es gibt keine Umschreibung mit *do*. Bei indirekten Fragen steht **kein Fragezeichen**.

		SUBJECT	VERB	
Fred:	'When **did**	Mary	**leave**	school?'
Fred **asks**	when	Mary	**left**	school.
Dan:	'**Does**	she	**like**	her job?'
Dan **asked if**		she	**liked**	her job.

Befehle und Bitten in der indirekten Rede — reporting orders and requests 4

Über einen Befehl oder ein Verbot wird in der indirekten Rede mit

tell + Objekt + *to*-Infinitiv

berichtet.

Hugh: '**Buy** two tickets for the musical tonight, Lisa.'
→ Hugh **told Lisa to buy** two tickets for the musical last night.

Bei negativen Sätzen steht *not* immer vor dem *to*-Infinitiv.

Hugh: '**Don't take** the very expensive seats.'
→ He **told her not to take** the very expensive seats.

Über Bitten wird in der indirekten Rede mit

ask + Objekt + *to*-Infinitiv

berichtet.

Diana: '**Could you help** me with my CV, please, Harry?'
→ Diana **asked Harry to help** her with her CV.

Ähnliche indirekte Sätze lassen sich bilden mit:
- *advise* (raten)
- *expect* (erwarten)
- *invite* (einladen)
- *warn* (warnen)

She **advised me not to miss** the exam.
He **expected me to visit** him the next day.
They **invited us to join** their party.
The teacher **warned us not to be** late again.

1 the passive

SUBJECT	VERB	OBJECT	
Marconi	**invented**	the radio	in 1898
The radio	**was invented**		**by** Marconi.

King George V opened the Science Museum in 1928.

The Science Museum was opened **by** King George V in 1928.

Das Passiv

Hat ein Aktivsatz ein Objekt (*the radio*), so kann man daraus einen Passivsatz bilden. Das Objekt des Aktivsatzes wird Subjekt des Passivsatzes.

Das Subjekt des Aktivsatzes ist der Verursacher der Handlung (*agent*). Er kann im Passivsatz mit *by* angehängt werden.

Ob man einen Aktivsatz oder einen Passivsatz verwendet, hängt davon ab, was betont werden soll. Im Aktivsatz wird das Subjekt (*King George V*) hervorgehoben. Ist das Objekt des Aktivsatzes (*The Science Museum*) das wichtigste, so verwendet man eher einen Passivsatz.

a tenses

SIMPLE PRESENT	The museum **is** (*… wird geschlossen*)	**closed** at 6 pm.
SIMPLE PAST	The museum **was** (*… wurde geschlossen*)	**closed** yesterday.
PRESENT PERFECT	The museum **has been** (*… ist geschlossen worden*)	**closed**.
PAST PERFECT	The museum **had been** (*… war geschlossen worden*)	**closed** earlier.
WILL-FUTURE	The museum **will be** (*… wird geschlossen werden*)	**closed** soon.

Zeitformen

Passivformen werden mit *be* + **Partizip Perfekt** (*past participle*) gebildet.

Beachte:
Im Deutschen verwenden wir „werden" für das Passiv und das Futur:

'Star Wars' is shown at 4 and at 8. (Passiv)
(wird … gezeigt)

ITV will show 'Star Wars' on Monday. (Futur)
(wird … zeigen)

b the passive: modal verbs

MODAL VERBS	The museum **should be** (*… sollte geschlossen werden*)	**closed**.
	The museum **might be** (*… könnte … geschlossen werden*)	**closed** earlier.

Modalverben im Passiv

Nach einem Modalverb (*can, may, must …*) bildet man das Passiv mit *be* + **Partizip Perfekt**.

Verlaufsformen im Passiv

the passive: progressive forms c

Im Passiv sind *progressive forms* nur im *present* und *past* üblich. Sie werden jeweils mit *being* gebildet:

PRESENT PROGRESSIVE PASSIVE

is/are/am + being + past participle

PAST PROGRESSIVE PASSIVE

was/were + being + past participle

Look, the moon landing **is being shown** again on TV.
(*... wird gerade ... wieder gezeigt*)

Some drinks **were being served** when we arrived.
(*... wurden gerade serviert*)

Verben mit zwei Objekten

Verben, die im Aktiv gewöhnlich mit zwei Objekten verbunden werden (*give*, *offer*, *tell*, *pay*, *promise*, *send*, *show*, *teach*, *lend*) bilden meist ein „**persönliches Passiv**"; d.h. das **indirekte Objekt** (Person) des **Aktivsatzes** wird zum **Subjekt des Passivsatzes**.

Es ist auch möglich, das direkte Objekt (Sache) des Aktivsatzes zum Subjekt des Passivsatzes zu machen. Das „persönliche Passiv" wird jedoch bevorzugt.

verbs with two objects d

SUBJECT	VERB	INDIRECT OBJECT	DIRECT OBJECT
They	showed	**us**	some books.
We	were shown		some books.

SUBJECT	VERB	INDIRECT OBJECT	DIRECT OBJECT
They	gave	us	**a guidebook**.
A guidebook	was given	to us.	

be said to

say kann im Passiv verwendet werden, um auszudrücken, dass es sich um ein verbreitetes Gerücht handelt.

Beachte die deutsche Übersetzung:
He is said to have a lot of money.
(**Man sagt,** er habe viel Geld. / **Er soll** viel Geld haben.)

Neben *say* können auch *believe*, *know*, *suppose*, *think*, ... so verwendet werden.

be said to e

Some people say that mobiles are unsafe.

Mobiles **are said to** be unsafe.

His father **is known to** have financial problems.

2 have something done

	HAVE	OBJECT	PAST PARTICIPLE
She	**'s having**	**her shoes**	**cleaned**.
They need to	**have**	**their phone**	**repaired**.

Etwas machen lassen

Man verwendet die Struktur

have + Objekt + *past participle*

um auszudrücken, dass **jemand etwas** von einer anderen Person **machen lässt**.

Vergleiche:
*Bill **has repaired** his computer.*
(hat … repariert)
*Bill **has** his computer **repaired**.*
(lässt … reparieren)

Beachte: Im informellen Sprachgebrauch kann auch *get something done* stehen:
*Why did you **get** your hair cut?*

UNIT 4

1 the infinitive

Do you know **where to find** India's Silicon Valley?
Lots of young Indians **want to work** in the US.
Are you **ready to help** me?
It's **time to do** some work now.

Where **does** she **come** from?
Indira **can spend** 10 months at the training camp.
Why don't they **let** their daughters **go** to school?
They always **make** them **do** housework.
You **had better look** for a proper job.
I'd rather not work as a servant.

Der Infinitiv

Es gibt zwei Arten des Infinitivs.

- Der *to*-Infinitiv (*to-infinitive*) steht nach bestimmten
  Fragewörtern,
  Verben,
  Adjektiven und
  Nomen
- Der Infinitiv ohne *to* (*infinitive without to*) steht nach Hilfs- und Modalverben,
  let (lassen),
  make (veranlassen),
  had better und
  would rather (vgl. S. 119).

a question word + to-infinitive

Vikram has decided **what to do** after school.
Do you know **how to make** Indian bread?
She wonders **whether to go** to Bombay or **to stay** in Madras.

He couldn't decide **which computer to buy**.
*Er konnte sich nicht entschließen, **welchen Computer er kaufen sollte**.*

Fragewort + to-Infinitiv

Nach Fragewörtern (*who*, *what*, *where*, *when*, *which*, *how*) und *whether* (= ob) kann der *to*-Infinitiv stehen.

Beachte: Im Deutschen übersetzt man diese Konstruktion immer mit einem Nebensatz.

Verb + to-Infinitiv

b

Der *to*-Infinitiv wird nach bestimmten Verben verwendet:

verb + to-infinitive

Maneka **decided** **to go** to the US.
She **promised** **to send** some money to her family.

VERBEN + TO-INFINITIV

agree	zustimmen	**forget**	vergessen	**promise**	versprechen
can afford	sich leisten können	**hope**	hoffen	**refuse**	sich weigern
choose	beschließen	**learn**	lernen	**seem**	scheinen
decide	sich entschließen	**manage**	schaffen	**try**	versuchen
expect	erwarten	**offer**	anbieten	**want**	wollen
fail	es nicht schaffen	**plan**	planen	**would like/love**	möchte gern

Beachte: den *to*-Infinitiv bei *be able to do* (tun können), *be allowed to do* (tun dürfen), *have to do* (tun müssen), *ought to do* (tun sollen).

Linda **wasn't able** **to do** the job properly.
Are we **allowed** **to go** now?
You **have to** **leave** now. You **ought to** **be** home in time.

Verb + Objekt + to-Infinitiv

c

Nach bestimmten Verben mit einem Objekt steht der *to*-Infinitiv:

verb + object + to-infinitive

They **expect** **her to speak** English well.
The teacher **helped** **the pupils to learn** English.

advise	raten	**force**	zwingen	**want**	wollen, dass
allow	erlauben	**help**	helfen	**warn**	warnen
ask	bitten	**invite**	einladen	**would like/love**	möchte(n) gern, gern (tun) wollen
cause	verursachen	**remind**	erinnern an		
encourage	ermutigen	**teach**	lehren		
expect	erwarten	**tell**	befehlen		

Beachte dass auf *want* und *would like/love* kein *that*-Satz folgt:
I would like you to work for me.
Ich **möchte**, **dass** Sie für mich arbeiten.

He wanted her to buy a hamster.

Nomen/Pronomen + to-Infinitiv

d

Ein *to*-Infinitiv wird oft nach Nomen, bestimmten Pronomen (*something, anything*) und Mengenbezeichnungen anstelle eines Relativsatzes verwendet:
*Is there **anything to drink**? = Is there **anything that I can drink**?*

noun/pronoun + to-infinitive

I must buy a **book** **to read**.
We've got plenty of **time** **to see** the museum.
May I have **something** **to drink**?
There's **lots** **to do**.

e adjective + to-infinitive

It's not **easy to learn** Hindi.
It's **more difficult to learn** Urdu.
Digvijay is **too ill to come** to school.
It's not **warm enough to wear** shorts.

Adjektiv + to-Infinitiv

Der *to*-Infinitiv kann nach den meisten Adjektiven und ihren Steigerungsformen stehen. Oft steht er auch in Verbindungen von Adjektiven mit *too* (zu) und *enough* (genug).

f used to

When I was younger, I **used to play** cricket a lot.
There **used to be** a village where the computer company is now.
I **didn't use to like** fish but now I do.
Did you **use to play** cricket at school?

used to

used + *to*-Infinitiv bezieht sich auf Gewohnheiten in der Vergangenheit (spielte früher immer) oder einen Zustand in der Vergangenheit.

- **Verneinte Form:** *didn't use* + *to*-Infinitiv
- **Fragen:** *did … use* + *to*-Infinitiv

He **used to work** a lot. (*Er arbeitete früher viel.*)
He **is used to working** a lot. (*Er ist es gewöhnt, viel zu arbeiten.*)

Beachte: *used to* + Infinitiv wird oft mit *be used to* +*ing*-Form (gewöhnt sein) verwechselt.

2 the ing-form

Die -ing-Form

Die *-ing*-Form kann als **Gerundium** (*gerund*) wie ein Nomen verwendet werden, d.h.:

Travelling can be very interesting.

- als **Subjekt**,

I like **travelling** very much.

- als **Objekt** (es steht dabei nach bestimmten Verben)

VERBEN + -ING-FORM

avoid	vermeiden	**give up**	aufgeben	**mention**	erwähnen
dislike	ungern tun	**go on**	weitermachen	**miss**	verpassen
enjoy	gern tun	**imagine**	sich vorstellen	**practise**	üben
finish	aufhören	**keep**	weitermachen	**suggest**	vorschlagen
mind	etwas dagegen haben	(*mind* kommt nur in Fragen und Verneinungen vor: *Do you **mind** opening the window? I don't **mind** helping you.*)			

I get a lot of pleasure **from travelling**.

- oder nach einer **Präposition**.

Taking photos can be very exciting.
My sister doesn't like **working at night**.

Das Gerund kann wie ein Verb durch ein **Objekt** oder durch eine **adverbiale Bestimmung** erweitert werden.

Die -ing-Form nach Präpositionen

the ing-form after prepositions

3

Nach einer Präposition (*at*, *of*, *for*, …) steht das folgende Verb in der *-ing*-Form. Die Präposition ist dabei mit einem

- **Adjektiv**
- **Nomen**
- **Verb** verbunden oder sie steht
- **allein**.

Are you **good at using** a computer?
We have the **opportunity of going** to Delhi.
He **apologized for being** late again.
Please phone me **before leaving** the house.

Adjektiv + Präposition + -ing-Form

adjective + preposition + ing-form

a

Julie is **used to working** hard.
I'm **afraid of losing** my job.

VERBINDUNGEN VON ADJEKTIV + PRÄPOSITION + -ING-FORM

be afraid of	Angst haben vor	**be good at**	gut sein in
be annoyed	verärgert sein über	**be interested in**	interessiert sein an
be bad at	schlecht sein in	**be keen on**	gerne tun
be crazy about	verrückt sein nach	**be nervous of**	Angst haben vor
be different from	sich unterscheiden von	**be proud of**	stolz sein auf
be excited about	aufgeregt sein wegen	**be tired of**	genug haben von
be famous for	berühmt sein für	**be used to**	gewöhnt sein an
be fond of	mögen	**be worried about**	sich Sorgen machen um

Nomen + Präposition + -ing-Form

nomen + preposition + ing-form

b

What's the **advantage of going** by plane?
He takes no **interest in reading** history books.

VERBINDUNGEN VON NOMEN + PRÄPOSITION + -ING-FORM

advantage of	Vorteil von	**interest in**	Interesse an
chance of	Gelegenheit zu	**opportunity of**	Gelegenheit zu
choice between	Auswahl zwischen	**reason for**	Grund für
danger of	Gefahr zu	**way of**	Art und Weise zu
hope of	Hoffnung auf		

Beachte: *way* und *chance* können auch mit dem *to*-Infinitiv verwendet werden:
This is the best way to do / way of doing it.
We had no chance to see / chance of seeing him.

c verb + preposition + ing-form

Verb + Präposition + -ing-Form

Do you **feel like going** to the movies?
He **worries about losing** his job.

VERBINDUNGEN VON VERB + PRÄPOSITION + -ING-FORM

agree with	einverstanden sein mit	**depend on**	abhängen von
apologize for	sich entschuldigen für	**feel like**	Lust haben auf
approve of	einverstanden sein mit	**insist on**	bestehen auf
believe in	glauben an	**look forward to**	sich freuen auf
complain about	sich beschweren über	**succeed in**	Erfolg haben mit
concentrate on	sich konzentrieren auf	**think of**	denken an
consist of	bestehen aus	**worry about**	sich Sorgen machen um

d preposition/conjunction + ing-form

Präposition/Konjunktion + -ing-Form

You must phone me **before going** on holiday.
On hearing the news of his death she started to cry.

Die *-ing*-Form kann im Anschluss an bestimmte **allein stehende Präpositionen** und **Konjunktionen der Zeit** stehen:

before leaving	vor dem Verlassen	**on arriving**	bei der Ankunft
after getting up	nach dem Aufstehen	**while talking**	während des Sprechens
since returning	seit der Rückkehr	**when riding**	als er/sie/… ritt

Sie folgt auch auf **andere** allein stehende **Präpositionen**:

in spite of trying/ despite trying	trotz des Versuchs	**without seeing**	ohne zu sehen
		by using	indem man … verwendet
instead of eating	anstatt zu essen	**for opening**	zum Öffnen

In spite of trying hard she failed the history test.
The corkscrew is **for opening** wine bottles.

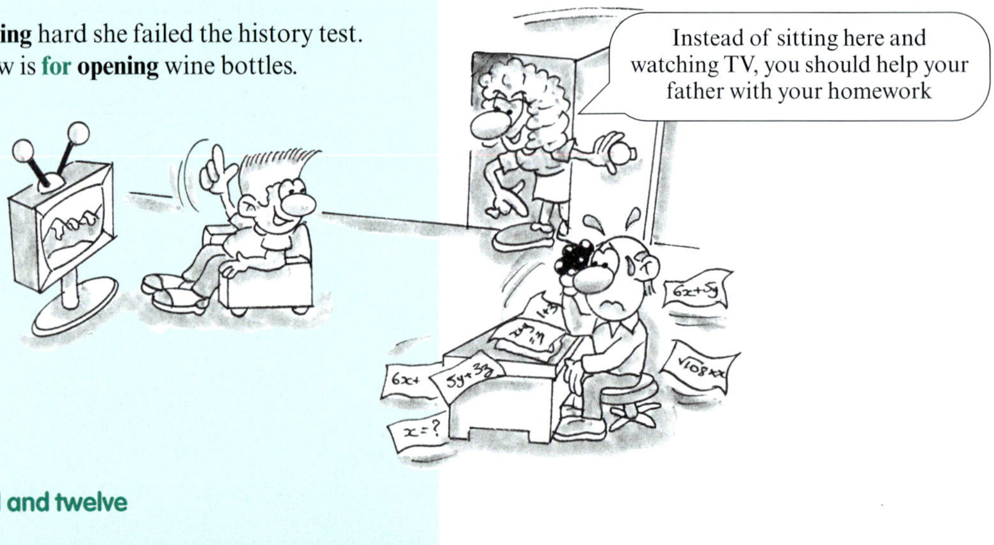

Die -ing-Form nach bestimmten Ausdrücken — the ing-form after certain expressions 4

Die *-ing*-Form steht nach den Ausdrücken:

be worth	(sich lohnen)
be no use	(keinen Sinn haben)
what about/how about	(wie wär's mit)

My old computer isn't **worth repairing**.
It's no **use complaining**.
I'm thirsty. **What about/How about stopping** for a drink?

Infinitiv oder -ing-Form — the infinitive or the ing-form 5

Nach einigen Verben kann sowohl der *to*-Infinitiv als auch die *-ing*-Form verwendet werden. Die Bedeutung bleibt dabei unverändert.

Mrs Patel **loves** watch**ing** TV.
to watch TV.
I **hate** driv**ing** at night.
to drive at night.

Dazu gehören: *start*, *begin*, *continue*, *love*, *like*, *prefer*, *hate*.

Bei folgenden Verben hängt der Anschluss davon ab, welche Bedeutung gemeint ist:

stop + *to*-Infinitiv	anhalten, um etwas zu tun
stop + *-ing*-Form	aufhören, etwas zu tun
forget + *to*-Infinitiv	vergessen, etwas zu tun
forget + *-ing*-Form	vergessen, dass man etwas getan hat
remember + *to*-Infinitiv	daran denken, etwas zu tun
remember + *-ing*-Form	sich (daran) erinnern, dass man etwas getan hat

He **stopped to** smoke a cigarette.
He **stopped** smok**ing**.

I **forgot to** buy something to drink.
I'll never **forget** see**ing** her for the first time.

You must **remember to** learn your words for your test.
I still **remember** writ**ing** my first English test.

He stopped smoking.

Irregular verbs Unregelmäßige Verben

INFINITIVE	SIMPLE PAST	PAST PARTICIPLE	
to be	was/were	been	sein
to beat	beat	beaten	schlagen
to become	became	become	werden
to begin	began	begun	anfangen, beginnen
to bend	bent	bent	biegen
to bet	bet/betted	bet/betted	wetten
to bite	bit	bitten	beißen
to blow	blew	blown	blasen
to break	broke	broken	brechen
to bring	brought	brought	bringen
to build	built	built	bauen
to burn	burnt/burned	burnt/burned	(ver)brennen
to buy	bought	bought	kaufen
to catch	caught	caught	fangen
to choose	chose	chosen	wählen
to come	came	come	kommen
to cost	cost	cost	kosten
to cut	cut	cut	schneiden
to dig	dug	dug	graben
to do	did	done	tun, machen
to draw	drew	drawn	ziehen, zeichnen
to dream	dreamt/dreamed	dreamt/dreamt	träumen
to drink	drank	drunk	trinken
to drive	drove	driven	fahren
to eat	ate	eaten	essen
to fall	fell	fallen	fallen
to feed	fed	fed	füttern
to feel	felt	felt	fühlen
to fight	fought	fought	kämpfen
to find	found	found	finden
to fly	flew	flown	fliegen
to forbid	forbade	forbidden	verbieten, untersagen
to forget	forgot	forgotten	vergessen
to freeze	froze	frozen	(ge)frieren
to get	got	got	bekommen
to give	gave	given	geben
to go	went	gone	gehen
to grow	grew	grown	wachsen, anbauen, werden
to hang	hung	hung	hängen
to hang	hanged	hanged	erhängen (töten)
to have	had	had	haben
to hear	heard	heard	hören
to hide	hid	hidden	(sich) verstecken
to hit	hit	hit	treffen, schlagen
to hold	held	held	halten
to hurt	hurt	hurt	verletzen
to keep	kept	kept	halten, behalten
to know	knew	known	wissen, kennen
to lay	laid	laid	legen
to lead	led	led	führen
to learn	learnt/learned	learnt/learned	lernen

INFINITIVE	SIMPLE PAST	PAST PARTICIPLE	
to leave	**left**	**left**	verlassen
to lend	**lent**	**lent**	leihen, borgen
to let	**let**	**let**	lassen, zulassen
to lie	**lay**	**lain**	liegen
to light	**lit**	**lit**	anzünden
to lose	**lost**	**lost**	verlieren
to make	**made**	**made**	machen
to mean	**meant**	**meant**	bedeuten, meinen
to meet	**met**	**met**	treffen, begegnen
to pay	**paid**	**paid**	bezahlen
to put	**put**	**put**	setzen, stellen
to quit	**quit**	**quit**	verlassen
to read	**read**	**read**	lesen
to ride	**rode**	**ridden**	reiten, fahren
to ring	**rang**	**rung**	klingeln, anrufen
to rise	**rose**	**risen**	ansteigen, aufgehen
to run	**ran**	**run**	laufen
to say	**said**	**said**	sagen
to see	**saw**	**seen**	sehen
to sell	**sold**	**sold**	verkaufen
to send	**sent**	**sent**	schicken, senden
to set	**set**	**set**	setzen, stellen
to shine	**shone**	**shone**	scheinen
to shoot	**shot**	**shot**	schießen
to show	**showed**	**shown/showed**	zeigen
to shut	**shut**	**shut**	schließen
to sing	**sang**	**sung**	singen
to sink	**sank**	**sunk**	sinken, untergehen
to sit	**sat**	**sat**	sitzen
to sleep	**slept**	**slept**	schlafen
to speak	**spoke**	**spoken**	sprechen
to spend	**spent**	**spent**	ausgeben, verbringen
to spill	**spilt/spilled**	**spilt/spilled**	verschütten
to spin	**spun**	**spun**	spinnen
to split	**split**	**split**	spalten, teilen
to spread	**spread**	**spread**	verbreiten
to stand	**stood**	**stood**	stehen
to steal	**stole**	**stolen**	stehlen
to stick	**stuck**	**stuck**	kleben, stecken bleiben
to sweep	**swept**	**swept**	fegen
to swim	**swam**	**swum**	schwimmen
to swing	**swung**	**swung**	schwingen
to take	**took**	**taken**	nehmen
to teach	**taught**	**taught**	unterrichten, lehren
to tell	**told**	**told**	erzählen
to think	**thought**	**thought**	denken, glauben
to throw	**threw**	**thrown**	werfen
to understand	**understood**	**understood**	verstehen
to wake	**woke**	**woken**	aufwecken, aufwachen
to wear	**wore**	**worn**	tragen
to win	**won**	**won**	gewinnen
to write	**wrote**	**written**	schreiben

English sounds Erklärung der Lautschriftzeichen

Vowels
Selbstlaute, Vokale

[iː]	eat, week, he
[i]	party, very, ready
[ɪ]	in, give, film
[e]	end, get, many
[æ]	add, man, black
[ʌ]	under, come
[ɑː]	ask, half, car
[ɒ]	often, what, coffee
[ɔː]	all, four, door
[ʊ]	put, good, woman
[u]	situation, unite, actual
[uː]	who, June, blue
[ɜː]	learn, girl, work
[ə]	again, policeman, sister
[eɪ]	eight, table, play
[aɪ]	I, nice, by
[ɔɪ]	boy, toilet
[əʊ]	old, road, know
[aʊ]	out, house, now
[ɪə]	we're, here, near
[eə]	wear, chair, there
[ʊə]	tour, pure, sure

Consonants
Mitlaute, Konsonanten

[p]	pen, speak, map
[b]	book, rabbit, job
[t]	table, letter, sit
[d]	desk, radio, old
[k]	car, basketball, back
[g]	get, bigger, bag
[f]	father, left, cliff
[v]	very, every, have
[θ]	thank, birthday, bath
[ð]	this, father, with
[s]	see, classes, dance
[z]	zoo, thousand, please
[ʃ]	shop, sugar, English
[ʒ]	television, usually
[tʃ]	child, kitchen, watch
[dʒ]	jam, June, arrange
[h]	help, who, home
[m]	mouse, number, film
[n]	name, window, pen
[ŋ]	sing, morning, long
[l]	like, blue, all
[r]	read, borrow, very
[j]	yes, you, year
[w]	walk, where, quiz

The English alphabet
Das englische Alphabet

a	[eɪ]
b	[biː]
c	[siː]
d	[diː]
e	[iː]
f	[ef]
g	[dʒiː]
h	[eɪtʃ]
i	[aɪ]
j	[dʒeɪ]
k	[keɪ]
l	[el]
m	[em]
n	[en]
o	[əʊ]
p	[piː]
q	[kjuː]
r	[ɑː]
s	[es]
t	[tiː]
u	[juː]
v	[viː]
w	['dʌbl juː]
x	[eks]
y	[waɪ]
z	[zed]

Erklärung der Symbole im Wörterverzeichnis

Com	=	Communication	Proj	=	Project	TYE	=	Test your English
Dict	=	Dictionary Work	Read	=	Reading	SP	=	Speaking Practice
Ex	=	Exercise	Rev	=	Revision	WP	=	Words and Pictures
Fol	=	Follow up	Sit	=	Situation	›	=	definition
Lit	=	Literature	T	=	Text	››	=	synonym
Pract	=	Practice	TP	=	Translation Practice	›‹	=	opposite

Unit 1

WP	**what's on?** [wɒts 'ɒn]	was läuft (im Kino/ Theater, …)?	***What's on*** *at the local cinema tonight?*
	box office ['bɒks ɒfɪs]	Theater-, Kinokasse	❯ *a place where you can buy tickets in a theatre or cinema*
	to **dream (of)** [dri:m] **dreamt/dreamed, dreamt/dreamed** [dremt, dremt]	träumen (von)	*She's **dreaming** of becoming a rock star.*

Unregelmäßige Verben

to **dream, dreamt, dreamt** *auch*: **dreamed, dreamed**	*träumen*	to **let, let, let**	*lassen*
		to **catch, caught, caught**	*fangen*
to **drive, drove, driven**	*fahren, treiben*	to **put, put, put**	*setzen, stellen, legen*
to **bend, bent, bent**	*biegen, beugen*	to **mean, meant, meant**	*bedeuten*
to **set, set, set**	*setzen*		

Alle unregelmäßigen Verben findest du auf Seite 114–115.

	matinee ['mætɪneɪ]	Nachmittagsvorstellung, Matinee	❯ *an afternoon performance in the theatre, cinema, etc*
	online ['ɒnlaɪn]	online	
	stage [steɪdʒ]	Bühne	*She was too nervous to go on **stage**.*
	steel [sti:l]	Stahl	*The bridge is made of **steel**.*
	worker ['wɜ:kə]	Arbeiter/in	*The steel **workers** are on strike.*
	clone [kləʊn]	geklontes Wesen, Klon	❯ *the exact copy of something or someone*
	PG [ˌpi: 'dʒi:]	betreut durch Erwachsene, Eltern	❯ *PG* steht für *parental guidance;* Kinder sollten Kinofilme, die so ausgezeichnet sind, nicht ohne die Betreuung von Eltern/Erwachsenen ansehen.
	to **race** [reɪs]	jagen, rasen	❯ *to move very fast*
	ring [rɪŋ]	Ring	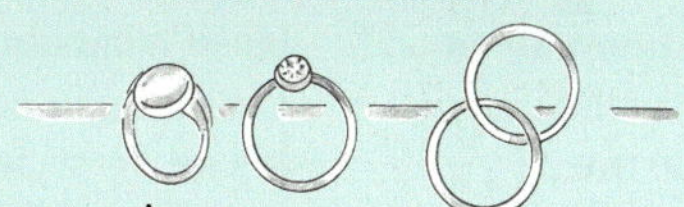
	acrobat ['ækrəbæt]	Akrobat/in	*You can see **acrobats** at a circus.*
	live [laɪv]	live, lebend	*Is the show **live** or recorded?*
	rock music ['rɒk mju:zɪk]	Rock (Musikrichtung)	
	Caribbean [ˌkærɪ'bi:ən]	Karibik; karibisch	
	samba ['sæmbə]	Samba (Tanz)	
Sit1	**so** [səʊ]	auch	*Mike is clever and **so** is his brother.*
	neither ['naɪðə]	auch nicht	*I don't like horror movies. ~ **Neither** do I.*
	nor [nɔ:]	auch nicht	*~ **Nor** do I*
Ex1	**kind (of)** [kaɪnd]	Art, Sorte, Gattung (von)	*What **kind of** music do you like? ~ Rock music.*
	to **continue** [kən'tɪnju:]	weitermachen, fortfahren mit	❯❯ *to go on (with)*
Sit2	to **ask out** [ˌɑ:sk 'aʊt]	einladen, ausführen (in ein Lokal)	❯ *to invite sb to go out with you*
Ex4	**chat show** ['tʃæt ʃəʊ]	Talkshow	❯❯ *talk show AE*
T1	**downstairs** [ˌdaʊn'steəz]	unten, die Treppe hinunter	*Come **downstairs**,*

to **chat** [tʃæt]	plaudern	› *to talk in a friendly way*
paper ['peɪpə]	Zeitung	›› *newspaper*
no way [ˌnəʊ 'weɪ]	kommt überhaupt nicht infrage	*Do you want me to help you? ~* ***No way!***
would rather [wʊd 'rɑːðə]	möchte lieber	***I'd rather*** *go shopping tomorrow.*
to **envy** ['envi]	beneiden	*Jill was beautiful and rich. All the other girls* ***envied*** *her.*
to **go on** [ˌgəʊ 'ɒn] **went, gone** [went, gɒn]	vor sich gehen, passieren	*What's going on?* = Was ist los?
what about do**ing?** ['wɒt əbaʊt]	wie wär's mit?	***What about*** *going to a party?*
circus ['sɜːkəs]	Zirkus	*You can see acrobats at a* ***circus.***
come on! [ˌkʌm 'ɒn]	sei vernünftig! komm schon!	***Come on****, you can do it.*
performance [pə'fɔːməns]	Aufführung, Vorstellung	*The evening* ***performance*** *will begin at 9 p.m.*
it's **no use doing sth** [ɪts nəʊ 'juːs]	es hat keinen Sinn, etwas zu tun	*It's* ***no use*** *waiting – she won't come.*
stuff [stʌf]	Zeug, Sachen; Material	›› *things*
electro [ɪ'lektrəʊ]	Electro (Musikrichtung)	
tech house ['tek haʊs]	Tech House (Musikrichtung)	
reggae ['regeɪ]	Reggae (Musikrichtung)	
it's **worth doing sth** [ɪts 'wɜːθ]	es lohnt sich, etwas zu tun	***Is it worth seeing*** *the new James Bond film?*

Expression + verb + -ing

What/how about … ?	**How/What about** watch**ing** *Lord of the Rings*?
It's worth …	Yes, **it** might **be worth** watch**ing**.
It's no use …	**It's no use** try**ing** to get tickets. Look, it says 'No tickets left'.

Nach *What/How about …*, *it's worth …* und *it's no use …* kann ein Verb in der *-ing*-Form folgen.

to **mind** [maɪnd]	etwas einzuwenden haben gegen	⚠ *mind* nur in Fragen und Verneinungen: ***Do you mind*** *opening the window? ~ No, I* ***don't mind.***
fortunately ['fɔːtʃənətli]	glücklicherweise	
upstairs [ˌʌp'steəz]	oben	›‹ *downstairs*
perfect ['pɜːfɪkt]	perfekt	›› *excellent, very good*
you **had better** [ju həd 'betə]	du solltest / man sollte besser	*Next time I tell you something you'****d better*** *listen.*

Expression + infinitive without to

Nach *would rather* und *had better* folgt ein Infinitiv ohne *to*:

Would you **rather stay** here or go to a gig?
I'd rather go out tonight.
I'd rather not stay at home and watch *Star Trek*.

Mit *would rather* wird ausgedrückt, was man bevorzugt tun würde.

I think she**'d better see** a doctor
You**'d better hurry** – it's late.
You**'d better not forget** your homework again.

Mit *had better* gibt man einen Rat oder fordert jemanden auf etwas zu tun.

Ex7	**vague** [veɪg]	vage, ungenau	› *not very clear, not exact*
	likely ['laɪkli]	wahrscheinlich	*Gary is the most **likely** winner of the race.* *He's **likely** to win.* (= Er wird wahrscheinlich gewinnen.)
Ex8	to **design** [dɪ'zaɪn]	entwerfen, konstruieren	*The dress was **designed** by Vivienne Westwood.*
	opera ['ɒprə]	Oper	
Ex9	to **prefer** [prɪ'fɜː]	vorziehen, lieber haben	*His grandfather always **preferred** tea to coffee.*

-rr-

to prefer	she preferred	preferring
to star	he starred	starring
to occur	it occurred	occurring

Nach einem einzelnen, betonten Vokal wird ein einzelner Endkonsonant verdoppelt.

	soul [səʊl]	Soul (Musikrichtung)	
Ex10	to **combine** [kəm'baɪn]	zusammenfügen, verbinden	› *to put different things together*
Ex11	to **thank sb for doing sth** ['θæŋk fə]	jmd. danken, etwas getan zu haben	*I must **thank her for** send**ing** the money.*
	excellent ['eksələnt]	ausgezeichnet	›› *very good*
	to **look forward to doing sth** [ˌlʊk 'fɔːwəd tə]	sich darauf freuen, etwas zu tun	***I'm** really **looking forward to** visit**ing** my pen-friend in the USA.*
Sit3	**mixed-up** [ˌmɪkst 'ʌp]	konfus, zerstreut, durcheinander	*She's just a crazy **mixed-up** kid.*
	the day before yesterday [ðə deɪ bɪˌfɔː 'jestədeɪ]	vorgestern	›› *two days ago*
	the day after tomorrow [ðə deɪ ˌɑːftə tə'mɒrəʊ]	übermorgen	›› *in two days*

the day before yesterday — **yesterday** — **today** — **tomorrow** — **the day after tomorrow** →

	to **change one's mind** [ˌtʃeɪndʒ wʌnz 'maɪnd]	seine Meinung ändern	› *to change your opinion about something*
	to **wonder** ['wʌndə]	sich fragen, gerne wissen wollen	›› *to ask oneself:* *I don't know the girl over there. I **wonder** who she is.*
Ex12	**trousers** ['traʊzəz]	Hose	⚠ *trousers* ist immer Plural: *Are those new **trousers**? ~ Yes, I bought **them** this morning.*

Sit4	**globe** [gləʊb]	Kugel, Erdball, Globus	
	birth [bɜːθ]	Geburt	›‹ *death*
	hygiene ['haɪdʒiːn]	Hygiene, Gesundheitspflege	
	Latin ['lætɪn]	Latein, Lateinisch	› *the language of the Romans*
	instead of doing sth [ɪn'sted əv]	anstatt etwas zu tun	*We should do something **instead of** just talk**ing** about it.*
	employer [ɪm'plɔɪə]	Arbeitgeber/in	
	behaviour [bɪ'heɪvjə]	Benehmen, Verhalten	*Can violence on TV start violent **behaviour**?*
T2	**mayor** [meə]	Bürgermeister/in	
	to **set up** [ˌset 'ʌp] **set, set** [set, set]	gründen, eröffnen	›› *to build*
	success [sək'ses]	Erfolg	*The party was a big/great **success**.*
	partly ['pɑːtli]	teilweise, zum Teil	›‹ *completely* *It was **partly** my fault.*
	thatched [θætʃt]	strohgedeckt	*thatched roof*
	roof [ruːf]	Dach	
	cannon ['kænən]	Kanone	
	to **catch fire** [ˌkætʃ 'faɪə] **caught, caught** [kɔːt, kɔːt]	Feuer fangen	› *to start burning*
	to **manage to** do sth ['mænɪdʒ]	es schaffen, es fertigbringen, etw zu tun	
	flame [fleɪm]	Flamme	*The theatre was in **flames** when they arrived.*
	to **put out** [ˌpʊt 'aʊt]	löschen, ausmachen	› *to make a fire, etc stop burning*
	career [kə'rɪə]	Laufbahn, Karriere	
	financial [faɪ'nænʃl]	finanziell	
	plot [plɒt]	Handlung (z. B. Film)	› *what happens in a story or play*
	complicated ['kɒmplɪkeɪtɪd]	kompliziert	› *difficult to understand*
	to **concentrate (on)** ['kɒnsntreɪt ɒn]	sich konzentrieren (auf)	*She tried to **concentrate on** her book.*
	throne [θrəʊn]	Thron	
	revenge [rɪ'vendʒ]	Rache	*He took **revenge** on his enemies.*
	such [sʌtʃ]	solche(r,s), so, derartig	

such a(n) und so

such a(n) und *so* sind sehr ähnlich in der Bedeutung, werden aber unterschiedlich verwendet:

She's **such a** nice **person**.
He's **such an idiot**.

Wir verwenden *such a(n)* vor einem Nomen.

She's **so nice**.
He's **so stupid**.

So steht vor einem Adjektiv (ohne Nomen).

half a(n), quite a(n), such a(n)

He arrived **half an** hour later.
She's **quite a** good cook.
Rex is **such a** lovely dog.

Half, *such* und *quite* stehen vor *a* oder *an*.

	to **drive** [draɪv] **drove, driven** [drəʊv, 'drɪvn]	(an)treiben	*His ideas **are driving** me mad.* (… machen mich verrückt/ treiben mich in den Wahnsinn)
	poison ['pɔɪzn]	Gift	*gift* = Geschenk Gift = *poison*
	to **prepare** [prɪ'peə]	zubereiten	› *to make/get ready*
	replica ['replɪkə]	Nachbildung, Rekonstruktion	
	method ['meθəd]	Methode, Verfahren	Betonung: ***method*** ●• › *a planned way of doing something*
	comment ['kɒment]	Bemerkung, Kommentar	Betonung: ***comment*** ●•
Ex15	**smell** [smel]	Geruch, Gestank	*Oh! What a **smell**!*
Ex18	**dry** [draɪ]	trocken	›‹ *wet*
	imaginary [ɪ'mædʒɪnəri]	frei erfunden, eingebildet	›‹ *real*
	it's no good [ɪts nəʊ 'gʊd]	es ist sinnlos	›› *it's no use*
Com	to **crash** [kræʃ]	abstürzen (Computer)	*If a computer **crashes**, it suddenly stops working.*
	relief [rɪ'li:f]	Erleichterung	*That's a **relief**!* = Mir fällt ein Stein vom Herzen.
	to **signal** ['sɪgnəl]	signalisieren, Zeichen geben	*The policeman **signalled** to the children to cross the road.*
	emotion [ɪ'məʊʃn]	Gefühl, Emotion	*Love and hate are **emotions**.*
	to **reassure** [ˌri:ə'ʃʊə]	beruhigen, versichern	› *to make someone feel less worried*
TYE	**industry** ['ɪndəstri]	Industrie	*heavy / light / computer / film **industry***
	caste [keɪst]	Kaste	› *one of the social classes in India*
	romance [rəʊ'mæns]	Romanze, Liebesgeschichte	› *a story about love*
	background ['bækgraʊnd]	Hintergrund	*In the **background** of this photo you can see some mountains.*
	tax [tæks]	Steuer	*The British colonists had to pay a **tax** on tea.*
	influence (on) ['ɪnfluəns ɒn]	Einfluss (auf), Auswirkung	
TYE3	**director** [də'rektə]	Regisseur/in; Direktor/in	› *the person who tells the actors what to do*
TYE4	**harbour** ['hɑ:bə]	Hafen	› *a place where ships can go and stay in*
	mainland ['meɪnlænd]	Festland	*There's a ferry service between the islands and the **mainland**.*
Read	to **separate** ['sepəreɪt]	(sich) trennen	› *to stop living together*
	suitcase ['su:tkeɪs]	Koffer	
	note [nəʊt]	Banknote, Geldschein	*Adrian found a ten-pound **note**.*
	labour ward ['leɪbə wɔ:d]	Entbindungsstation, Kreißsaal	
	spaghetti [spə'geti]	Spaghetti	***Spaghetti** is my favourite food.* (= Spaghetti sind …)
	jar [dʒɑ:]	Krug, Gefäß, Marmeladenglas	
	untidy [ʌn'taɪdi]	unordentlich	›‹ *tidy*
	nightmare ['naɪtmeə]	Albtraum	› *a very frightening dream; a very bad situation*
	upside down [ˌʌpsaɪd 'daʊn]	verkehrt herum, auf dem Kopf stehend	

to **pass** [pɑːs]	vorbeigehen, vorbeifahren	›› *to go by*
to **change** [tʃeɪndʒ]	wechseln	*Can you **change** a £10 note?*
lift [lɪft]	Aufzug, Lift	›› *elevator AE*
permission [pəˈmɪʃn]	Erlaubnis	*She gave us **permission** to leave early.*
pleased [pliːzd]	erfreut	›› *happy*
to **screw your face up** [ˈskruː jɔː feɪs ʌp]	das Gesicht verziehen	
normal [ˈnɔːml]	normal	›› *ordinary*
nurse [nɜːs]	Krankenschwester/ Krankenpfleger	
to **let go (of)** [ˌlet ˈɡəʊ] **let, let** [let, let]	loslassen	
the pains [ðə ˈpeɪnz]	die Wehen	
head end [ˈhed end]	Kopfende	
to **pant** [pænt]	keuchen, hecheln	
sigh [saɪ]	Seufzer	*After the test he gave a long **sigh** of relief.*
skinny [ˈskɪni]	dürr	›› *very thin*
purple [ˈpɜːpl]	purpurrot	
bad-tempered [ˌbædˈtempəd]	schlecht gelaunt	
belly [ˈbeli]	Bauch	
to **stare at** [ˈsteər ət]	anstarren	*What **are** you **staring at**?*
to **gibber** [ˈdʒɪbə]	stammeln, brabbeln	
gap [ɡæp]	Lücke	

Mind the gap 1 — Tipps zum Bearbeiten von mixed grammar-Übungen

Was muss man tun, wenn ein Verb in Klammern steht?

◆ Das Verb muss in die richtige Zeitstufe gesetzt werden → nach Signalwörtern im Satz suchen!

He usually (go) ______ to the movies on Friday night.
He usually (go) **goes** to the movies on Friday night.

Signalwörter für simple present:
always, usually, often, sometimes, every day, …

Listen, Kirsty (practise) ______ the guitar.
Listen, Kirsty (practise) **is practising** the guitar.

Signalwörter für present progressive:
at the moment, (right) now, just, look!, listen!, …

In 1987 my father (buy) ______ a sports car.
In 1987 my father (buy) **bought** a sports car.

Signalwörter für simple past:
in 1989, five years ago, yesterday, last month, when, …

We (be/never) ______ to India.
We (be/never) **have never been** to India.

Signalwörter für present perfect:
just, ever, never, yet, so far, since/for (seit), …

After Sam (finish) ______ his job, he watched TV.
After Sam (finish) **(had) finished** his job, he watched TV.

Signalwörter für past perfect:
before, after, … + im Hauptsatz simple past

Next year we (spend) ______ our holiday in the US.
Next year we (spend) **'ll spend** our holiday in the US.

Signalwörter für future:
tomorrow, next year/month/…, soon, in 2015, …

Unit 2

WP	**web** [web]	Netz	*a spider's web* *the worldwide web*
	designer [dɪ'zaɪnə]	Designer/in	
	to **require** [rɪ'kwaɪə]	benötigen, erfordern	›› *to need*
	required [rɪ'kwaɪəd]	verlangt, gefordert, erforderlich	›› *necessary*
	engineering [ˌendʒɪ'nɪərɪŋ]	Technik	› *designing and making machines, bridges, etc*
	diploma [dɪ'pləʊmə]	Diplom	
	recruitment agency [rɪ'kru:tmənt ˌeɪdʒənsi]	Arbeitsvermittlung	
	mechanic [mɪ'kænɪk]	Mechaniker/in	*A **mechanic** can repair machines and cars.*
	apprentice [ə'prentɪs]	Auszubildende/r, Lehrling	› *a young worker who is learning a job or trade*
	assistant [ə'sɪstənt]	Assistent/in, Verkäufer/in	*A shop **assistant** helps customers in a shop.*
	travel agency ['trævl ˌeɪdʒənsi]	Reisebüro	› *a company that plans holidays for people*
	skill [skɪl]	Fertigkeit, Geschicklichkeit	*You need computing **skills** for that job.*
	customer ['kʌstəmə]	Kunde/Kundin	*A **customer** buys things from a shop.*
	to **train** [treɪn]	trainieren, schulen, unterweisen	› *to learn the skills of a job*

Lernen

Sandra is **training** to be a nurse. = *eine **praktische Ausbildung** machen*
Michael is **studying** music at university. = *etwas aus **Büchern und in Kursen** lernen*
How long have you been **learning** English? = *lernen **allgemein***

	training ['treɪnɪŋ]	Ausbildung, Schulung, Training	
	experience [ɪk'spɪəriəns]	Erfahrung	
	advantage [əd'vɑ:ntɪdʒ]	Vorteil	› *something useful*
	to **ship** [ʃɪp]	versenden, verfrachten, verschiffen	› *to send something by ship*
	CV [ˌsi: 'vi:]	Lebenslauf	› 'CV' steht für lat.: 'curriculum vitae'
	department [dɪ'pɑ:tmənt]	Abteilung	› *one of the parts of a big company, shop or university*
	veterinary ['vetnri]	tierärztlich, Veterinär-	
	to **apply to sb for sth** [ə'plaɪ fə]	sich bei jdm. bewerben um, für	*She **applied to** a computer company for the job of a mechanic.*
	nursery ['nɜ:səri]	Kindertagesstätte	
Sit1	**electrical** [ɪ'lektrɪkl]	elektrisch, Elektro-	
	GCSE [ˌdʒi: si: es 'i:]	General Certificate of Secondary Education	› Prüfung, die Schüler in England, Wales, und Nordirland im Alter von 16 Jahren ablegen. Normalerweise wird die Prüfung in mehreren Fächern absolviert.

exam [ɪg'zæm]	Prüfung	› *a spoken or written test*
education [ˌedʒu'keɪʃn]	Erziehung	
qualification [ˌkwɒlɪfɪ'keɪʃn]	Qualifikation	
interview ['ɪntəvju:]	Gespräch, Interview	*a job interview* = ein Vorstellungsgespräch
to **report** [rɪ'pɔ:t]	berichten	› *to tell someone what has been happening*
T1 **abroad** [ə'brɔ:d]	im Ausland, ins Ausland	*She's never lived **abroad** before. He often goes **abroad** on business.*
yeah [jeə]	ja (*umg.*)	
to **choose to do sth** [tʃu:z]	beschließen, etwas zu tun	*She **chose to** learn French at school.*
advantage of doing sth [əd'vɑ:ntɪdʒ əv]	Vorteil, etwas zu tun	*The **advantage of** living in the country is that it's cheaper.*
to **suggest** [sə'dʒest]	vorschlagen	› *to give someone an idea*
foreigner ['fɒrənə]	Ausländer/in	› *someone from another country*
banking ['bæŋkɪŋ]	Bankbranche	
to **spend** [spend] **spent, spent** [spent, spent]	verbringen (Zeit)	*He **spends** all his time with his computer.*
to **improve** [ɪm'pru:v]	verbessern, sich bessern	›› *to become better, to make better*
scholarship ['skɒləʃɪp]	Stipendium	
to **attend** [ə'tend]	besuchen (Schule), teilnehmen	*All children between the ages of 5 and 16 must **attend** school.*

Besuchen

Lots of people **visit** the Tower every year.	= *besuchen, besichtigen*
Did he **attend** the meeting?	= *Veranstaltung besuchen*
He goes to **see** his mother every week.	= *jdn. freundschaftlich besuchen*

certificate [sə'tɪfɪkət]	Urkunde	*a birth / school **certificate***
credit ['kredɪt]	Kredit	› *sum of money lent by a bank*
administration [ədˌmɪnɪ'streɪʃn]	Verwaltung	› *controlling and managing a business, etc*
colleague ['kɒli:g]	Kollege/Kollegin	› *someone you work with*
to **get to know** [get tə 'nəʊ]	kennen lernen	*She's very nice when you **get to know** her.*
it doesn't agree with sb [ə'gri: wɪð]	jdm. nicht bekommen, es nicht vertragen	*If a type of food or drink **does not agree with you**, it makes you feel ill.*
practical ['præktɪkl]	praktisch	›› *useful*
green card [ˌgri:n 'kɑ:d]	Aufenthaltsgenehmigung	› Man muss sich als Ausländer von der US-Einwanderungsbehörde eine *green card* ausstellen lassen, wenn man längerfristig arbeiten möchte.
discussion [dɪ'skʌʃn]	Diskussion, Besprechung	
bill [bɪl] *BE*	Rechnung	› *a list that shows how much money you have to pay*
to **get on someone's nerves** [ˌget ɒn sʌmwʌnz 'nɜ:rvz] **got, got** [gɒt, gɒt]	jdm. auf die Nerven gehen	

	to **miss** [mɪs]	vermissen	*He **missed** his girlfriend.*
	ups and downs [ˌʌps ən 'daʊnz]	Höhen und Tiefen (des Lebens)	› *the good and bad things in life*
	to **be bitten by the bug** [bi ˌbɪtn baɪ ðə 'bʌg]	es hat einen gepackt	› *to be very interested in*
	willing ['wɪlɪŋ]	bereitwillig, gewillt	› *happy to do something*
	to **regret** [rɪ'gret]	bedauern, bereuen	› *to feel sorry: He **regrets** that he was unfriendly to her.*
Ex5	**following** ['fɒləʊɪŋ]	folgend	›› *next*
Ex8	**idiom** ['ɪdiəm]	Redewendung, idiomatischer Ausdruck	› *'to spill the beans' is an idiom meaning 'to make known a secret'.*
Ex9	**hairdresser** ['heədresə]	Friseur/in	
	make-up artist [ˌmeɪkʌp 'ɑːtɪst]	Visagist/in	
Ex10	**similar** ['sɪmələ]	ähnlich	›› *almost the same*
	Yours faithfully [jɔːz 'feɪθfəli]	Mit freundlichen Grüßen (Brief)	
	application [ˌæplɪ'keɪʃn]	Bewerbung	
	Ms [mɪz]	Anrede für verheiratete oder ledige Frau	
	Yours sincerely [jɔːz sɪn'sɪəli]	Mit freundlichen Grüßen (Brief)	
Ex11	**curriculum vitae** [kəˌrɪkjələm 'viːtaɪ]	Lebenslauf	› *CV*
	nationality [ˌnæʃə'næləti]	Staatsangehörigkeit, Nationalität	*She has British **nationality**.*
	date of birth [ˌdeɪt əv 'bɜːθ]	Geburtsdatum	*Please write your name, address and **date of birth** on the form.*
	marital status [ˌmærɪtl 'steɪtəs]	Familienstand	*What is your **marital status**: single or married?*
	single ['sɪŋgl]	allein stehend, unverheiratet	›‹ *married*
	to **obtain** [əb'teɪn]	erhalten, erzielen, sich verschaffen	›› *to get* ⚠ *obtain* klingt etwas förmlich!
	advanced [əd'vɑːnst]	fortgeschritten	
	vocational [vəʊ'keɪʃənl]	Berufs-	***Vocational** training teaches you the skills you need to do a special job.*
	studies ['stʌdiz]	Studium	⚠ *studies* steht immer im Plural!
	waitress ['weɪtrɪs]	Kellnerin	› *a woman who serves food and drink in a restaurant*
Ex12	**mind map** ['maɪnd mæp]	Mindmap	
Sit2	**change** [tʃeɪndʒ]	Änderung	
	copy ['kɒpi]	Kopie, Exemplar	*We will send you a **copy** of the report.*
	order ['ɔːdə]	Befehl	
	to **advise** [əd'vaɪz]	den Rat geben, raten	› *to tell somebody what they should do*
Sit3	**tourism** ['tʊərɪzəm]	Tourismus, Fremdenverkehr	
Ex14	to **drop out of** [ˌdrɒp 'aʊt əv]	(die Schule o. Ä.) abbrechen	*Four students **dropped out** of the course after two weeks.*
T2	to **grow up** [grəʊ 'ʌp] **grew, grown** [gruː, grəʊn]	aufwachsen, erwachsen werden	› *to become older or an adult* *She **grew up** in Scotland.*

	lawyer ['lɔ:jə]	Rechtsanwalt/ Rechtsanwältin	*She wants to see her **lawyer** before she says anything.*
	primitive ['prɪmətɪv]	primitiv, urzeitlich	›› *simple*
	existing [ɪg'zɪstɪŋ]	vorhanden, existierend	
	boss [bɒs]	Chef/in	*Linda was the **boss** of a large company.*
	personal ['pɜ:sənl]	persönlich	***personal** computer / problems / letters / life / service*
	operating system ['ɒpəreɪtɪŋ ˌsɪstəm]	Betriebssystem	*DOS stands for disk **operating system**.*
	producer [prə'dju:sə]	Produzent/in	*a film / Hollywood / movie producer; gas / oil producers*
	to **update** [ˌʌp'deɪt]	aktualisieren, auf den neuesten Stand bringen	› *to make something more modern*
	household ['haʊshəʊld]	Haushalt	*It was a **household** word / name. = it was famous*
	hi-tech [ˌhaɪ'tek]	technisch hoch entwickelt	› *using the most advanced machines and methods*
	to **turn on** [ˌtɜ:n 'ɒn]	anschalten	
	to **turn off** [ˌtɜ:n 'ɒf]	ausschalten	
	tactic ['tæktɪk]	Taktik, taktischer Zug	
	none [nʌn]	keine(r, s)	› *not one (of a group of three or more)*
	competitor [kəm'petɪtə]	Konkurrent/in	*We must keep this new idea a secret from our **competitors**.*
	per cent [pə'sent]	Prozent	
	importance [ɪm'pɔ:tns]	Bedeutung	› *how important something or someone is*
	browser ['braʊzə]	Browser	
	rival ['raɪvl]	Konkurrenz-, Rivale/Rivalin	*They were business **rivals**.* ›› *competitor*
	to **connect** [kə'nekt]	verbinden	*Can I **connect** my printer to your computer?*
	instant ['ɪnstənt]	sofort, augenblicklich	
	available [ə'veɪləbl]	verfügbar	*The new software is not yet **available**.*
	global ['gləʊbl]	weltweit, global	›› *worldwide*
	globalization [ˌgləʊbəlaɪ'zeɪʃn]	Globalisierung	
Ex17	**unfair** [ˌʌn'feə]	unfair, ungerecht	›‹ *fair*
	meeting ['mi:tɪŋ]	Treffen, Zusammenkunft	
Ex19	to **switch off** [ˌswɪtʃ 'ɒf]	abschalten	›› *turn off*
Ex20	**telesales** ['teliseɪlz]	Verkauf per Telefon	› *telephoning people in order to try to sell them things*
Com	to **disagree with sb** [ˌdɪsə'gri:]	sich mit jdm. nicht einig sein	
	direct [də'rekt]	direkt	›‹ *indirect*
	a matter of opinion [ˌmætər əv ə'pɪniən]	Ansichtssache	
Ex21	**well off** [ˌwel 'ɒf]	wohlhabend, reich, gut dran	

well off *better off* *best off*

	barrier ['bæriə]	Schranke, Barriere	
	to **compete with/ against** [kəm'pi:t]	konkurrieren mit, kämpfen gegen	*They can't **compete with** us on price. The two businesses **are competing against** each other.*
	efficient [ɪ'fɪʃnt]	leistungsfähig, effizient	*If something is **efficient**, it works well.*

	power ['paʊə]	Macht, Kraft, Fähigkeit	*The huge **power** of television can be frightening.*
	to **communicate** [kə'mjuːnɪkeɪt]	in Verbindung stehen	*They only **communicate** by e-mail.*
TYE	**military** ['mɪlətri]	Militär, militärisch	
	scientist ['saɪəntɪst]	Naturwissenschaftler/in	› *someone who works or is trained in science*
	development [dɪ'veləpmənt]	Entwicklung	*There have been a lot of computer **developments** in the last ten years.*
	hacker ['hækə]	Computerhacker/in	
	file [faɪl]	Datei; Akte	
	to **destroy** [dɪ'strɔɪ]	zerstören	*Fire **destroyed** the building.*
Read	**high flier** [ˌhaɪ 'flaɪə]	Senkrechtstarter/in, Hochbegabte/r	› *someone who is extremely successful in their job or in school*
	helicopter ['helɪkɒptə]	Hubschrauber	
	shoulder ['ʃəʊldə]	Schulter	
	rescue ['reskjuː]	Rettung	*A **rescue** team brought the injured man down the mountain.*
	pilot ['paɪlət]	Pilot/in	Betonung: ***pilot*** ●•
	on standby [ɒn 'stændbaɪ]	in Bereitschaft	› *ready to help instantly*
	blonde [blɒnd]	blond (Frau)	
	to **give as good as you get** [ˌgɪv əz ˌgʊd əz ju 'get]	sich kräftig wehren	*She can **give as good as she gets.***
	girlie ['gɜːli]	mädchenhaft	
	boot [buːt]	Stiefel	
	orange ['ɒrɪndʒ]	orange	
	jumpsuit ['dʒʌmpsuːt]	Overall	
	to **matter** ['mætə]	von Bedeutung sein, darauf ankommen	› *to be important* *Money is the only thing that **matters** to him.*
	patient ['peɪʃnt]	Patient/in	
	survival [sə'vaɪvl]	Überleben	
	oncoming ['ɒnkʌmɪŋ]	aus der Gegenrichtung	***oncoming** car / traffic*
	neck [nek]	Hals	
	injury ['ɪndʒəri]	Verletzung	*Beckham can't play today because of an **injury** to his foot.*
	stomach ['stʌmək]	Magen	›› *belly*
	bloated ['bləʊtɪd]	aufgedunsen	
	internal [ɪn'tɜːnl]	innerlich, innere(r/s)	› *inside your body*
	rupture ['rʌptʃə]	Bruch, Riss	
	fatal ['feɪtl]	tödlich, mit tödlichem Ausgang	*a **fatal** accident / illness / injury*
	to **act** [ækt]	handeln, tätig sein	› *to do something*
	physiology [ˌfɪzi'ɒlədʒi]	Physiologie	
	physical ['fɪzɪkl]	körperlich	***physical** exercise / activity / development*
	to **achieve** [ə'tʃiːv]	erreichen, schaffen, erzielen	› *to succeed in doing something*
	trapped [træpt]	gefangen, eingeschlossen	*They were **trapped** in the burning building.*
	to **crawl** [krɔːl]	kriechen, krabbeln	*Look out! There's a spider **crawling** up your arm.*
	to **push oneself too far** ['pʊʃ wʌnself ˌtuː 'fɑː]	zu weit gehen	

Mind the gap 2 — Tipps zum Bearbeiten von mixed grammar-Übungen

Was muss man tun, wenn ein Verb in Klammern steht?

◆ Die Zeitstufe der übrigen Satzteile ist zu beachten:

If you eat too many sweets, you (damage) ______ your teeth.
If you eat too many sweets, you (damage) **damage** your teeth.

if-clause – type I: If + simple present, will/can/…+ infinitive

If you (be) ______ a teacher, you wouldn't talk like that.
If you (be) **were** a teacher, you wouldn't talk like that.

if-clause – type II: If + simple past, would/could/… + infinitive

I don't know what I (do) ______ if you hadn't helped me.
I don't know what I (do) **would have done** if you hadn't helped me.

if-clause – type III: If + past perfect, would/could/… + have + past participle

◆ Das Verb muss im Passiv stehen:

The picture (paint) ______ by van Gogh 90 years ago.
The picture (paint) **was painted** by van Gogh 90 years ago.

Du musst den *by-agent* im Satz suchen und den Sinn des Satzes beachten.

◆ Das Verb steht nach einer Präposition:

After (read) ______ the comic, he switched on the TV.
After (read) **reading** the comic, he switched on the TV.

Nach einer Präposition steht das folgende Verb meist in der *-ing*-Form.

◆ Ein entsprechendes Wort der Wortfamilie ist gesucht:

Her (know) ______ of English is excellent.
Her (know) **knowledge** of English is excellent.

Du musst auf den Sinnzusammenhang achten!

Unit 3

WP	**fascinating** ['fæsɪneɪtɪŋ]	faszinierend, fesselnd	› *very interesting*
	satellite ['sætəlaɪt]	Satellit	*Last week the US launched a new weather **satellite**.*
	steam [sti:m]	(Wasser-)Dampf	*150 years ago most engines were driven by **steam**.*
	scientific [ˌsaɪən'tɪfɪk]	(natur)wissenschaftlich	*a **scientific** discovery / study, **scientific** research*
	experiment [ɪk'sperɪmənt]	Experiment	› *a scientific test*
	medicine ['medsn]	Medizin	› *the study of diseases*
	glimpse [glɪmps]	flüchtiger Blick	*She caught a **glimpse** of him in the crowd.*
	photography [fə'tɒgrəfi]	Fotografieren	
	chemistry ['kemɪstri]	Chemie	
	everyday ['evrideɪ]	alltäglich, Alltags-	*The internet has become part of **everyday** life.*
	nuclear ['nju:kliə]	nuklear, atomar, Atom-, Kern-	
	material [mə'tɪəriəl]	Material, Stoff	*Wood, stones and metal are building **materials**.*
	telecommunications [ˌtelikəˌmju:nɪ'keɪʃnz]	Telekommunikation	
	farming ['fɑ:mɪŋ]	Landwirtschaft	

an alarm clock

a wrist watch

a phonograph

a space capsule

	clock [klɒk]	Uhr	
	virtual ['vɜːtʃuəl]	virtuell	›‹ *real*
	basement ['beɪsmənt]	Kellergeschoss	
	phonograph ['fəʊnəʊgrɑf]	Phonograph	
	space capsule ['speɪs ˌkæpsjuːl]	Raumkapsel	
	difference engine ['dɪfrəns ˌendʒɪn]	mechanische Rechenmaschine zur Lösung von Differenzialgleichungen	
Sit1	to **orbit** ['ɔːbɪt]	umkreisen	*The earth takes a year to **orbit** the sun.*
	planet ['plænɪt]	Planet	*Earth, Venus and Mars are **planets**.*
	artificial [ˌɑːtɪ'fɪʃl]	künstlich, Kunst-	
	Russian ['rʌʃn]	Russe/Russin; russisch	
	space probe ['speɪs prəʊb]	Raumsonde	
	surface ['sɜːfɪs]	Oberfläche	*These plants float on the **surface** of the water.*
	to **forecast** ['fɔːkɑːst]	voraussagen, vorhersehen	› *say what you think will happen in the future*
	to **spy (on)** [spaɪ]	nachspionieren, bespitzeln	› *to watch something or somebody secretly*
Ex1	**version** ['vɜːʃn]	Version, Fassung	
	orbit ['ɔːbɪt]	Umlaufbahn	
Ex2	**spacecraft** ['speɪskrɑːft] pl spacecraft	Raumfahrzeug, -schiff	*A **spacecraft** can travel in space.*
	astronaut ['æstrənɔːt]	Raumfahrer/in; Astronaut/in	› *a person who works in a spacecraft*
	lunar module [ˌluːnə 'mɒdjuːl]	Mondfähre	
Sit2	to **blast off** [ˌblɑːst 'ɒf]	in den Weltraum schießen	›› *to take off* *The rocket **blasted off** in the early morning.*
	to **dock** [dɒk]	andocken, koppeln	*If two spacecraft **dock**, they are joined together in space.*
	laboratory [lə'bɒrətri]	Laboratorium, Labor	
	solar panel [ˌsəʊlə 'pænl]	Sonnenkollektor	
	off course [ˌɒf 'kɔːs]	nicht auf Kurs	› *going in the wrong direction*
	asteroid ['æstərɔɪd]	Asteroid	› *a small planet which goes round the sun* (kleiner Planet)
Ex3	**attendant** [ə'tendənt]	Aufseher/in, Wärter/in	*a museum / car park / flight **attendant*** (= Flugbegleiter/in)
T1	**science fiction** [ˌsaɪəns 'fɪkʃn]	Science-Fiction	
	businessman ['bɪznəsmæn] **businessmen** ['bɪznəsmən]	Geschäftsmann	› *a person who buys and sells things*
	cosmonaut ['kɒzmənɔːt]	Kosmonaut/in	› *a Russian astronaut*
	return ticket [rɪˌtɜːn 'tɪkɪt]	Rückfahrkarte	› *a ticket for a journey to a place and back again*

including [ɪn'klu:dɪŋ]	einschließlich, inbegriffen	
accommodation [əˌkɒmə'deɪʃn]	Unterkunft	***Accommodation*** *is included in the price of your holiday.*
bargain ['bɑ:gɪn]	Schnäppchen, guter Kauf	› *something that is very cheap*
paradise ['pærədaɪs]	Paradies	› *a perfect place for someone*
delay [dɪ'leɪ]	Verzögerung, Aufschub	*Our flight had a* ***delay*** *of three hours.*
billion ['bɪliən]	Milliarde	› *one thousand million*
to **waste** [weɪst]	vergeuden, verschwenden	*to* ***waste*** *time / food / money / paper / …*
used to do sth ['ju:s tə]	etwas früher getan haben	*He* ***used to*** *smoke, but now he has stopped.*

used to oder be/get used to

She **used to** like cats but one attacked her and she doesn't anymore.
I **didn't use to** like him much when we were at school.

used to + Infinitiv bedeutet, dass man früher immer etwas getan hat, jetzt aber nicht mehr

I'm used to the noise from the traffic. **I'm not used to** getting up early.

to be used to + noun/-ing-form heißt, dass man etwas gewohnt ist

You can **get used to** it. You'll soon **get used to** living here.

to get used to bedeutet, dass man sich an etwas gewöhnt

luggage ['lʌgɪdʒ] *BE*	Gepäck	› *bags, suitcases, etc for travelling*
thought [θɔ:t]	Gedanke	
to **vary** ['veəri]	variieren, sich verändern	›› *to change*
plus [plʌs]	plus	›‹ *minus*
shorts [ʃɔ:ts]	kurze Hose, Shorts	*Football players wear* ***shorts.***
spacesuit ['speɪssu:t]	Raumanzug	› *clothing which is worn by a person who travels in space*
space shuttle ['speɪs ˌʃʌtl]	Raumfähre	
long-term [ˌlɒŋ'tɜ:m]	langfristig, Langzeit-	***long-term*** *effects / unemployment*
resident ['rezɪdənt]	Bewohner/in, Einwohner/in	› *someone who lives in a place*
crew [kru:]	Besatzung, Crew, Mannschaft	› *a group of people who work together on a ship, plane, spacecraft*
commander [kə'mɑ:ndə]	Kommandant/in	
system ['sɪstəm]	System	› *a group of things that work together*
to **carry out** [ˌkæri 'aʊt]	aus-, durchführen	*They* ***carried out*** *a number of experiments.*
weightlessness ['weɪtləsnəs]	Schwerelosigkeit	
research [rɪ'sɜ:tʃ]	Forschung, wissenschaftliche Untersuchung	*medical / scientific* ***research, research*** *on animals*
effect [ɪ'fekt]	Wirkung, Effekt	› *what happens because of something*
Ex5 **info box** ['ɪnfəʊ bɒks]	Infobox	

Ex7	**incorrect** [ˌɪnkə'rekt]	falsch, unrichtig	›‹ *correct*
Ex8	**scissors** ['sɪzəz]	Schere	
	washing machine ['wɒʃɪŋ ˌməʃi:n]	Waschmaschine	
	sunglasses ['sʌnglɑ:sɪz]	Sonnenbrille	

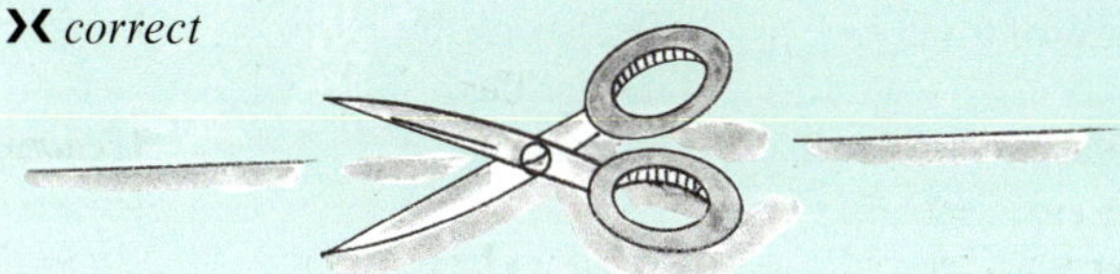

Pair nouns

I've bought **some** sunglasses. Where are **the** scissors?	Paarwörter bezeichnen Dinge, die aus **zwei gleichen Teilen** bestehen. Sie können **nur im Plural** verwendet werden. Man kann sie nicht zusammen mit *a/an* oder einer Zahl verwenden.
I need **a pair of** jeans and **two pairs of** shorts.	Um eine genaue Anzahl anzugeben, kann man *a/one pair of*, *two/three/… pairs of* verwenden.

Weitere Paarwörter: *trousers BE / pants AE* (Hose), *shorts*, *jeans*, *pyjamas BE / pajamas AE* (Schlafanzug), *glasses*, *headphones* (Kopfhörer), *scissors* (Schere), *tights* (Strumpfhose).

Ex9	**such as** ['sʌtʃ əz]	wie zum Beispiel	›› *for example*

Group nouns

Our team **is/are** playing very well.	Sammelnamen bezeichen immer **eine Gruppe von Leuten**. Bei Sammelnamen im Singular kann das folgende **Verb im Singular** (*is*) oder **im Plural** (*are*) stehen.
The family **has** lived here for 200 years.	Sieht man die **Gruppe als Einheit**, so verwendet man das Verb im **Singular**.
The family **have** all left the house.	Meint man eher die **einzelnen Mitglieder der Gruppe**, so verwendet man das Verb im **Plural**.

Beachte: Im *AE* wird normalerweise nur der **Singular** verwendet.

Weitere Sammelwörter: *army*, *choir* (Chor), *audience*, *band*, *class*, *club*, *company*, *couple*, *crew*, *crowd*, *gang*, *government*, *group*, *party* (Partei), *public* (Öffentlichkeit), *tribe*

Ex10	**central heating** [ˌsentrəl 'hi:tɪŋ]	Zentralheizung	
	coal [kəʊl]	Kohle	
	lamp [læmp]	Lampe, Leuchte	
Sit 3	**device** [dɪ'vaɪs]	Gerät, Vorrichtung	
	to **regard as** [rɪ'gɑ:d əz]	betrachten (als), halten (für)	*Lots of people **regard** Dennis Tito as a hero.*
	battery ['bætəri]	Batterie	
	bulb [bʌlb]	Glühbirne, -lampe	
	inventor [ɪn'ventə]	Erfinder/in	*An **inventor** plans and thinks of something new.*
	necessity [nə'sesəti]	Notwendigkeit, Bedürfnis	*Food and clothes are **necessities** of life.*
	case [keɪs]	Fall	

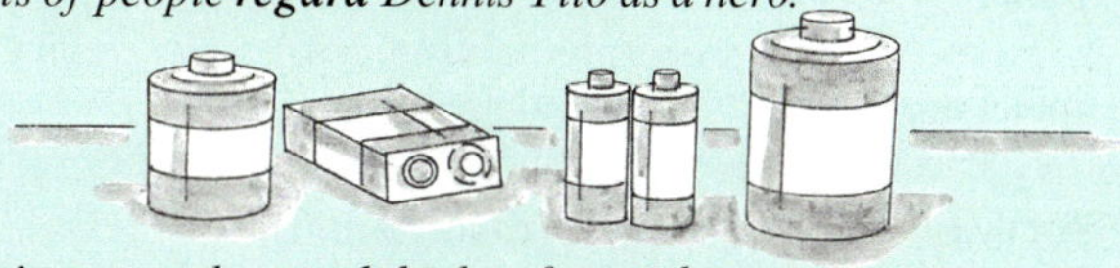

	desire [dɪ'zaɪə]	Verlangen, Wunsch, Begierde	› *a feeling that you want something very much*
Ex11	**housework** ['haʊswɜ:k]	Hausarbeit	*We usually do the **housework** at weekends.* Hausaufgaben = *homework; housework* = Hausarbeit
Ex12	**proverb** ['prɒvɜ:b]	Sprichwort	*'An apple a day keeps the doctor away' is a **proverb**.*
Sit4	**competition** [ˌkɒmpə'tɪʃn]	Wettbewerb	
	congratulations [kənˌgrætʃu'leɪʃnz]	Glückwünsche, ich gratuliere	***Congratulations** on your new job.*
	bicycle ['baɪsɪkl]	Fahrrad	›› *bike*
	brake [breɪk]	Bremse	
	to **trigger** ['trɪgə]	auslösen	› *to make something start to happen*
	to **slow down** [ˌsləʊ 'daʊn]	(sich) verlangsamen, langsamer werden	› *to become slower, to make something slower*
	to **fit** [fɪt]	einbauen, ausrüsten mit	› *to put a small piece of equipment into a place*
	to **reduce** [rɪ'dju:s]	vermindern, reduzieren	› *to make something less or smaller*
	to **solve** [sɒlv]	lösen	› *to find the correct answer to a problem*
	solution [sə'lu:ʃn]	Lösung	*There are no simple **solutions** to the problem.*
	to **replace** [rɪ'pleɪs]	ersetzen	› *to put one thing in place of another thing*
T2	**cast** [kɑ:st]	Gipsverband	
	cerebral palsy [ˌserəbrəl 'pɔ:lzi]	zerebrale Bewegungsstörung	
	operation [ˌɒpə'reɪʃn]	Operation	*He's going to have an **operation** on his knee.*
	to **itch** [ɪtʃ]	jucken, brennen	
	to **ventilate** ['ventɪleɪt]	belüften, ventilieren	› *to let fresh air into a room, etc*
	narrow ['nærəʊ]	eng, schmal	›‹ *wide*
	tube [tju:b] *BE*	Röhre, Röhrchen, Schlauch	
	to **attach** [ə'tætʃ]	anfügen, befestigen, verbinden mit	› *to connect one thing to another*
	light [laɪt]	leicht	›‹ *heavy*
	pump [pʌmp]	Pumpe	
	to **power** ['paʊə]	antreiben, betreiben	*Most motors **are powered** electrically.*
	volt [vəʊlt]	Volt	
	Velcro ['velkrəʊ]	Klettband	
	apprenticeship [ə'prentɪʃɪp]	Lehrzeit, Lehre	*He's serving an **apprenticeship** as a baker.* (… macht eine Lehre)
	institute ['ɪnstɪtju:t]	Institut	
	to **encourage** [ɪn'kʌrɪdʒ]	ermutigen	*Peter's friends **encouraged** him to apply for the job.*
	therapy ['θerəpi]	Therapie, Behandlung	Betonung: ***therapy*** ●••
	to **act on** ['ækt ɒn]	handeln nach, sich richten nach	
	cot death ['kɒt deθ]	plötzlicher Kindstod	
	sleep [sli:p]	Schlaf	*I didn't get much **sleep** last night.*
	garment ['gɑ:mənt]	Kleidungsstück	› *a piece of clothing* ⚠ *garment* klingt förmlich!
	to be **asleep** [bi ə'sli:p]	schlafen	*He's still **asleep**. Don't wake him.*

sleep oder be asleep

I normally **sleep** on my back.
Did you **sleep** well?

Be quiet! The baby **is asleep**.
I always **fall asleep** in front of the TV. (*schlafe ein*)

Normalerweise verwendet man *is asleep* statt *is sleeping* wenn jemand gerade schläft.

	comfortable ['kʌmftəbl]	bequem, angenehm	
	ambition [æm'bɪʃn]	Ehrgeiz, Ziel	*It's Sita's **ambition** to be a doctor.*
Ex17	to **fit** [fɪt]	passen zu	› *to be right for*
Ex18	**coal mine** ['kəʊlmaɪn]	Kohlenbergwerk	
	telescope ['telɪskəʊp]	Teleskop	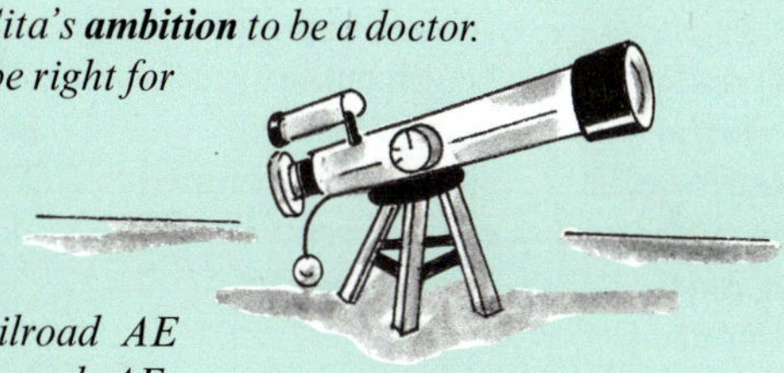
Com	to **dash** [dæʃ]	flitzen, sich beeilen	
	railway ['reɪlweɪ] *BE*	Eisenbahn	›› *railroad AE*
Ex20	**penfriend** ['penfrend]	Brieffreund/in	›› *pen pal AE*
TYE	**pioneer** [ˌpaɪə'nɪə]	Pionier/in, Bahnbrecher/in	
	aeroplane ['eərəpleɪn], **aircraft** ['eəkrɑ:ft] pl aircraft	Flugzeug	›› *plane*
	non-stop [ˌnɒn'stɒp]	ohne Zwischenlandung, pausenlos, Nonstop-	› *without stopping*
	immediate [ɪ'mi:diət]	sofortig, umgehend	›› *instant*
	immediately [ɪ'mi:diətli]	sofort	›› *at once*
	solo ['səʊləʊ]	Solo-, allein	*a **solo** flight, a **solo** performance*
	household name ['haʊshəʊld ˌneɪm]	Name, den jede/r kennt	
	to **admire** [əd'maɪə]	bewundern	› *to have a very high opinion of someone*
	navigator ['nævɪgeɪtə]	Navigator/in	
Read	**failure** ['feɪljə]	Scheitern	›‹ *success*
	pipeline ['paɪplaɪn]	Rohrleitung, Pipeline	
	to **irrigate** ['ɪrɪgeɪt]	bewässern	
	motorized ['məʊtəraɪzd]	motorisiert	*a **motorized** bike*
	toilet ['tɔɪlət]	Toilette	
	saddle ['sædl]	Sattel	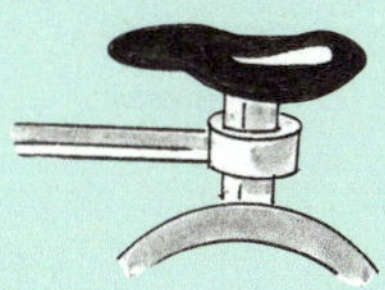 
	funnel ['fʌnl]	Trichter	
	waste [weɪst]	Abfall, Exkrement	*human waste* = Exkremente
	to **pass** [pɑ:s]	durchfließen, durchgehen	›› *to go through*
	container [kən'teɪnə]	Behälter, Gefäß, Container	*Baskets, boxes, bags, cans, jars and bottles are **containers**.*
	cyclist ['saɪklɪst]	Radfahrer/in	› *someone who rides a bike*
	way [weɪ]	weit	*way out* = weit weg
	error ['erə]	Irrtum, Fehler, Versehen	›› *a mistake*
	spokesman ['spəʊksmən]	Sprecher, Wortführer	

to **collapse** [kə'læps]	zusammenbrechen, einen Kollaps erleiden	› *to fall down*
X-ray ['eksreɪ]	Röntgenaufnahme	
centimetre ['sentɪmiːtə]	Zentimeter	
nail [neɪl]	Nagel	
accidental [ˌæksɪ'dentl]	zufällig, unbeabsichtigt	
nail gun ['neɪl gʌn]	Nagelpistole	
hearing ['hɪərɪŋ]	Hören, Gehör	*hearing aid* = Hörhilfe, Hörgerät
to **suppose** [sə'pəʊz]	annehmen, vermuten	› *to think that something is probably true*
to **explode** [ɪk'spləʊd]	explodieren	*A bomb **had exploded** in the next street.*
changing room ['tʃeɪndʒɪŋ ruːm]	Umkleideraum	
naked ['neɪkɪd]	nackt	› *not covered by clothes*

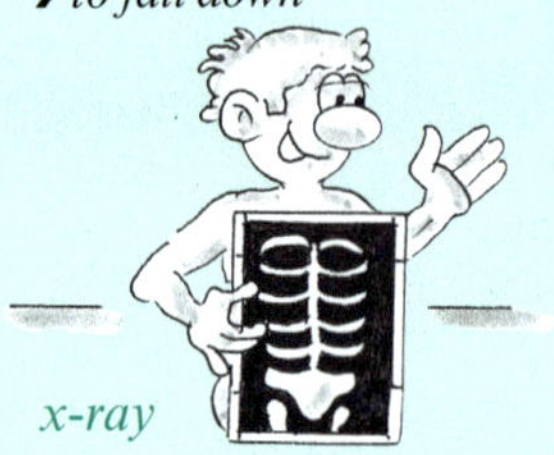

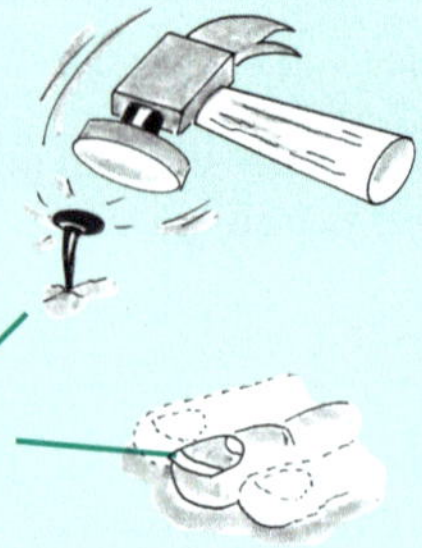

Mind the gap 3 — Tipps zum Bearbeiten von mixed grammar-Übungen

Was muss man tun, wenn ein Adjektiv oder Adverb in Klammern steht?

◆ Das Adjektiv bleibt oder wird zum Adverb:

We spent a (beautiful) ______ afternoon in the park.
We spent a (beautiful) **beautiful** afternoon in the park.
Das Adjektiv bleibt:
*A **great** novel. It is **good**. Your new dress looks **good**. The milk smells **sour**.*

It was (extreme) ______ hot.
It was (extreme) **extremely** hot.

He drove (careful) ______.
He drove (careful) **carefully**.

Das Adjektiv wird in ein Adverb umgewandelt:
*He drives **carefully**. It's **extremely** hot. He answered **extremely** quickly.*

◆ Ein entsprechendes Wort der Wortfamilie ist gesucht:

The neighbours complained about the (noisy) ______.
The neighbours complained about the (noisy) **noise**.
Du musst auf den Sinnzusammenhang achten.

◆ Das Adjektiv muss gesteigert werden:

The test was (difficult) ______ than I had thought.
The test was (difficult) **more difficult** than I had thought.
Regeln der Steigerung beachten:
*big – **bigger** – **biggest**; difficult – **more** difficult – **most** difficult; older **than***

◆ Die Stellung des Adverbs ist zu beachten:

(you/ever/apply) ______ for a job?
(you/ever/apply) **Have you ever applied** for a job?
Nach dem Hilfs- oder Modalverb, aber vor dem Vollverb: *He's **always** late. Pete **often** plays volleyball.*

Unit 4

WP	**heart** [hɑːt]	Herz, Zentrum	*Our hotel was in the* ***heart*** *of the city.*
	to **rule** [ruːl]	herrschen über, beherrschen	*Britain once* ***ruled*** *over a large empire.*
	relative ['relətɪv]	relativ, verhältnismäßig	*The test was* ***relatively*** *easy.*
	official [ə'fɪʃl]	Beamte/r, Beamtin	*a government* ***official***
	to **control** [kən'trəʊl]	beherrschen, steuern	*to control* = beherrschen, steuern; kontrollieren = *to check*
	servant ['sɜːvənt]	Diener/in, Dienstbote/ Dienstbotin	› *someone who works in another person's house, and cooks, cleans, etc. for them*
	nation ['neɪʃn]	Nation	›› *country*
	democracy [dɪ'mɒkrəsi]	Demokratie	› *a country with a government that the people choose*
	textile ['tekstaɪl]	Textil-, Stoff-	
	machinery [mə'ʃiːnəri]	Machinen-, Maschinenbau	
	living ['lɪvɪŋ]	Lebensunterhalt	*He earns his* ***living*** *as a farmer.*
	to **own** [əʊn]	besitzen	› *to have something that is yours*
	to **afford** [ə'fɔːd]	sich leisten	*We can't* ***afford*** *to go abroad this summer.*
	poverty ['pɒvəti]	Armut	*Many people in India live in* ***poverty****.*
	Hindi ['hɪndi]	Hindi (Sprache in Indien)	
	official [ə'fɪʃl]	offiziell	
Sit 1	**youth** [juːθ]	Jugend	› *young men and women*
	hobby ['hɒbi]	Hobby	
Sit2	**primary** ['praɪməri]	hauptsächlich, primär	*primary education* = Grundschulausbildung ›› *first, earliest*
	care [keə]	Sorge, Sorgfalt, Pflege, Obhut	› *to take care of = to look after*
	to **open up** [ˌəʊpən 'ʌp]	sich auftun, sich erschließen	› *to become possible*
	to **enable** [ɪ'neɪbl]	befähigen, ermöglichen	*The new software* ***enables*** *you to protect your computer.*
	to **persuade sb to do sth** [pə'sweɪd]	jdn. überreden, etwas zu tun	*We* ***persuaded Claire to come*** *with us.*
	to **force sb to do sth** [fɔːs]	jdn. zwingen, etwas zu tun	*They* ***forced her to marry*** *a man from another village.*
T1	**soul** [səʊl]	Seele	
	waiting room ['weɪtɪŋ ruːm]	Wartesaal, Wartezimmer	› *a room where people can wait*
	jewel ['dʒuːəl]	Juwel	*jewels* = Schmuck, Juwelen
	as a result of [əz ə rɪ'zʌlt əv]	als Folge von	*He died* ***as a result of*** *his injuries.*
	to **pass a law** [ˌpɑːs ə 'lɔː]	ein Gesetz verabschieden	
	rule [ruːl]	Herrschaft	*India was once under British* ***rule****.*
	non-violent [ˌnɒn 'vaɪələnt]	gewaltfrei, gewaltlos	
	to **obey** [ə'beɪ]	gehorchen	› *to do what someone tells you to do*
	follower ['fɒləʊə]	Anhäger/in	

	sympathy ['sɪmpəθi]	Mitgefühl, Mitleid, Verständnis	› *understanding of other people's feelings*
	Muslim ['mʊzlɪm]	muslimisch; Muslim/in	› *someone whose religion is Islam*
	Christian ['krɪstʃən]	christlich; Christ/in	*the **Christian** Church / religion*
	low [ləʊ]	niedrig	›‹ *high*
	untouchable [ʌn'tʌtʃəbl]	Unberührbare/r	*The **untouchables** belong to the lowest caste in India.*
	to **spin** [spɪn]		*to **spin** wool, to **spin** a web*
	spun, spun [spʌn, spʌn]	spinnen	
	cloth [klɒθ]	Tuch	
	to **establish** [ɪ'stæblɪʃ]	gründen, einrichten	›› *to set up*
	salt [sɔːlt]	Salz	
	to **boil** [bɔɪl]	sieden, kochen	*to boil* = in Wasser kochen, sieden *to cook* = durch Erhitzen zubereiten
	to **introduce** [ˌɪntrə'djuːs]	einführen	› *to bring something in for the first time*
	protest ['prəʊtest]	Protest	
	march [mɑːtʃ]	Marsch	*The soldiers were tired after the long **march**.*
	marcher ['mɑːtʃə]	Teilnehmer/in des Marsches	
	to **refuse to do sth** [rɪ'fjuːz]	sich weigern, etwas zu tun	*He **refused to discuss** the matter.*
	to **fail to do sth** [feɪl]	es nicht schaffen, etwas zu tun	*Doctors **failed to save** the man's life.*
	attitude ['ætɪtjuːd]	Haltung, Einstellung	› *what you think about something*
	impossible [ɪm'pɒsəbl]	unmöglich	›‹ *possible*
Fol	to **worship** ['wɜːʃɪp]	(an)beten, Andacht verrichten	› *to pray to a god in a church, temple, mosque, etc*
	belief [bɪ'liːf]	Glaube	***belief** in God / democracy*
	holy ['həʊli]	heilig	*the **Holy** Bible*
	evil ['iːvl]	böse, schlecht, übel	› *bad and cruel*
	mosque [mɒsk]	Moschee	*Muslims worship in a **mosque**.*
	to **behave** [bɪ'heɪv]	sich verhalten, sich benehmen	*Did the children **behave** well?*
	hope [həʊp]	Hoffnung	*They have given up **hope** of finding the missing child.*
	birthplace ['bɜːθpleɪs]	Geburtsort	› *the house or area where a person was born*
Sit3	to **sweep** [swiːp] **swept, swept** [swept, swept]	fegen	*to **sweep** the floor / street / stairs*
	to **cope with** ['kəʊp wɪð]	fertigwerden mit	› *to do a difficult job*
	racism ['reɪsɪzəm]	Rassismus	› *the belief that some races are better than others*
Ex10	**refugee** [ˌrefju'dʒiː]	Flüchtling	
Sit4	**race** [reɪs]	Rasse	
	riot ['raɪət]	Aufstand, Aufruhr	
	to **suffer (from)** ['sʌfə]	leiden (an), erleiden	*Lots of people in Africa **suffer from** Aids.*
	calypso [kə'lɪpsəʊ]	Calypso (Musikrichtung)	
	to **drown** [draʊn]	ertrinken, überschwemmt werden	*Two children **drowned** after falling into the river.*

	jungle ['dʒʌŋgl]	Dschungel; *hier* Jungle (Musikrichtung)	
T2	**unemployed** [ˌʌnɪm'plɔɪd]	arbeitslos	› *without a job*
	ignorant ['ɪgnərənt]	unwissend	
	unfriendly [ʌn'frendli]	unfreundlich	›‹ *friendly*
	hostel ['hɒstl]	Wohnheim	› *a place where people can get cheap rooms*
	nigger ['nɪgə]	'Nigger'	⚠ Beleidigende Bezeichnung für Farbige
	to **accept** [ək'sept]	annehmen, akzeptieren	*They **accepted** the plan.*
	shit [ʃɪt]	Scheiße	⚠ Schimpfwort: *Don't give me that kind of **shit**.*
	mind your own business [ˌmaɪnd jɔːr əʊn 'bɪznəs]	kümmere dich um deine Angelegenheiten	
	to **care (about)** [keə]	sich kümmern, sich Sorgen machen um	*The only thing he **cares about** is money.*
	to **doubt** [daʊt]	bezweifeln	› *to think that something may not be true*
	prejudiced ['predʒudɪst]	voreingenommen, befangen, mit vorgefasster Meinung	*I think he's **prejudiced** against blacks.*
	not … at all [ət 'ɔːl]	überhaupt nicht	*I did**n't** enjoy the film **at all**.*
	politics ['pɒlətɪks]	Politik	*She became quite interested in **politics**.*
	prime minister [ˌpraɪm 'mɪnɪstə]	Premierminister/in	
	African ['afrɪkən]	afrikanisch; Afrikaner/in	
	to **grow** [grəʊ] **grew, grown** [gruː, grəʊn]	werden	*It **grew** dark and began to rain.*
	wave [weɪv]	Welle	
	to **investigate** [ɪn'vestɪgeɪt]	nachforschen, Ermittlungen anstellen	*The police **are investigating** the murder.*
	racist ['reɪsɪst]	rassistisch; Rassist/in	
	cabinet ['kæbɪnət]	Kabinett (Politik)	
Ex16	**cleaner** ['kliːnə]	Raumpfleger/in	› *a person whose job is to clean other people's houses*
Com	**doubt** [daʊt]	Zweifel	*There is no **doubt** that we did the right thing.*
Ex19	**dialect** ['daɪəlekt]	Dialekt	
TYE	**township** ['taʊnʃɪp]	Township (Südafrika)	› *a town in South Africa where black people live*
	shack [ʃæk]	Hütte, Baracke	
	tap [tæp]	(Wasser-)Hahn	
	apartheid [ə'pɑːthaɪt]	Apartheid, Rassentrennung	
	uprising ['ʌpraɪzɪŋ]	Aufstand, Volkserhebung	›› *revolt*
	congress ['kɒŋgres]	Kongress	
	unemployment [ˌʌnɪm'plɔɪmənt]	Arbeitslosigkeit	› *having no job*
	AIDS [eɪdz]	Aids	
	politician [ˌpɒlə'tɪʃn]	Politiker/in	

TYE5	**grandmother** ['grænmʌðə]	Großmutter	› *the mother of your father or mother*

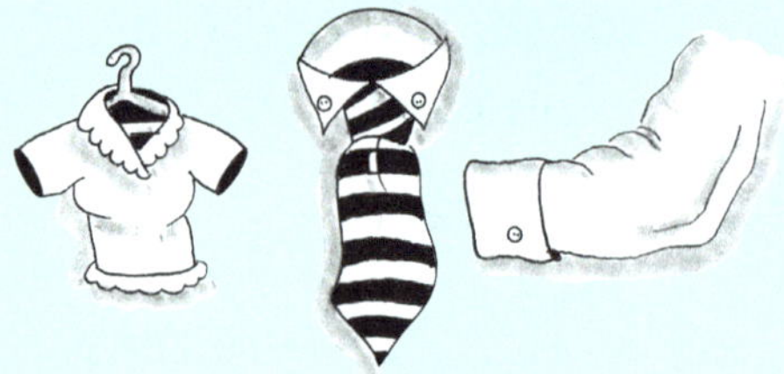

Read	**blouse** [blaʊz]	Bluse	
	tie [taɪ]	Krawatte	
	sleeve [sli:v]	Ärmel	
	mood [mu:d]	Laune, Stimmung	*She's in a good* ***mood****. (= she's happy and friendly)* *He's always in a bad* ***mood****. (= he's angry and unfriendly)*
	what's up? [wɒts 'ʌp]	was ist los?	›› *What's the matter?*
	to **nod** [nɒd]	nicken	
	calm [kɑ:m]	ruhig, still	*It's important to keep* ***calm*** *in an emergency.*
	dunno = don't know [də'nəʊ] *umg.*	weiß nicht	
	butcher ['bʊtʃə]	Metzger, Fleischer	⚠ Aussprache: ['bʊtʃə]
	to **say good riddance** [ˌseɪ gʌd 'rɪdns]	froh sein, dass jd. weg ist	
	mama ['mæmə]	Mama	›› *mum*
	to **stab** [stæb]	(nieder)stechen, erstechen	*He was* ***stabbed*** *to death in a racist attack.*
	to **empty** ['empti]	(aus)leeren	› *to take everything out*
	to **set fire to** [ˌset 'faɪə tə]	anzünden, in Brand stecken	› *to make something start burning*
	sari ['sɑ:ri]	Sari (Kleidungsstück)	
	to **order** ['ɔ:də]	bestellen	*He* ***ordered*** *a coffee and a sandwich.*
	to **wipe** [waɪp]	(ab)wischen	*She* ***wiped*** *her hands on her trousers.*
	cheek [tʃi:k]	Wange, Backe	

	lezzie ['lezi] *umg.*	Lesbe	
	to **bet** [bet] **bet, bet** [bet]	wetten	*I* ***bet*** *that we're too late.*
	virgin ['vɜ:dʒɪn]	Jungfrau, jungfräulich	
	to **have in common** [ˌhəv ɪn 'kɒmən]	etwas gemein haben mit	› *to have the same interests or ideas as another person*
	donkey ['dɒŋki]	Esel	
	connection [kə'nekʃn]	Verbindung, Zusammenhang	*a direct/strong* ***connection*** *with sth*
	eh [eɪ]	nicht wahr	
	to **wink** [wɪŋk]	blinzeln, zwinkern	*to wink* = zwinkern, winken = *to wave (your hand)*
	papa [pə'pɑ:]	Papa	›› *dad*

Mind the gap 4 — Tipps zum Bearbeiten von mixed grammar-Übungen

Was muss man tun, wenn nur Lücken (ohne Angaben in Klammern) vorhanden sind?

Tom is ___ old ___ his girlfriend Kirsty. → Tom is **as** old **as** his girlfriend Kirsty.

Steigerung oder Vergleich werden vervollständigt:
__as__ tall __as__ … ; older __than__ … ; the __most__ beautiful girl; …

A cyclist is a person ___ rides a bike. → A cyclist is a person **who** rides a bike.

Ein Relativpronomen fehlt:
the girl __who__ came … ; the train __that/which__ left … ; the girl __whose__ mother phoned …

Gerry saw ___ in the mirror. → Gerry saw **himself** in the mirror.

Ein Reflexivpronomen fehlt:
I cut __myself__ with a knife; help __yourself__ to some tea

Would you like green socks or blue ___? → Would you like green socks or blue **ones**?

Das Stützwort *one/ones* fehlt:
a German car and a French __one__

You won't find him, ___? → You won't find him, **will you**?

Ein Frageanhängsel fehlt:
He's British, __isn't he__? She speaks Italian, __doesn't she__?
We aren't going, __are we__? He didn't phone, __did he__?

Are you interested ___ politics? → Are you interested **in** politics?

Eine Präposition fehlt:
good __at__ English; wait __for__ the bus; success __in__ writing; …

Projects

Proj1	to **struggle** ['strʌgl]	kämpfen, sich abmühen	›› *to fight*
	determined [dɪ'tɜːmɪnd]	entschlossen	› *very certain that you want to do something*
	dramatic [drə'mætɪk]	dramatisch	
	actress ['æktrəs]	Schauspielerin	› *a woman or girl who acts in plays or films*
	follow-up ['fɒləʊ ʌp]	Fortsetzungs-	
	review [rɪ'vjuː]	Rezension, Kritik	*critic* = Kritiker/in, Kritik = *review*
	to **film** [fɪlm]	filmen	
	topic ['tɒpɪk]	Thema	›› *subject*
Proj3	**related to** [rɪ'leɪtɪd tə]	verwandt (mit); zusammenhängend	›› *connected with*

	artist ['ɑːtɪst]	Künstler/in	› *a person who paints pictures / writes poems / …*
	musician [mjuː'zɪʃn]	Musiker/in	› *someone who plays a musical instrument or writes music*
	lyrics ['lɪrɪks]	Songtext	
	domino ['dɒmɪnəʊ]	Dominospielstein	
Proj4	**aspect** ['æspekt]	Aspekt, Seite	
	wildlife ['waɪldlaɪf]	Tierwelt	*We watched a documentary on African* ***wildlife****.*
	familiar (with) [fə'mɪliə wɪð]	gewohnt, bekannt, vertraut (mit)	*to look / sound / taste* ***familiar*** *Are you* ***familiar with*** *the software they use?*
	dictionary ['dɪkʃənri]	Wörterbuch	*You can find the new word in your* ***dictionary****.*
	fellow ['feləʊ]	Kumpel, Kamerad	
	penguin ['peŋgwɪn]	Pinguin	

Revision

Rev1	**chemical** ['kemɪkl]	chemisch	
Rev3	**second** ['sekənd]	Sekunde	*There are sixty* ***seconds*** *in a minute.*
	economical [ˌiːkə'nɒmɪkl]	wirtschaftlich, sparsam	
Rev4	to **delay** [dɪ'leɪ]	verzögern, aufschieben	*The plane* ***was delayed*** *by bad weather.*
Rev5	**safety** ['seɪfti]	Sicherheit	›‹ *danger*
	countryside ['kʌntrisaɪd]	Landschaft	› *land that is outside cities and towns*
	barbed wire [ˌbɑːbd 'waɪə]	Stacheldraht	
	to **declare** [dɪ'kleə]	erklären; verzollen	*He* ***declared*** *that he wasn't the thief. Have you got anything to* ***declare****?*
	landing ['lændɪŋ]	Landung	
	parachute ['pærəʃuːt]	Fallschirm	
Rev6	**database** ['deɪtəbeɪs]	Datenbank	
	secret ['siːkrɪt]	Geheimnis	*to keep a* ***secret****; to tell somebody a* ***secret***
	timeline ['taɪmlaɪn]	Zeitleiste	
	to **return** [rɪ'tɜːn]	zurückgeben	› *to give sth back, to take sth back*
Rev7	**headmaster** [ˌhed'mɑːstə]	Schuldirektor	
	ambitious [æm'bɪʃəs]	ehrgeizig	› *determined to be successful*
Rev8	**smartcard** ['smɑːtkɑːd]	Smartcard	
	to **attract** [ə'trækt]	anziehen, reizen	*The new product* ***has attracted*** *a lot of interest.*
	aloud [ə'laʊd]	laut	
Rev9	**towel** ['taʊəl]	Handtuch	› *a cloth for drying your body*
	to **wish** [wɪʃ]	wünschen	
	mark [mɑːk]	Kratzer, Markierung; Note	*mark* = Markierung, Note; Marke, Briefmarke = *stamp*
Rev10	**navy** ['neɪvi]	Marine, Kriegsmarine	› *the warships belonging to a country*
	tattoo [tə'tuː]	Tätowierung	
	forever [fə'revə]	für immer	
	rose [rəʊz]	Rose	

Literature

British Isles [ˌbrɪtɪʃ ˈaɪlz]	Britische Inseln	
ruler [ˈruːlə]	Herrscher/in	› *a leader of a country*
tale [teɪl]	Geschichte, Erzählung	›› *story*
reader [ˈriːdə]	Leser/in; Lesebuch, Lektüre	› *someone who reads* › *a book for reading in class*
society [səˈsaɪəti]	Gesellschaft; Verein	*The criminal is a danger to* ***society****.*
midsummer [ˌmɪdˈsʌmə]	Mittsommer	
manners [ˈmænə]	Manieren, Umgangsformen	*It's bad* ***manners*** *to talk with your mouth full.*
traveller [ˈtrævələ]	Reisende/r	› *a person on a journey*
tiny [ˈtaɪni]	winzig	›› *very small*
giant [ˈdʒaɪənt]	Riese/Riesin	*Goliath was a* ***giant****.*
relationship [rɪˈleɪʃnʃɪp]	Beziehung, Verbindung; Verwandtschaft	
pride [praɪd]	Stolz	*He took* ***pride*** *in his success.*
prejudice [ˈpredʒudɪs]	Vorurteil	
sense [sens]	Sinn, Gefühl, Verstand	*She has a good* ***sense*** *of direction.*
sensibility [ˌsensəˈbɪləti]	Empfindsamkeit	› *the ability to understand deep feelings*
upper [ˈʌpə]	obere(r, s)	›‹ *lower*
workhouse [ˈwɜːkhaʊs]	Armenhaus	*In the 19th century poor people were often sent to a* ***workhouse****.*
pickpocket [ˈpɪkpɒkɪt]	Taschendieb/in	› *someone who steals things from people's pockets*
nasty [ˈnɑːsti]	ekelhaft, scheußlich	›› *very bad*
employee [ɪmˈplɔɪiː]	Arbeitnehmer/in, Beschäftigte/r	› *a person who is paid to work for sb*
poetry [ˈpəʊətri]	Lyrik, Dichtung	›› *poems*
hate [heɪt]	Hass	›‹ *love*
mathematics [ˌmæθəˈmætɪks]	Mathematik	›› *maths*
to **educate** [ˈedʒukeɪt]	unterrichten, erziehen	› *to teach someone at a school, university, etc*
fable [ˈfeɪbl]	Fabel	› *a short story that teaches something*
to **be supposed to do** [bi səˈpəʊzd tə duː]	tun sollen	› *to be expected to do*
eventually [ɪˈventʃuəli]	schließlich, endlich	›› *finally, at last*
dictatorship [dɪkˈteɪtəʃɪp]	Diktatur	
fiction [ˈfɪkʃn]	Erzählliteratur	› *literature that describes imaginary people and events*
thriller [ˈθrɪlə]	Thriller, Krimi	› *an exciting story or film about crime*
mousetrap [ˈmaʊstræp]	Mausefalle	

Speaking Practice

speech [spiːtʃ]	Rede	*to make a speech* = eine Rede halten
by heart [baɪ ˈhɑːt]	auswendig	*I've learned this song **by heart**.*
e.g. [ˌiː ˈdʒiː]	z.B.	› *for example*
difficulty [ˈdɪfɪkəlti]	Schwierigkeit	›› *problem*
to **react** [riˈækt]	reagieren	
prompt [prɒmpt]	Stichwort, Stimulus	

Translation Practice

rough [rʌf]	grob	
context [ˈkɒntekst]	Kontext, Textzusammenhang	*Can you guess the meaning of the word from the **context**?*
adventurous [ədˈventʃərəs]	abenteuerlich	› *full of exciting and dangerous things*
banker [ˈbæŋkə]	Bankier, Bankfachmann/frau	
spy [spaɪ]	Spion/in	› *a person who tries to get secret information about another country, company or person*
collection [kəˈlekʃn]	Sammlung	› *a number of things that have been collected*
various [ˈveəriəs]	verschieden, unterschiedlich	›› *different*
grammar [ˈgræmə]	Grammatik	
to **modernize** [ˈmɒdənaɪz]	modernisieren	› *to make something more modern*
pleasant [ˈpleznt]	angenehm, erfreulich	›› *nice, friendly*
to **breathe (in)** [briːð]	(ein)atmen	*She **was breathing** heavily after her long run.*
to **electrify** [ɪˈlektrɪfaɪ]	elektrifizieren	
speed [spiːd]	Geschwindigkeit	› *how fast something goes*

List of names Liste der Eigennamen

Boys/Men

A
Aaron ['eərən]
Adam ['ædəm]
Arthur ['ɑːθə]

B
Ben [ben]
Bob [bɒb]
Brian ['braɪən]

D
Daniel ['dænjəl]
Darren ['dærən]
Declan ['deklən]

E
Ed [ed]

F
Frank [fræŋk]

G
George [dʒɔːdʒ]
Greg [greg]

H
Harold ['hærəld]
Hector ['hektə]
Hugh [hjuː]

J
James [dʒeɪmz]
Jamie ['dʒeɪmi]
Joe [dʒəʊ]
John [dʒɒn]
Jordan ['dʒɔːdn]
Josh [dʒɒʃ]

L
Lloyd [lɔɪd]
Luke [luːk]

M
Mark [mɑːk]
Matthew ['mæθjuː]
Michael ['maɪkl]
Mike [maɪk]

N
Nick [nɪk]

O
Oliver ['ɒlɪvə]

P
Paul [pɔːl]
Peter ['piːtə]

R
Raymond ['reɪmənd]
Richard ['rɪtʃəd]
Ryan ['raɪən]

S
Simon ['saɪmən]
Stephen ['stiːvn]

T
Tim [tɪm]
Tom [tɒm]
Tony ['təʊni]
Trevor ['trevə]
Tyler ['taɪlə]

V
Vikram ['vɪkrəm]
Vincent ['vɪnsənt]

Girls/Women

A
Amber ['æmbə]
Amy ['eɪmi]
Angela ['ændʒələ]
Angie ['ændʒi]
Anita [ə'niːtə]
Antoinette [ˌæntwə'net]

C
Catherine ['kæθrɪn]
Charlotte ['ʃɑːlət]
Chloe ['kləʊi]
Claire [kleə]

D
Donna ['dɒnə]
Dorothy ['dɒrəθi]

E
Emily ['eməli]
Emma ['emə]

G
Gemma ['dʒemə]

H
Hannah ['hænə]
Harriet ['hæriət]
Helen ['helən]

I
Indira ['ɪndɪrə]
Isobel ['ɪzəbel]

J
Jane [dʒeɪn]
Jamie-Louisa [ˌdʒeɪmi lu'iːzə]
Jess [dʒes]
Jessica ['dʒesɪkə]
Joanna [dʒəʊ'ænə]
Jody ['dʒəʊdi]
Julie ['dʒuːli]

K
Kate [keɪt]
Keesha ['kiːʃə]
Kirsty ['kɜːsti]
Kizzy ['kɪzi]

L
Lauren ['lɔːrən]
Linda ['lɪndə]
Lisa ['liːsə]
Louise [luː'iːz]
Luka ['luːkə]

M
Meena ['miːnə]
Melissa [mə'lɪsə]

N
Natalie ['nætəli]
Nicola ['nɪkələ]

O
Olivia [ə'lɪviə]

P
Pinkie ['pɪŋki]

R
Rachel ['reɪtʃl]
Rebecca [rɪ'bekə]

S
Sarah ['seərə]
Sophie ['səʊfi]
Susan ['suːzn]
Susanna [su'zænə]

T
Tessa ['tesə]
Tiffany ['tɪfəni]
Tina ['tiːnə]

V
Viv [vɪv]

Family names

A
Adams ['ædəmz]

B
Baker ['beɪkə]
Bates [beɪts]
Bun [bʌn]

C
Chandra ['ʃændrə]
Chatterjee ['tʃætədʒiː]
Crosby ['krɒzbi]

D
Dobson ['dɒbsn]
Draper ['dreɪpə]

E
Earnshaw ['ɜːnʃɔː]
Easter ['iːstə]

G
Gibbs [gɪbz]
Gilbert ['gɪlbət]
Green [griːn]

H
Hain [heɪn]
Harris ['hærɪs]
Heywood ['heɪwʊd]
Hillary ['hɪləri]
Holmes [həʊmz]

J
Johnson ['dʒɒnsn]

K
Kelsey ['kelsi]
Kitchener ['kɪtʃənə]

L
Long [lɒŋ]
Love [lʌv]

P
Pandit ['pændɪt]
Patten ['pætn]
Pedrick ['pedrɪk]
Pike [paɪk]
Plumpton ['plʌmptən]

R
Roberts ['rɒbəts]
Rose [rəʊz]
Rosen ['rəʊzn]

S
Senby ['senbi]
Singh [sɪŋ]
Sithole ['sɪthəʊl]
Smart [smɑːt]
Smith [smɪθ]
Snow [snəʊ]

T
Taylor ['teɪlə]

W
Webster ['webstə]
Whitehouse ['waɪthaʊs]
Wood [wʊd]

Famous people

A

John Alcock [ˌdʒɒn ˈælkɒk] brit. Pilot
Paul Allen [ˌpɔːl ˈælən] Freund und Kollege von Bill Gates
American HIFI am. Pop- und Rockgruppe
Jane Austen [ˌdʒeɪn ˈɒstɪn] brit. Schriftstellerin (1775–1817)

B

The Beatles [ˈbiːtlz] brit. Popgruppe von 1962–70
David Beckham [ˌdeɪvɪd ˈbekəm] brit. Fußballspieler (*1975)
Victoria Beckham [vɪkˌtɔːriə ˈbekəm] Mitglied der 'Spice Girls' (*1975)
Eric Arthur Blair [ˌerɪk ˌɑːθə ˈbleə] = George Orwell
William Bligh [ˌwɪljəm ˈblaɪ] Kapitän der HMS Bounty
Paul Boateng [ˌpɔːl ˈbwɑːteŋ] erster farbiger Kabinettminister in GB (*1951)
James Bond [ˌdʒeɪmz ˈbɒnd] Figur in den Büchern von Ian Fleming
Brontë sisters [ˈbrɒnti sɪstəz] brit. Schriftstellerinnen: Charlotte (1816–55), Emily (1818–48) und Anne (1820–49) Brontë
Arthur Brown [ˌɑːθə ˈbraʊn] brit. Pilot
Buffalo Bill [ˌbʌfələʊ ˈbɪl] berühmter Büffeljäger im am. Westen, ging später mit einer 'Wild West Show' auf Tournee
James Burbage [ˌdʒeɪmz ˈbɜːbɪdʒ] Gründer des ersten Londoner Theaters

C

Lewis Caroll [ˌluːɪs ˈkærəl] brit. Schriftsteller und Mathematikprofessor in Oxford (1832–98)
Geoffrey Chaucer [ˌdʒefri ˈtʃɔːsə] brit. Dichter (ca. 1343–1400), Autor der 'Canterbury Tales'
Fletcher Christian [ˌfletʃə ˈkrɪstʃən] erster Offizier auf der Bounty
Agatha Christie [ˌægəθə ˈkrɪsti] brit. Schriftstellerin (1890–1976), erfand Detektive wie Miss Marple oder Hercule Poirot
Christopher Columbus [ˌkrɪstəfə kəˈlʌmbəs] ital. Entdecker (1451–1506)
Sir Sean Connery [ˌʃɔːn ˈkɒnərɪ] schott. Schauspieler (*1930)
Michael Crichton [ˌmaɪkl ˈkraɪtn] am. Autor (*1942) von 'Dinopark' und 'Timeline'

D

Daniel Defoe [ˌdænjəl dɪˈfəʊ] brit. Schriftsteller (1660–1731), gilt als der erste Romanautor in England
Leonardo DiCaprio [ˌliːəʊˈnɑːdəʊ di ˈkæpriəʊ] am. Schauspieler (*1974)
Charles Dickens [ˌtʃɑːlz ˈdɪkɪnz] brit. Romanautor (1812–70), der 'Oliver Twist' verfasste
Sir Arthur Conan Doyle [ˌɑːθə ˌkəʊnən ˈdɔɪl] brit. Schriftsteller (1859–1930)

E

Amelia Earhart [əˌmiːliə ˈɪəhɑːt] am. Flugpionierin (1897–1937)
Clint Eastwood [ˌklɪnt ˈiːstwʊd] am. Schauspieler (*1930)
Thomas Alva Edison [ˌtɒməs ˌælvə ˈedɪsn] bedeutender am. Erfinder (1847–1931),
Elizabeth I, Virgin Queen [ɪˈlɪzəbəθ, ˌvɜːdʒɪn ˈkwiːn] englische Königin (1533–1603)

F

Ian Fleming [ˌiːən ˈflemɪŋ] brit. Autor (1908–64), schrieb Romanvorlagen für die ersten James-Bond-Filme
Mayhew Folger [ˌmeɪhjuː ˈfəʊldʒə] am. Kapitän
Freestylers [ˈfriːstaɪləz] am. Rockband

G

Liam Gallagher [ˌliːəm ˈgæləhə] Sänger der Popgruppe Oasis (*1972)
Kasturba Gandhi [kəˌstɜːbə ˈgɑːndi] Mohandas Gandhis Frau
Mohandas (Mahatma) Gandhi [məˌhɑːtmə ˈgɑːndi] ind. Politiker und Nationalheld (1869–1948)
Bill Gates [ˌbɪl ˈgeɪts] (*1955) Pionier der am. Computertechnologie, gründete das Industrieimperium Microsoft
Yuri Gidzenko russ. Kosmonaut
Graham Greene [ˌgreɪəm ˈgriːn] brit. Schriftsteller (1904–91), schrieb u.a. 'Der dritte Mann'

H

Devon Harris [ˌdevn ˈhærɪs] Mitglied des jamaikanischen Bobteams bei den Olympischen Spielen
Anne Hathaway [ˌæn ˈhæθəweɪ] Ehefrau Shakespeares
Frank Hawks [ˌfræŋk ˈhɔːks] am. Pilot
Ernest Hemingway [ˌɜːnɪst ˈhemɪŋweɪ] am. Schriftsteller (1899–1961), schrieb 'Der alte Mann und das Meer'
Herbert Hoover [ˌhɜːbət ˈhuːvə] Chef des FBI von 1924–1972
James Hunter [ˌdʒeɪmz ˈhʌntə] brit. Rhythm and Blues Sänger

I

Paul Ince [ˌpɔːl ˈɪns] erster farbiger Fußball-Mannschaftsführer in England

J

Jerome K. Jerome [dʒəˌrəʊm keɪ dʒəˈrəʊm] brit. Schriftsteller (1859–1927), schrieb 'Drei Männer in einem Boot'
Amy Johnson [ˌeɪmi ˈdʒɒnsn] am. Pilotin

K

Martin Luther King [ˌmɑːtɪn ˌluːθə ˈkɪŋ] farbiger am. Bürgerrechtsführer (1929–1968)
Sergei Krikalev russ. Kosmonaut

L

Stephen Laurence [ˌstiːvn ˈlɒrəns]
Jerome H. Lemelson [dʒəˌrəʊm eɪtʃ ˈlemlsən] am. Erfinder
Charles A. Lindbergh [ˌtʃɑːlz eɪ ˈlɪndbɜːg] am. Flugpionier (1902–1974)

M

Nelson Mandela [ˌnelsn mænˈdeɪlə] Präsident Südafrikas (*1918)
Bob Marley [ˌbɒb ˈmɑːli] Reggae-Sänger (1945–81) aus Jamaica
Margaret Mitchell [ˌmɑːgrət ˈmɪtʃəl] am. Autorin (1900–1949), schrieb 'Vom Winde verweht'
Krysta Morlan [ˌkrɪstə ˈmɔːlən] junge am. Erfinderin
Iris Murdoch [ˌaɪrɪs ˈmɜːdɒk] brit. Autorin (1919–99)

N

Parminder K. Nagra [ˌpɑːmɪndə keɪ ˈnɑːgrə] Schauspielerin
Fred Noonan [ˌfred ˈnuːnən] am. Navigator

O

George Orwell [ˌdʒɔːdʒ ˈɔːwel] brit. Schriftsteller (1903–50), schrieb 'Farm der Tiere' und '1984'

P

Hector Petersen [ˌhektə ˈpiːtəsən] erstes Opfer der Rassenunruhen in Soweto 1976

R

Patrick Robinson [ˌpætrɪk ˈrɒbɪnsən] Mitglied des jamaikanischen Bobteams bei den Olympischen Spielen

S

Haile Selassie [ˌhaɪli səˈlæsi] letzter Kaiser von Äthiopien (1930–74)
William Shakespeare [ˌwɪljəm ˈʃeɪkspɪə] brit. Dichter und Dramatiker (1564–1616)
Bill Shepherd [ˌbɪl ˈʃepəd] am. Astronaut
Antoinette Sithole [ˌæntwəˈnet ˈsɪthəʊl] Schwester von Hector Petersen
The Strokes [strəʊks] am. Popgruppe
Wilmer Stultz [ˌwɪlmə ˈstʊlts] am. Pilot
Jonathan Swift [ˌdʒɒnəθən ˈswɪft] irischer Autor (1667–1745), wurde mit 'Gulliver's Travels' bekannt
Meera Syal [ˌmɪərə ˈsaɪəl] brit. Autorin, Schauspielerin u. Sängerin (*1963)

T

Ras Tafari [ˌræs təˈfɑːri] Taufname von Haile Selassie
Dennis Tito [ˌdenɪs ˈtiːtəʊ] erster Weltraumtourist (*1940)
John R. R. Tolkien [ˌdʒɒn ˈtɒlkiːn] brit. Schriftsteller (1882–1973), wurde mit 'Der Herr der Ringe' und 'Der kleine Hobbit' bekannt
Sue Townsend [ˌsuː ˈtaʊnzend] brit. Autorin (*1959)
Mark Twain [ˌmɑːk ˈtweɪn] am. Schriftsteller (1835–1910) = S. L. Clemens, schrieb 'Tom Sawyer' und 'Huckleberry Finn'

V

Suzanne Vega [su,zæn 'vi:gə] am. Pop-Folk-Sängerin (*1959)

W

Randall Wallace [,rændl 'wɒlɪs] am. Drehbuchautor und Regisseur
Sam Wanamaker [,sæm 'wɒnəmeɪkə] am. Schauspieler (1919–93)
Wellington ['welɪŋtən] brit. Soldat und Politiker (1769–1852)
Kate Winslet [,keɪt 'wɪnslət] brit. Schauspielerin (*1975)
Orville Wright [,ɔ:vɪl 'raɪt] am. Flugpionier

Other names

A

AA Magazine [,eɪ ,eɪ ,mægə'zi:n] Name einer Autozeitschrift
Air India [,eər 'ɪndiə] indische Luftfahrtgesellschaft
Alice in Wonderland [,ælɪs ɪn 'wʌndəlænd] Kinderbuch (1865) von Lewis Caroll
Allah ['ælə, ə'lɑ:] arab. 'Gott'
Altair 8800 ['ælteə] früher Computer
ANC [,eɪ en 'si:] Afrikanischer Nationalkongress
Anglo-Saxon [,æŋgləʊ 'sæksn] angelsächsisch
Animal Farm [,ænɪml 'fɑ:m] 'Farm der Tiere', Roman von George Orwell
Apollo Victoria [ə,pɒləʊ vɪk'tɔ:riə] Musicaltheater in London
Apollo XI [ə,pɒləʊ ɪ'levn] Apollo-Mission, die 1969 zur Mondlandung führte
Attack of the Clones [ə,tæk əv ðə 'kləʊnz] am. Film (2002) von George Lucas: 'Star Wars – Episode II: Angriff der Klonkrieger'
Ayodha heilige Stadt der Hindus

B

BASIC ['beɪsɪk] Computersprache
Bend it like Beckham [,bend ɪt laɪk 'bekəm] brit. Film (2002): 'Kick it like Beckham'
Beowulf ['beɪəʊwʊlf] altenglische Dichtung (8. Jhd)
Binglish ['bɪŋglɪʃ] Mischung aus Bengali und Englisch
The Blitz [ðə 'blɪts] Periode intensiver deutscher Bombenangriffe auf englische Städte im 2. Weltkrieg
Bombay Dreams [,bɒmbeɪ 'dri:mz] von Andrew Lloyd Webber produziertes Musical, das in 'Bollywood' spielt
John Book [,dʒɒn 'bʊk] von Harrison Ford gespielte Figur aus dem Film 'Der einzige Zeuge'
Booker Prize ['bʊkə praɪz] Literaturpreis, der jährlich für den besten brit. Roman vergeben wird
Braveheart ['breɪvhɑ:t] Roman von Randall Wallace
Brick Lane Festival [,brɪk leɪn 'festɪvl] Festival in London
British Young Inventor of the Year [,brɪtɪʃ jʌŋ ɪn'ventər əv ðə jɪə] Junge/r Erfinder/in des Jahres in GB
Buckingham Palace [,bʌkɪŋəm 'pæləs] Buckingham-Palast

C

Cambridge First Certificate [,keɪmbrɪdʒ ,fɜ:st sə'tɪfɪkət] Englischprüfung für Nichtmuttersprachler, durchgeführt von der Universität Cambridge
Camden Palace [,kæmdən 'pæləs] große Disco in London
Canterbury Tales ['kæntəbəri teɪlz] langes Erzählgedicht von G. Chaucer
Cape Kennedy [,keɪp 'kenədi] Weltraumbahnhof in Florida
CARE-India [,keər 'ɪndiə] Hilfsorganisation in Indien
Carl-Duisberg Gesellschaft gemeinnützige Organisation für internationale Weiterbildung und Personalentwicklung
Casino Royale [kə,si:nəʊ rɔɪ'ɑ:l] Thriller von Ian Fleming
A Christmas Carol [ə ,krɪsməs 'kærəl] Erzählung von Charles Dickens
Cirque Eloize [sɜ:k ,eləʊ'i:z] kanadischer Zirkus
Claudius ['klɔ:diəs] Onkel Hamlets
Cold War [,kəʊld 'wɔ:] 'Kalter Krieg', Ost-West-Konflikt (1945–90) zwischen der Nato und dem Warschauer Pakt
Covent Garden [,kɒvənt 'gɑ:dn] ehemaliger Obst- u. Gemüsemarkt Londons
Bob Crachit [,bɒb 'krætʃɪt] Figur aus 'A Christmas Carol' von Ch. Dickens

D

David Copperfield [,deɪvɪd 'kɒpəfi:ld] Roman von Charles Dickens
Diwali [dɪ'wɑ:li] Lichtfest der Hindus
The Dorchester ['dɔ:tʃɪstə] Hotel in London
Dr No [,dɒktə 'nəʊ] Titel des ersten James-Bond-Films (1962)
Dussehra indisches Fest

E

East India Company [,i:st ɪndiə 'kʌmpəni] ostindische Handelsgesellschaft, die im 18. Jh. für die Verwaltung Indiens zuständig war
East Is East [,i:st ɪz 'i:st] brit. Filmkomödie (1999)
Emma ['emə] Roman von Jane Austen
Empire Windrush [,empaɪə 'wɪndrʌʃ] Schiff, das 1948 die ersten Einwanderer aus Jamaica nach Großbritannien brachte
ET [,i: 'ti:] am. Film (1982) von Steven Spielberg

F

The Fast and the Furious [ðə ,fɑ:st ən ðə 'fjʊəriəs] am. Action Thriller (2001)
Huckleberry Finn [,hʌklbərɪ 'fɪn] Roman(figur) bei Mark Twain
The Full Monty [ðə ,fʊl 'mɒnti] brit. Komödie (1997): 'Ganz oder gar nicht'

G

Gertrude ['gɜ:tru:d] Mutter Hamlets
Globe Theatre [,gləʊb 'θɪətə] Theater in London
Gone with the Wind [,gɒn wɪð ðə 'wɪnd] 'Vom Winde verweht', Roman von Margaret Mitchell
Grendel ['grendl] Monster, bedroht in 'Beowulf' das dänische Königreich
Lemuel Gulliver [,lemjuəl 'gʌlɪvə] Figur in Swifts Roman 'Gulliver's Travels'
Gulliver's Travels [,gʌlɪvəz 'trævlz] Roman von Jonathan Swift

H

Hamlet ['hæmlət] Schauspiel von William Shakespeare
Harry Potter and the Chamber of Secrets [,hæri 'pɒtər ən ðə ,tʃeɪmbər əv 'si:krɪts] Roman von J. K. Rowling: 'Harry Potter und die Kammer des Schreckens'
Heathcliff ['hi:θklɪf] Figur aus 'Wuthering Heights' von Emily Brontë
Henry V [,henri ðə 'fɪfθ] Schauspiel von William Shakespeare
Highlander ['haɪləndə] am. Film (1986)
Hinglish ['hɪŋglɪʃ] Mischung aus Hindi und Englisch
HMS Bounty [,eɪtʃemes 'baʊnti] brit. Schiff, das durch eine Meuterei berühmt wurde
Sherlock Holmes [,ʃɜ:lɒk 'həʊmz] Detektivfigur in den Büchern von Sir Arthur Conan Doyle
The Hunt for Red October [ðə ,hʌnt fə red ɒk'təʊbə] am. Thriller (1990): 'Jagd auf Roter Oktober'

I

International Space Station/ISS [,ɪntənæʃnəl 'speɪs steɪʃn] Internationales Raumfahrtprojekt
Interpol ['ɪntəpɒl] Internationale Kriminalpolizeiliche Organisation
Interworld Communications [,ɪntəwɜ:ld kə,mju:nɪ'keɪʃnz] Name einer Organisation

J

Jurassic Park [dʒu'ræsɪk pɑ:k] 'Dinopark', Roman von Michael Crichton

L

Lagaan [lə'gɑ:n] indischer Film (2001)
Lemelson-MIT Invention Apprenticeship [,lemlsən em aɪ ,ti: ɪn,venʃn ə'prentɪʃɪp] Programm zur Förderung junger Erfinder in den USA
Lilliput ['lɪlɪpʌt] Land, das von Gulliver in 'Gulliver's Travels' besucht wurde
The Lion King [ðə ,laɪən 'kɪŋ] am. Musical: 'Der König der Löwen'
Lockheed Electra [,lɒkhi:d ɪ'lektrə] Flugzeug, mit dem Amelia Earhard zu ihrem Flug um die Welt aufbrach

London Aeroplane Club [ˌlʌndən 'eərəpleɪn klʌb] Flugsportclub in London
London School of Samba [ˌlʌndən ˌsku:l əv 'sæmbə] Tanzgruppe
Lord of the Rings [ˌlɔ:d əv ðə 'rɪŋz] Titel eines Buches von J. R. R. Tolkien
Lyceum Theatre [laɪˌsi:əm 'θɪətə] Musicaltheater in London

M

Madame Tussaud's [ˌmædəm tə'sɔ:dz] Londoner Wachsfigurenkabinett
Man Friday [ˌmæn 'fraɪdeɪ] Figur in Defoes Roman 'Robinson Crusoe'
Manchester United [ˌmæntʃɪstə ju'naɪtɪd] brit. Fußballverein
Mariner I [ˌmærɪnə 'wʌn] Weltraumsonde (1962)
Mars [mɑ:z] Mars
Massachusetts Institute of Technology [ˌmæsə'tʃu:sɪts ˌɪnstɪtju:t əv tek'nɒlədʒi] am. Universität in Cambridge, Massachusetts
Metropolitan Railway [ˌmetrəˌpɒlɪtən 'reɪlweɪ] Londoner Untergrundbahn
A Midsummer Night's Dream [ə ˌmɪdsʌmə 'naɪts dri:m] Komödie von William Shakespeare
Miss Marple [mɪs 'mɑ:pl] Figur in den Kriminalromanen von A. Christie
MITS [ˌem aɪ ti: 'es] Computerfirma
Adrian Mole [ˌeɪdriən 'məʊl] Figur in den Romanen von Sue Townsend
The Mousetrap [ðə 'maʊstræp] Theaterstück von A. Christie, das seit 1959 ununterbrochen in London aufgeführt wird
Mr Universe [ˌmɪstə 'ju:nɪvɜ:s] Mr Universum
MS-DOS [ˌemes 'dɒs] Betriebssystem

N

The Name of the Rose [ðə ˌneɪm əv ðə 'rəʊz] europ. historischer Kriminalfilm (1986): 'Der Name der Rose'
Nasa ['næsə] am. Raumfahrtbehörde
National Geographic Gold Medal [ˌnæʃnəl ˌdʒi:ə'græfɪk ˌgəʊld 'medl] Auszeichnung der Zeitschrift 'National Geographic'
Nineteen Eighty-Four [ˌnaɪnti:n ˌeɪti 'fɔ:] '1984', Roman von George Orwell
Notting Hill Carnival [ˌnɒtɪŋ ˌhɪl 'kɑ:nɪvl] multikulturelle Karnevalsveranstaltung in London

O

Old English [ˌəʊld 'ɪŋglɪʃ] Sprache der germanischen Invasoren, die sich ab 400 AD in England ansiedelten
The Old Man and the Sea [ði əʊld ˌmæn ən ðə 'si:] Erzählung E. Hemingways
Oliver Twist [ˌɒlɪvə 'twɪst] Roman von Charles Dickens
Ophelia [ə'fi:liə] Freundin Hamlets

P

Hercule Poirot [ˌhɜ:kju:l 'pwɑ:rəʊ] Figur in den Kriminalromanen von A. Christie
Harry Potter [ˌhæri 'pɒtə] Figur in den Romanen von J. K. Rowling
Pride and Prejudice [ˌpraɪd ən 'predʒudɪs] Roman von Jane Austen
Prince of Wales Theatre [prɪns əv ˌweɪlz 'θɪətə] Musicaltheater in London

Q

The Quiet American [ðə ˌkwaɪət ə'merɪkən] Roman von Graham Greene: 'Der stille Amerikaner'

R

Radio Liffey Live [ˌreɪdiəʊ 'lɪfi laɪv] Radiosender in Dublin
Rama ['rɑ:mə] indischer Gott
Ravana [rə'vɑ:nə] indischer Gott
Richard III [ˌrɪtʃəd ðə 'θɜ:d] Theaterstück von William Shakespeare
Robinson Crusoe [ˌrɒbɪnsən 'kru:səʊ] Figur und Roman von Daniel Defoe
Romeo and Juliet [ˌrəʊmiəʊ ən 'dʒu:liət] Schauspiel von William Shakespeare
Russian Revolution [ˌrʌʃn ˌrevə'lu:ʃn] Oktoberrevolution 1917 in Russland

S

Sadler's Wells [ˌsædləz 'welz] Tanz- und Musiktheater in London
Science Museum [ˌsaɪəns mju'zi:əm] Naturwissenschaftliches Museum in London
Ebenezer Scrooge [ˌebəni:zə 'skru:dʒ] Figur aus 'A Christmas Carol' von Ch. Dickens
The Sea, The Sea [ðə ˌsi: ðə 'si:] Roman von Iris Murdoch
Sense and Sensibility [ˌsens ənd ˌsensə'bɪləti] Roman von Jane Austen
Silbury ['sɪlbəri] Name eines Supermarkts
Simputer [sɪm'pju:tə] preisgünstiger Computer aus Indien
Soviet Union [ˌsəʊviət 'ju:niən] Sowjetunion
Spanglish ['spæŋglɪʃ] Mischung aus Spanisch und Englisch
Sputnik One [ˌspʊtnɪk 'wʌn] sowjetischer Satellit, der 1957 in den Weltraum geschossen wurde

T

Taino ['taɪnəʊ] Ureinwohner Jamaikas
A Tale of Two Cities [ə ˌteɪl əf tu: 'sɪtiz] Roman von Charles Dickens
Three Men in a Boat [θri: ˌmen ɪn ə 'bəʊt] Roman von Jerome K. Jerome: 'Drei Männer in einem Boot'
Timeline ['taɪmlaɪn] Roman von Michael Crichton
Tintagel Castle [tɪnˌtædʒəl 'kɑ:sl] Burgruine an der Nordküste Cornwalls
Titanic [taɪ'tænɪk] am. Liebesfilm (1997) mit Kate Winslet und Leonardo DiCaprio
Tower of London [ˌtaʊər əv 'lʌndən] Befestigungsanlage im Osten der City of London
Twelfth Night [ˌtwelfθ 'naɪt] Komödie von William Shakespeare

U

U-boat ['ju:bəʊt] deutsches U-Boot
Udaan Training Camp [ju'dɑ:ən 'treɪnɪŋ kæmp] Bildungsprojekt in Indien
Universal Studios [ˌju:nɪvɜ:sl 'stju:diəʊz] Filmstudios in Hollywood
University College Los Angeles [ˌju:nɪˌvɜ:səti ˌkɒlɪdʒ lɒs 'ændʒəli:z] Universität in Los Angeles
The Untouchables [ði ʌn'tʌtʃəblz] am. Actionfilm (1987): 'Die Unbestechlichen'

V

Venus ['vi:nəs] Venus

W

Dr Watson [ˌdɒktə 'wɒtsn] Assistent von Sherlock Holmes in den Romanen von Sir Arthur Conan Doyle
Wellcome Wing ['welkəm wɪŋ] Abteilung des Science Museum in London, gewidmet der modernen Wissenschaft und Technik
World War II [ˌwɜ:ld 'wɔ: tu:] Zweiter Weltkrieg (1939–1945)
World's Children's Prize for the Rights of the Child [wɜ:ldz ˌtʃɪldrənz 'praɪz fə ðə ˌraɪts əv ðə 'tʃaɪld] Auszeichnung für die Rechte der Kinder
Wuthering Heights ['wʌðərɪŋ haɪts] Roman von Emily Brontë

Place names

A

Alaska [ə'læskə] US-Bundesstaat
Arima ['ærimə] Stadt auf Trinidad
Antarctic [ænt'ɑ:ktɪk] Antarktis
Ashbury ['æʃbəri] brit. Ortsname
the Atlantic (Ocean) [ði ətˌlæntɪk 'əʊʃn] der Atlantik

B

Bangalore [ˌbæŋgə'lɔ:] Stadt in Indien
Birmingham ['bɜ:mɪŋəm] Industriestadt in Mittelengland
Blenheim Palace [ˌblenɪm 'pæləs] Landsitz in der Nähe von Oxford, wo Winston Churchill geboren wurde
Bollywood ['bɒliwʊd] Filmstadt in Bombay, Indien
Bombay [ˌbɒm'beɪ] Stadt in Indien, Mumbai
Brazil [brə'zɪl] Brasilien
Brighton ['braɪtn] Küstenort in Südengland
Bristol ['brɪstl] Industrie- und Hafenstadt im Südwesten Englands
Brixton ['brɪkstən] Stadtteil im Süden Londons

C

Calgary ['kælgəri] Stadt in Alberta, Kanada
California [ˌkælə'fɔ:niə] US-Bundesstaat
Cambourne ['kæmbɔ:n] Ort in Cornwall
Camden Town [ˌkæmdən 'taʊn] Stadtteil im Norden Londons

Canterbury ['kæntəbəri] Stadt in Kent, England
Cape of Good Hope [ˌkeɪp əv gʊd 'həʊp] Kap der Guten Hoffnung, an der Südostspitze Afrikas
Cape Town [ˌkeɪp 'taʊn] Kapstadt in Südafrika
Chelmsford ['tʃelmzfəd] Ort in Essex
Colchester ['kəʊltʃɪstə] Ort in Essex
Colorado [ˌkɒlə'rɑːdəʊ] US-Bundesstaat
Cornwall ['kɔːnwəl] Urlaubsgebiet im äußersten Südwesten Englands
Cowlinge ['kaʊlɪŋ] Ort in Suffolk, England

D

Darwin ['dɑːwɪn] Stadt in Australien
Delaware ['deləweə] Bundesstaat der USA
Delhi ['deli] Hauptstadt Indiens
Dublin ['dʌblɪn] Hauptstadt der Republik Irland
Dunure Castle [də'njʊə kɑːsl] Burg im Südwesten Schottlands
Durban ['dɜːbən] Hafenstadt in Südafrika

E

Eastern Transvaal Mountains [ˌiːstən ˌtrænsvɑːl 'maʊntənz] Gebirge im Ost-Transvaal, Südafrika
Ecuador ['ekwədɔː] Ekuador
Edinburgh ['edɪnbərə] Hauptstadt Schottlands
Eilean Donan Castle [ˌelən 'dɒnən kɑːsl] Burg in Schottland
El Alamein [el 'æləmeɪn] Ort in Ägypten, wo im Zweiten Weltkrieg die entscheidende Schlacht auf dem afrikanischen Kriegsschauplatz stattfand
El Paso [el 'pæsəʊ] Stadt in Texas, USA
English Channel [ˌɪŋglɪʃ 'tʃænl] Ärmelkanal zwischen Frankreich und England
Essex ['esɪks] Verwaltungsbezirk in England

F

Falkland Islands ['fɔːklənd ˌaɪləndz] brit. Inselgruppe im Südwest-Atlantik
Florida ['flɒrɪdə] US-Bundesstaat

G

Glasgow ['glɑːsgəʊ] Großstadt in Westschottland
Glastonbury ['glæstənbəri] Stadt in Südwest-England
Great Britain [ˌgreɪt 'brɪtn] Großbritannien

H

Hastings ['heɪstɪŋz] Stadt an der Südostküste Englands; in der Nähe fand (1066) die Battle of Hastings statt
Hawaii [hə'waɪi] US-Bundesstaat
Highgate ['haɪgeɪt] Stadtteil vonLondon
Hollywood ['hɒliwʊd] Stadt und Filmzentrum in den USA
Hyderabad ['haɪdərəbæd] Stadt in Indien

J

Johannesburg [dʒəʊ'hænɪsbɜːg] größte Stadt Südafrikas

K

Kalikata [ˌkælɪ'kɑːtə] Kalkutta, Stadt in Indien
Kansas ['kænzəs] US-Bundesstaat
Kingston ['kɪŋstən] Hauptstadt von Jamaika
Kumale Street ['kuːmɑːlə striːt] Straße in Soweto, Südafrika

L

Lake Washington [leɪk 'wɒʃɪŋtən] See in der Nähe von Seattle
Larkhill Road ['lɑːkhɪl rəʊd] Straße in Camborne, Cornwall
Le Bourget [lə bʊə'ʒeɪ] Flughafen bei Paris
Leeds [liːdz] Stadt in England
London ['lʌndən] Hauptstadt von Großbritannien
Los Angeles [lɒs 'ændʒəliːz] Stadt in den USA

M

Madras [mə'drɑːs] Stadt in Indien
Malabar Hill ['mæləbɑː hɪl] Berg in der Nähe von Bombay
Manchester ['mæntʃɪstə] Großstadt im Nordwesten Englands
Marine Drive [mə'riːn draɪv] Küstenpromenade in Bombay
Miami [maɪ'æmi] Stadt in Florida, USA
Midlands ['mɪdləndz] die Midlands, Mittelengland
Milchester ['mɪltʃɪstə] brit. Ortsname
Mississippi [ˌmɪsɪ'sɪpi] Fluss und US-Bundesstaat
Missouri [mɪ'sʊəri] US-Bundesstaat
Montego Bay [mɒnˌtiːgəʊ 'beɪ] Stadt in Jamaika
Moscow ['mɒskəʊ] Moskau, Hauptstadt Russlands
Mumbai [ˌmʌm'beɪ] Bombay, Stadt in Indien

N

Namibia [nə'mɪbiə] Staat in Afrika
New Jersey [njuː 'dʒɜːzi] US-Bundesstaat
New Mexico [njuː 'meksɪkəʊ] US-Bundesstaat
New York (City) [ˌnjuː jɔːk 'sɪti] größte Stadt in den USA
Normandy ['nɔːməndi] Region im Nordwesten Frankreichs

O

Oldthorpe ['əʊldθɔːp] brit. Ortsname
Orlando West [ɔːˌlændəʊ 'west] Stadtteil in Soweto, Südafrika
Oxford ['ɒksfəd] Universitätsstadt in Südengland

P

the Pacific (Ocean) [ðə pəˌsɪfɪk 'əʊʃn] der Pazifik
Paris ['pærɪs] Hauptstadt Frankreichs
Pearl Harbor [ˌpɜːl 'hɑːbə] Hafenstadt auf Hawaii, USA
Pitcairn Island [ˌpɪtkeən 'aɪlənd] Insel im Pazifik
Porbandar ['pɔːbəndɑː] Ort in Indien
Port-of-Spain [ˌpɔːt əv 'speɪn] Hauptstadt von Trinidad und Tobago
Pretoria [prɪ'tɔːriə] Hauptstadt von Südafrika

R

Rio de Janeiro [ˌriːəʊ də ʒə'nɪərəʊ] Stadt in Brasilien
Rome [rəʊm] Hauptstadt von Italien

S

San Fernando [ˌsæn fɜː'nændəʊ] Stadt auf Trinidad
San Francisco [ˌsæn frən'sɪskəʊ] Stadt in Kalifornien
Santa Fe [ˌsæntə 'feɪ] Hauptstadt von New Mexico
Seattle [si'ætl] Stadt in den USA
Singleton Park ['sɪŋgltən pɑːk] Name eines Parks
Sneyd Park ['sniːd pɑːk] Stadtteil von Bristol
Southampton [saʊθ'hæmptən] Stadt in England
Soweto [sə'wetəʊ] Township in der Nähe von Johannesburg
Spanish Town [ˌspænɪʃ 'taʊn] Stadt in Jamaika
Stanford University [ˌstænfəd ˌjuːnɪ'vɜːsəti] private Universität in Kalifornien
Star City [ˌstɑː 'sɪti] Sternenstadt, Weltraumzentrum in Russland
Stratford-on-Avon [ˌstrætfəd ɒn 'eɪvn] Geburtsstadt Shakespeares in Mittelengland
Suffolk ['sʌfək] Verwaltungsbezirk in England

T

Tahiti [tə'hiːti] Insel im Südpazifik
Thames [temz] Englands bedeutendster Fluss
Tilbury ['tɪlbəri] Docks in London
Tobago [tə'beɪgəʊ] Insel in der Karibik
Trinidad ['trɪnɪdæd] Insel in der Karibik

U

Uttar Pradesh [ˌʊtə prə'deʃ] Bundesstaat in Nordindien

V

Vacaville ['vækəvɪl] Ort in der Nähe von San Francisco, USA
Venezuela [ˌvenə'zweɪlə] Venezuela
Virginia [və'dʒɪniə] US-Bundesstaat

W

Washington ['wɒʃɪŋtən] US-Bundesstaat
West End [ˌwest 'end] westlicher Teil der Londoner Innenstadt
Windsor Castle [ˌwɪnzə 'kɑːsl] Burganlage in Windsor, westlich von London
Wood Green [ˌwʊd 'griːn] Stadtteil im Norden Londons

Y

Yugoslavia [ˌjuːgəʊ'slɑːviə] Jugoslawien

INDEX

Dd

Gg

Qq

Rr

Unit 1 Extra Pages

paradise ['pærədaɪs] Paradies
to **remain** [rɪ'meɪn] bleiben
inhabitant [ɪn'hæbɪtənt] Bewohner
such as ['sʌtʃ əz] wie zum Beispiel
smallpox ['smɔ:lpɒks] Pocken
to **long (for)** [lɒŋ] sich sehnen (nach)
rhythm and blues [ˌrɪðəm ən 'blu:z] Rhythm and Blues (Musikrichtung)

ska [skɑ:] Ska (Musikrichtung)
oppression [ə'preʃn] Unterdrückung
to **influence** ['ɪnfluəns] beeinflussen
DJing [ˌdi: 'dʒeɪɪŋ] DJing
Rasta(farian) [ˌræstə'feəriən] Rastafari; Rasta-
faith [feɪθ] Glaube
to **worship** ['wɜ:ʃɪp] beten, Andacht verrichten

dignity ['dɪgnəti] Würde
to **stress** [stres] betonen
identity [aɪ'dentəti] Identität
belief [bɪ'li:f] Glaube
wool [wʊl] Wolle
dreadlocks ['dredlɒks] Locken der Rastas
natural ['nætʃrəl] natürlich, naturgegeben

salt [sɔ:lt] Salz
society [sə'saɪəti] Gesellschaft, Verein
to **smoke** [sməʊk] rauchen
marijuana [ˌmærə'wɑ:nə] Marihuana
religious [rɪ'lɪdʒəs] religiös
cool runnings [ku:l 'rʌnɪŋz] Friedliche Reise!
bobsled ['bɒbsled] Bob
to **bobsled** ['bɒbsled] Bob fahren
ice [aɪs] Eis
heart [hɑ:t] Herz, Zentrum
competition [ˌkɒmpə'tɪʃn] Wettbewerb
sprinter ['sprɪntə] Sprinter/in, Kurzstreckenläufer/in

sponsor ['spɒnsə] Sponsor/in, Geldgeber/in
medal ['medl] Medaille
racist ['reɪsɪst] rassistisch; Rassist
mph [ˌem pi: 'eɪtʃ] Meilen pro Stunde
finishing line ['fɪnɪʃɪŋ laɪn] Ziellinie
can't help doing sth [kɑ:nt 'help] müssen einfach tun
slapstick ['slæpstɪk] Klamauk, Slapstick
high-tech [ˌhaɪ 'tek] High-Tech-
to manage ['mænɪdʒ] fertig bringen, schaffen
respect [rɪ'spekt] Respekt, Achtung
to **deal with** ['di:l wɪð] sich beschäftigen mit
poverty ['pɒvəti] Armut
expression [ɪk'spreʃn] Ausdruck
peaceful ['pi:sfl] friedlich
to **react** [ri'ækt] reagieren
to **stand up for** [ˌstænd 'ʌp fə] eintreten für
  stood up, stood up [ˌstud 'ʌp]
preacher ['pri:tʃə] Prediger/in
heaven ['hevn] Himmel
high [haɪ] 'high', berauscht

to **keep on doing sth** [ˌki:p 'ɒn] mit etwas weitermachen
to **struggle on** [ˌstrʌgl 'ɒn] weiterkämpfen
to **be sick and tired of** [bi ˌsɪk ən 'taɪəd əv] es gründlich satt haben
ism and skism [ˌɪzəm ənd 'skɪzəm] System von abstrakten Ideen, Überzeugungen

almighty [ɔ:l'maɪti] allmächtig
we gonna [wi 'gɒnə] wir werden

Unit 2 Extra Pages

to **take time out** [teɪk ˌtaɪm 'aʊt] Pause machen, Auszeit nehmen
permanent ['pɜ:mənənt] ständig, permanent
to **think of doing sth** ['θɪŋk əv] daran denken, etwas zu tun
voluntary ['vɒləntri] freiwillig
sort [sɔ:t] Art, Sorte
conservation [ˌkɒnsə'veɪʃn] Naturschutz, Erhaltung

mind your own business [maɪnd jɔ:r ˌəʊn 'bɪznəs] kümmere dich um deine Angelegenheiten
experience of doing [ɪk'spɪəriəns əv] Erfahrung, etwas zu tun
to **respect** [rɪ'spekt] achten, respektieren
ignorant ['ɪgnərənt] unwissend
particular [pə'tɪkjələ] spezielle/r/s
giraffe [dʒə'rɑ:f] Giraffe
leaf [li:f] Blatt
  leaves [li:vs]
wildlife ['waɪldlaɪf] Tierwelt
hut [hʌt] Hütte
to **be prepared for** [bi prɪ'peəd fə] vorbereitet sein auf
remote [rɪ'məʊt] abgelegen, weit entfernt
celebrity [sə'lebrəti] Berühmtheit

Ex 1

punctuation [ˌpʌŋktʃu'eɪʃn] Zeichensetzung
capital letter ['kæpɪtl letə] Großbuchstabe
abbreviation [əˌbri:vi'eɪʃn] Abkürzung

Ex 3

immediate [ɪ'mi:diət] sofortig, umgehend
disadvantage [ˌdɪsəd'vɑ:ntɪdʒ] Nachteil

Ex 5

symbol ['sɪmbl] Symbol, Zeichen
humble ['hʌmbl] bescheiden

Unit 3 Extra Pages

such as ['sʌtʃ əz] wie zum Beispiel
politics ['pɒlətɪks] Politik
minister ['mɪnɪstə] Minister/in
variety [və'raɪəti] Vielfalt, Sorte

official [ə'fɪʃl] — offiziell
Afrikaans [ˌæfrɪ'kɑːns] — Afrikaans (Sprache in Südafrika)

to **influence** ['ɪnfluəns] — beeinflussen
jewel ['dʒuːəl] — Juwel
Hindi ['hɪndi] — Hindi (Sprache in Indien)

sister-in-law ['sɪstər ɪn lɔː] — Schwägerin
to **tease** [tiːz] — necken, verspotten
Bengali [ben'gɔːli] — Bengali (Sprache in Indien)

to **hold on (to)** [ˌhəʊld 'ɒn tə] — festhalten (an)
held, held ˌheld]
culture ['kʌltʃə] — Kultur
as well as [əz 'wel əz] — und auch noch, ebenso wie

to **pronounce** [prə'naʊns] — aussprechen
consonant ['kɒnsənənt] — Konsonant, Mitlaut
vacuum cleaner ['vækjuəm kliːnə] — Staubsauger
rapper ['ræpə] — Rapper/in (Musik)

Unit 4 Extra Pages

mutiny ['mjuːtəni] — Meuterei
extreme [ɪk'striːm] — extrem, äußerst
sailor ['seɪlə] — Seemann, Matrose
on board [ɒn 'bɔːd] — an Bord
breadfruit ['bredfruːt] — Brotfrucht
HMS [ˌeɪtʃ em 'es] — das Schiff Ihrer Majestät

cape [keɪp] — Kap
tip [tɪp] — Spitze
angel ['eɪndʒəl] — Engel
to **accuse** [ə'kjuːz] — anklagen, beschuldigen

tense [tens] — angespannt
decision [dɪ'sɪʒn] — Entscheidung
bastard ['bɑːstəd] — Bastard, Scheißkerl
mutineer [ˌmjuːtə'nɪə] — Meuterer
legend ['ledʒənd] — Legende
remote [rɪ'məʊt] — abgelegen, weit entfernt

midshipman ['mɪdʃɪpmən] — Leutnant zur See
islander ['aɪləndə] — Insulaner/in, Inselbewohner/in

Poems

gravestone ['greɪvstəʊn] — Grabstein
to **sip** [sɪp] — nippen an, schlürfen
cider ['saɪdə] — Apfelwein
sweet [swiːt] — süß
straw [strɔː] — Strohhalm, Stroh
it's all the go [ɪts ˌɔːl ðə 'gəʊ] — es ist der große Hit
jaw [dʒɔː] — Kinnlade, Kiefer
ma-in-law ['mɑː ɪn lɔː] — Schwiegermama
jersey ['dʒɜːzi] — Pullover
diet ['daɪət] — Diät
tall story[ˌtɔːl 'stɔːri] — Lügengeschichte

sole [səʊl] — einzig, Allein-
survivor [sə'vaɪvə] — Überlebende/r
atomic [ə'tɒmɪk] — atomar, nuklear, Atom-

joker ['dʒəʊkə] — Witzbold, Spaßvogel
prompt [prɒmpt] — prompt, unverzüglich
it goes to show [ɪt ˌgəʊz tə 'ʃəʊ] — es zeigt doch nur

Song

clumsy ['klʌmzi] — ungeschickt, schwerfällig

not … anymore [nɒt eni'mɔː] — nicht mehr

Geographical names

Country	Adjective	Language	People
Africa Afrika	African	African	African
America Amerika	American	American English	American
Asia Asien	Asian		Asian
Austria Österreich	Austrian	German	Austrian
Australia Australien	Australian	Australian English	Australian
Bavaria Bayern	Bavarian	German	Bavarian
Belgium Belgien	Belgian	French/Flemish	Belgian
Brazil Brasilien	Brazilian	Portuguese	Brazilian
Britain Großbritannien	British	English	Briton *pl.* the British
Canada Kanada	Canadian	Canadian English	Canadian
Caribbean Karibik	Caribbean	Caribbean	Caribbean
China China	Chinese	Chinese	Chinese (man/woman), *pl.* the Chinese
Cuba Kuba	Cuban	Spanish	Cuban
Czech Republic (the) Tschechische Republik	Czech	Czech	Czech
Denmark Dänemark	Danish	Danish	Dane
England England	English	English	Englishman/woman, *pl.* the English
Europe Europa	European		European
Finland Finnland	Finish	Finish	Fin
France Frankreich	French	French	Frenchman/woman, *pl.* the French
Germany Deutschland	German	German	German
Greece Griechenland	Greek	Greek	Greek
Hungary Ungarn	Hungarian	Hungarian	Hungarian
India Indien	Indian		Indian
Indonesia Indonesien	Indonesian	Indonesian	Indonesian
Iran Iran	Iranian	Persian	Iranian
Ireland Irland	Irish	English, Irish, Gaelic	Irishman/woman, *pl.* the Irish
Israel Israel	Israeli	Hebrew	Israeli
Italy Italien	Italian	Italian	Italian
Jamaica Jamaika	Jamaican	English	Jamaican
Japan Japan	Japanese	Japanese	Japanese (man/woman), *pl.* the Japanese
Korea Korea	Korean	Korean	Korean
Mexico Mexiko	Mexican	Spanish	Mexican
Netherlands (the) Niederlande	Dutch	Dutch	Dutchman/woman, *pl.* the Dutch
New Zealand Neuseeland	New Zealand	English	New Zealander
Norway Norwegen	Norwegian	Norwegian	Norwegian
Pakistan Pakistan	Pakistani		Pakistani
Philippines Philippinen	Philippine	Filipino, English	Filipino
Poland Polen	Polish	Polish	Pole
Portugal Portugal	Portuguese	Portuguese	Portuguese (man/woman), *pl.* the Portuguese
Russia Russland	Russian	Russian	Russian
San Salvador San Salvador	Salvadoran	Spanish	San Salvadorian
Scandinavia Skandinavien	Scandinavian		Scandinavian
Scotland Schottland	Scottish	English	Scot (Scotsman/woman) *pl.* the Scots, the Scottish
South Africa Südafrika	South African	Afrikaans, English	South African
Sweden Schweden	Swedish	Swedish	Swede
Switzerland Schweiz	Swiss		Swiss
Spain Spanien	Spanish	Spanish	Spaniard, *pl.* the Spanish
Tahiti Tahiti	Tahitian	Tahitian, English, French	Tahitian
Turkey Türkei	Turkish	Turkish	Turk
United States of America Vereinigte Staaten von Amerika	American	American English	American
United Kingdom Vereinigtes Königreich	British	(British) English	Briton *pl.* the British
Vietnam Vietnam	Vietnamese	Vietnamese	Vietnamese, *pl.* the Vietnamese
Wales Wales	Welsh	English, Welsh	Welshman/woman, *pl.* the Welsh
West Indies Westindindische Inseln	West Indian		West Indian

other useful words

Angles, the die Angeln
Bengali (Sprache in Indien und Pakistan)
Celt Kelte, Keltin
Hispanic Hispano-Amerikaner/in; hispanisch
Hindi Hindi (Sprache in Indien)
Hindu Hindu
Indian Indianer/in; indianisch
Muslim Muslim/in, muslimisch
Norman Normanne, Normannin; normannisch
Roman Römer/in; römisch
Saxon Sachse, Sächsin; sächsisch
Urdu (Sprache in Indien und Pakistan)

Umschlagfotos David Graham

Innenumschlag vorn **Archiv für Kunst und Geschichte, Berlin; Library of Congress, Washington** (2), **Mary Evans Picture Library, London** (11); **Marion Schweitzer, München** (Rex Features)

Innenumschlag hinten **Archiv für Kunst und Geschichte, Berlin** (3); **Mary Evans Picture Library, London** (3); **British Museum, London** (2); **©www.britainonview.com; Oxford University Press**

Fotos **action press, Hamburg:** S.9/B. Kammerer, S.68/All Action, S.69/Mallo Press (3), S.89/All Action, S.93/G. Ohlenbostel/Isopress Senepart/S.Wallocha; **Adidas Deutschland, Herzogenaurach:** S.44; **African National Congress:** S.66/ANC logo used by friendly permission of the ANC; **Agence France Press, Büro Berlin:** S.61/N. Asfouri; **Amir Khan Productions:** S.18; **AP Photos, Frankfurt/Main:** S.50/Schlesinger Library - Radcliffe College; **Jim Banks**: S.46/Jim Banks for the Lemelson MIT Program; **John Birdsall Photography, Nottingham**: S.83; **Bristol Grammar School**, S.47; **Franziska Bürgi, Zürich:** S.4, S.72, S.73; **Janet Chipps, London:** S.21; **COMSTOCK, Luxemburg:** S.93; **Corbis, Düsseldorf:** S.4/AFP, S.18/C. Karnow, S.30/D. Wilson, S.31/W. Whitehurst, S.44/Bettmann, S.48/LWA-D. Tardiff/G.B. Diebold, S.50, S.51, S.54/T. Stewart/A. Garg, S.55/L. Taylor, S.58/Sygma/Bradford T & A, S.60/Hulton Archive, S.61/N. Wheeler/D. Cumming, Eye Ubiquitos; S.69/D. Cumming, Eye Ubiquitos; S.71/J. Albertson, S.91/Bettmann (2)/B. Smith); S.93/C. Savage; **COREL Library:** S.11, 54, 73, 80, 82, 85; **Das Fotoarchiv, Essen:** S.53/J. Tack/W. Schmidt, S.75/W. Schmidt, S.76/J. Tack, S.93/J. Scheibner; **Deutscher Fernsehdienst, Hamburg:** S.4/Die Bounty, S.58/Gandhi, S.70/Cool Runnings, S.78-79-80/Die Bounty, S.84/Kick It Like Beckham; **Deutsches Museum, München:** S.48; **dpa-Bildarchiv, Berlin:** S.30/Getty Newsmaker, S.38/ESA, S.40/A. Nemenov/EPA-S.Chirikov, S.41/Consolidated NASA, S.42/EPA-PA Space Telescope Science Institute, S.59/epa-afp-Panthak/D'souza/Lehtikuva Oy, S.66/ANP/epd-Henner Frankenfeld; **Udo Diekmann, Berlin:** S.48 (2) mit freundlicher Genehmigung des Deutschen Museums, München; **Environmental Images, London:** S.82; **Getty Images, München:** S.3/C. Salvo/Stone, S.21/C. Salvo, S.21/M. Yates/T. Vine/J. Pumfrey/S.Cohen; S.32/B. Forster/T. Vine, S.34/Telegraph Library/Stone, S.45/R. Chapple, S.53/Hulton Archive, S.56-57/Hulton Archive, S.58/Hulton Archive, S.81/Hulton Archive, S.83/D. Cox, S.90/Hulton Archive, S.93/T. Arruza/F. Herholdt; **Getty Images Creative, Hamburg:** S.21, S.59; **The Globe Theatre, London:** S.14-15/Shakespeare's Globe/J. Tramper (4); **Béatrice Graham, Paris:** S.16; **David Graham, Paris**: S.3, 5, 6, 7, 8, 9, 10, 12, 14, 21, 22, 23, 24, 25, 27, 28, 29, 39, 42, 62, 83 (2), 84, 88; **Laif, Köln:** S.21/Wieland, S.44/Granser/Wieland, S.93/Wegner; **Library of Congress, Washington:** S.10; **Malta Airport:** S.75; **Mary Evans Picture Library, London:** S.69, S.87, S.90-91(8), S.95; **Sandra McAdam, Mbabane:** S.72 (2), S.73 (4); **Redferns Picture Library**, London: S.10; **Reuters AG, Frankfurt/M.:** S.63/I. Hodgson, S.85/New Media Inc.-J. Ngwenya; **Helen Rose:** S.36; **Heidi Schirrmacher, Berlin:** S.85; **Barbara Schumacher, Hannover:** S.77; **Marion Schweitzer, München:** S.67; **Science Museum, London:** S.34, 37, 39; **The Shakespeare Centre Library, Stratford-upon-Avon:** S.14; **Shakespeare's Globe, London:** S.14-15/John Tramper; **Marco Soldati, Zürich:** S.72; **Sportimage, Hamburg:** S.70/GEPA-G. Cooper, **Caroline Tauxe, Lausanne:** S.72 (2), S.85; **Sabine Theuring, Berlin:** S.75 (2); **TRIGON Film, Schweiz:** S.18; **Andreia Verdasca, London:** S.73 (3); **Verein Junger Freiwilliger, Berlin:** S.72 (2); **Dirk Walther, London:** S.26; **Elke Zahn, Bayreuth:** S.24

Illustrationen **Carlos Borrell:** S.53; **Christina de la Mare:** S.35; **Kathrin Schwertner:** S.13, 17, 33, 43, 49, 65

Cartoons **Peter Muggleston** (Anhang); **Wendy Sinclair** (Raben)

Buchumschläge S.20:*The Growing Pains of Adrian Mole*, Penguin Books, 2002; S.68: *Anita and Me* ©reproduction courtesy of Harper Collins Publishers, London; S.76: *The Official Spanglish Dictionary*, Fireside, Simon & Schuster, USA; S.90:*The Canterbury Tales*, British Library, London; *Macbeth*, Arden. London; *Robinson Crusoe*, John C. Winston, Philadelphia, 1925; *Gulliver's Travels*, John C. Winston, Philadelphia, 1930; *Beowulf*, Nelson Thornes, Cheltenham, 2001; Grafik aus *Beowulf*, Laszlo Matulay, Henry Holt & Co., New York, 1947; *Pride and Prejudice*, Harper Collins, USA, 1999; *Wuthering Heights*, Dover Publications, New York, 1996; S.91: *Alice in Wonderland*, Chronicle Books, USA, 2000; *A Murder is Announced*, Audio Partners, Auburn, 2002; *1984*, Harcourt Inc, USA, 1983; *Animal Farm*, Penguin Books, London, 1951; *The Sea, The Sea,* Chatto & Windus, London, 1978; *Moonraker*, Penguin Books, New York, 2003

Texte S.20: *The Growing Pains of Adrian Mole* von Sue Townsend, 1991; S.36: *Angel of Mercy* von Jay Gromadzka, AA Magazine autumn/winter 2000; S.46: http://web.mit.edu/invent; S.68: *Anita and Me* von Meera Syal, Flamingo, Harper Collins Publishers, London, 1997; S.71: *Get up, stand up* von Bob Marley und Peter Tosh, 1973 Cayman Music Inc/Stuck on Music, Rolf Budde Musikverlag GmbH, Berlin; S.81: *Mississippi said to Missouri* und *I was going to buy my sister* von Michael Rosen, reprinted by permission of pfd on behalf of Michael Rosen; S.82: *Tall story* von Brian Patten, Puffin Books, 1986; *Where is the forest?* von John Foster, 1995 aus *Standing on the Sidelines* (Oxford University Press), mit Genehmigung des Autors; S.83: *Luka*, Suzanne Vega, AGF Music Ltd Waifersongs Ltd., EMI Music Publishing Germany GmbH, Hamburg

Human beings have always needed to communicate ideas. They wanted to tell their descendants who we are and where we came from ...

Words, words, words ... and some pictures

Paintings like these were found all over Europe. They tell stories about how early man hunted animals.

In the Middle East the first books were written on clay tablets.

The Egyptians began to write on papyrus. They use system of pictures and symbols. In other areas peo wrote on the skins of animals such as sheep or go

The German Johann Gutenberg invented a way of printing words using separate letters. Each letter could be used again and again.

Dr Samuel Johnson's A Dictionary of the English Language was published in 1755. It defined 43,000 words. For more than 70 years it was the most important book if you wanted to find out about the meaning of words. Then in 1828 An American Dictionary of the English Language by Noah Webst was published. At the time this was the most complete dictionary in both America and Britain.